THE SUNDAY TIMES

BUSINESS ENTERPRISE GUIDE

The Business Enterprise Handbook

COLIN BARROW, ROBERT BROWN, LIZ CLARKE

RECOMMENDED BY
INSTITUTE OF DIRECTORS

KOGAN PAGE

Contents

About this book

The book is divided into three parts. Part 1 is concerned with establishing where your business is now – its current strengths and weaknesses. Part 2 looks at where you would like to take the business and the strategies you could pursue. Part 3 looks at how you will achieve your growth objectives – and helps you to document the transition by way of a new business plan (as shown in Figure A.1).

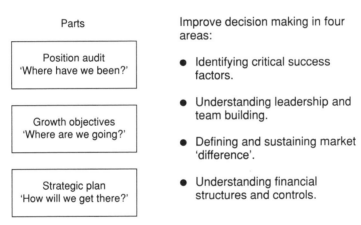

Figure A.1 *The Business Enterprise Handbook*: the three parts

In each of the book's parts, the core interlocking management disciplines are covered:

- people and management;
- financial management and control;
- marketing management.

E-business issues are addressed within each of the above areas, as we believe that for most businesses the Internet has potential as an enabling technology, rather than being a stand-alone topic.

Each chapter contains a wealth of examples and case studies to illustrate the points being made. Checklists and questionnaires are provided to help you put the ideas advanced into practice in your business immediately. At the end of each chapter there is an assignment task to help you review the issues raised in the light of your own experiences in your business. We firmly believe that all management theory is only useful insofar as you can apply it to profitable purpose in your business. The assignments will also be useful for instructors on other training programmes to steer their students through the course.

Any uncredited material is drawn either from the authors' private conversations or from case studies published by Cranfield School of Management. All the material featured in the case studies was accurate when it first went to press.

Introduction

Entrepreneurship, whilst still not exactly respectable – that would be too much to expect – is, however, becoming prolific and universal. There are now over 22 million independently-owned businesses in Europe. Tens and probably hundreds of millions more small- and medium-sized enterprises, SMEs as they have become known, operate in the United States, Russia, Eastern Europe, China, India and throughout Asia. More than one in fifteen of all Europeans, Japanese and Americans in work own and run a business of their own.

Whilst there are millions of small businesses starting up, many survive only a relatively short time. Corporate life generally is on the decline. Less than a third of the United States' leading companies operating 30 years ago still exist today. But over half of all independently owned ventures have ceased trading within five years of starting up. One comprehensive study of all 814,000 firms started up in the United States in a particular year followed their destinies for eight years. That research indicated that only 18 per cent were failures, in that the founders had no real say in the final event. A higher proportion opted for a voluntary closure, or sold out or in some other way changed their ownership, perhaps moving from a partnership to trading through a limited company (as shown in Figure 0.0.1).

Nevertheless, few of the survivors are either profitable or likely to achieve much growth. A major study by David Storey concluded that significant growth is confined to fewer than 4 per cent of UK owner-managed firms. This view is supported by other studies in the United States and elsewhere.

At Cranfield we review the growth performance of independent firms in the UK each year. We look at the accounts of some 15,000 independent UK firms, with turnover between £1 million and £50 million, to see how they have peformed over the preceding four years. Our latest study shows that less than 1,000 of these firms achieved substantial profitable growth. And that was during a period of reasonable growth in the economy at large (as shown in Figure 0.0.2).

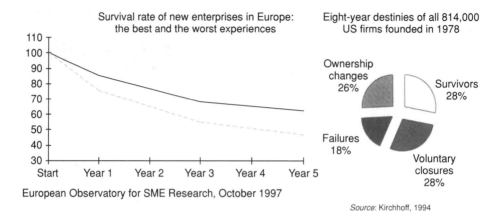

Survival rate of new enterprises in Europe: the best and the worst experiences

European Observatory for SME Research, October 1997

Eight-year destinies of all 814,000 US firms founded in 1978

Ownership changes 26%

Survivors 28%

Failures 18%

Voluntary closures 28%

Source: Kirchhoff, 1994

Figure 0.0.1   SME survival rates, Europe and USA

Barely 300 of these 'profitable' growers were in good financial shape – that is liquid and solvent, and so able to face the uncertain economic future.

Inevitably, having so few businesses able to achieve profitable growth raises questions as to what goes wrong. Some owner–managers obviously set their sights too low. In the mid-1990s, whilst the founder of the Oxford-based Internet Bookshop built up and sold a business for £10 million within five years, his counterpart at Amazon built a near identical business worth US$2 billion over the same period. One financed his venture on his credit card, whilst the other raised US$11 million venture capital. One located in his home town, the other set up in Seattle, a hub of the US book trade, and a home to some of the most creative database and Internet technology.

14,955 Firms

267 Firms

- Of which 960 have grown profit and sales by at least 25 per cent compound over the past four years.
- Of which 532 have made at least £100,000 profit.
- Of which 411 have made at least a 5 per cent return on sales and a 15 per cent return on capital.
- And 267 are liquid and appropriately geared (current ratio at least 1:1, and no more debt than equity).

Source: Cranfield, 2000

Figure 0.0.2   UK independent businesses with between £1m and £50m annual turnover: their growth and profitability over the four years to 1999

Internet businesses have set new standards for business growth (as shown in Figure 0.0.3). The old stager Oxford University Press has done well still to be around after more than 500 years. But its average growth has been only 1 per cent or so. IBM, a much younger, though still venerable, business has only managed 3 per cent growth over the past ten years. But for its hiccup a few years ago that figure would have been nearer 10 per cent. Microsoft, in the vanguard of the new economy, has been growing at 40 per cent per annum and still is. But the pressure to perform weighs heavily on the Internet sector. Yahoo!, for example, would have to grow at 95 per cent a year over the next ten years to justify its recent share price.

Although few Internet firms are profitable most are growing fast.

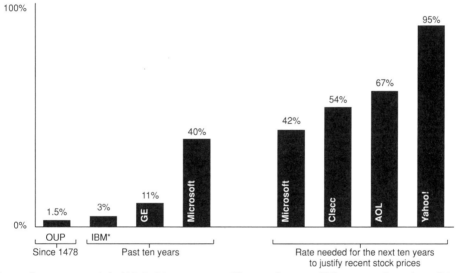

Source: Company accounts for historic data   *Over past four years IBM's compound growth was 9%

Figure 0.0.3   Old vs new

Would that all entrepreneurs were as bold as the typical Internet business founder. During one particularly good period of economic growth in the UK a study revealed that 55 per cent of owner-managed firms had no plans for growth at all.

Other businesses are prevented from growing because they still operate as a one-man band, despite often having dozens of employees. The founders of such firms either do not recognise the need to build a management team, or are incapable of doing so successfully. Most bosses of their own firms work long hours. Nearly a third admit to working 60 hours a week or more. This is in sharp contrast to employees in small firms, where only 3 per cent work the same long hours. Yet there is no evidence of a direct correlation between excessive work and excessive profit.

RBR

Rory Sweet and Ben White, both in their early 30s, built up their company RBR Networks starting out in a London basement with just £600. Within four years they had sold the company to a South African software and Internet provider for £25 million. Sweet admits that neither he nor his partner had a background in computing and confessed that 'half the time we didn't get up until 11 am and only worked until 1 pm.' Their 45 employees ran the business, whilst the founders planned the strategy. As well as taking their staff out for a curry to celebrate the company's success, Sweet and White set aside £1.5 million as a loyalty bonus for their team.

Unfortunately not many owner–managers can let go of the day-to-day work as Sweet and White seemed to. Once a management team is in place things ought to change. Sadly they do not. Most owner–managers become meddlers once they have managers. They actually work more hours, spending the extra time checking and overseeing the work they are already paying others handsomely to do.

The result of this meddling is much unhappiness all round. Overheads soar and motivation plummets. All too frequently the boss has picked the wrong team (in which case there is a recruitment problem) or alternatively the team is not being managed and motivated properly. More likely still the boss simply does not know how to stop working and start thinking.

To grow a business successfully three tasks have to be implemented. The day-to-day business **operation** has to be carried out effectively. Business **improvements** have to be carried out to make today's business better. A business **strategy** has to be developed to point the business in the best direction.

By far the most important task for the owner–manager is to plan the future strategy of the business. Ninety per cent of the potential to add value to a growing business lies in shaping its future competitive strategy *now* and on making the business better. If owner–managers spend any of their time on this at all, it tends to be barely 10 per cent. They seem to prefer to spend 90 per cent of their time on day-to-day operations. Without any clear strategic direction it is hardly surprising that many SMEs (and a few not so small firms) are either standing still or going round in circles.

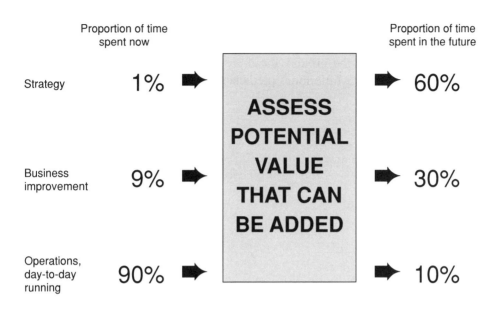

Figure 0.0.4 Refocusing the MD's activities

Our observations at Cranfield indicate that whilst most owner–managers spend most of their time on the wrong tasks, given the right skills, knowledge and encouragement they could redirect their energies to good effect. This book is for those entrepreneurs who want to grow and develop their businesses and themselves, but are realistic about the difficulties they are likely to encounter.

At Cranfield we have worked with over 400 successful owner–manager firms, and carefully observed the performance of thousands more. We have also studied all the relevant research into business growth, and the lack of it, and conducted and published many studies ourselves. Over the past 15 years, with the help of participants on our Business Growth and Development Programme, we have distilled what we believe to be the essence of how to achieve profitable growth. We have also charted the problems owner–managers are likely to encounter, whilst suggesting ways to anticipate and overcome those problems.

This book is the core text for the Cranfield programme and as such has helped hundreds of our programme participants to achieve their ambitions. Many have grown spectacularly, even during difficult times, and created businesses worth millions and in some cases hundreds of millions of pounds. Others have raised millions in new capital to fund expansion at home and abroad. Some have sold up and others have started quite different ventures from those they originally owned.

Our role in producing this book is akin to that of a map-maker. We did not design the terrain, nor in any real sense are we travelling across it. But we do hope that by charting the ground ahead we will make what is already a very hazardous occupation a little more predictable, profitable and fun for those on the road to growth.

Part 1

Where are we now?

The chapters in Part 1 are intended to help you establish the current position of your business. Just as a plan for a journey, for example, would be useless unless you had a clear idea of where you were starting out from, any business strategy needs a similar reference base.

Entrepreneurs have an almost irrepressible desire to move directly from spotting an opportunity to exploiting it or attempting to do so. This is rather like seeing a road sign to an interesting destination and immediately following it, without first checking that you have sufficient fuel to complete the journey, or whether there are even more appropriate and exciting destinations just beyond the horizon.

It is no great surprise, therefore, to find that a large proportion of management time is spent putting right yesterday's mistakes. Tom Frost, a former chief executive of NatWest, is on record as saying that mistakes account for between 25 and 40 per cent of the total cost in a service business. The following chapters pose the sort of questions that need asking to establish your strengths and weaknesses, and the opportunities and threats across the key areas of your business and its current and potential markets.

In business school jargon, the activity of taking stock is known as the position audit.

Phases of organisational growth

All business growth and development calls for change. The problem is that change is not always incremental. Children do not grow seamlessly from being babies to adulthood, but pass through phases: infancy, adolescence, teenage and so on. Businesses must also move through phases if they are to grow success-fully. Each phase is punctuated by a 'crisis', a word which derives from the Chinese and translates loosely as 'dangerous opportunity'.

Researchers such as L E Greiner (1972) and Churchill and Lewis (1983) have identified each distinctive phase in a firm's growth pattern, and provided an insight into the changes in organisational structure, strategy and behaviour that are needed to move successfully on to the next phase of growth (as shown in Figure 1.0.1). An inability to recognise the phases of growth and to manage transition through them is probably the single most important reason why most owner-managed firms fail to achieve their true potential, let alone their founders' dreams.

Typically a business starts out taking on any customers it can get, operating informally, with little management and few controls. The founder, who usually provides all the ideas, all the drive, makes all the decisions and signs the cheques, becomes overloaded with administrative detail and operational problems. Unless the founder can change the organisational structure, any further growth will leave the business more vulnerable. The crises of leadership, autonomy and control loom large.

Over time, the successful owner–manager tackles these crises: finds a clear focus, builds a first-class team, delegates key tasks, appraises performance, institutes control and reporting systems and ensures that progress towards objectives is monitored and rewarded. The firm itself consistently delivers good results.

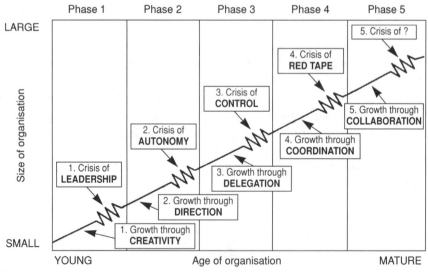

Source: Greiner, 1972

Figure 1.0.1   Organisational phases of growth

Each phase of growth calls for a different approach to managing the business. Sometimes strong leadership is required, at others a more consultative approach. Some phases call for more systems and procedures, some for more cooperation between staff. Unfortunately, most founders try to run their business in much the same way as it gets bigger as they did when it was small. They end up with a big small company, rather than the small big company that is required if successful growth is to be achieved. They believe the problems of growth can be solved by taking on another sales person, a few hundred square metres of space or another bank loan. This approach is rather like suggesting that the transition from infancy to adulthood can be accomplished by nothing more significant than providing larger clothes.

Let us now look more closely at each of the five growth phases, bearing in mind that, in practice, most independent businesses pursuing growth are somewhere between Phases 1 and 3.

Phase 1: growth through creativity

Any business starting up does so because somebody (perhaps you) has a good idea about providing a product or service for which they believe there is demand. If the idea is successful the business can grow or evolve with equal success. The founder of the company is at the heart of everything. Assuming the business has been successful and shows steady growth – a description which fits a minority of start-ups, as most will already have failed by this stage – there comes a time when the person who started the business with their creative ideas and personal, informal style of operation can no longer cope effectively. The person who provided all the drive, all the ideas and made all the decisions becomes overloaded with administrative detail and operational problems.

Unless the founder can change the organisational structure of his or her firm and put in place a management team, any further growth will leave the business vulnerable: it will be incapable of becoming a substantial firm with a life independent from that of its founder. Those companies who do not make it through to the next phase of growth will either experience a cycle of 'one step forward and two steps back' or gentle decline will set in. The end of this first growth phase, which can take anything from two or three years to several decades in extreme cases, is signalled by a crisis of leadership.

Phase 2: growth through direction

In a crisis of leadership, a business requires a strong leader who is able to make tough decisions about priorities and provide the clear, single-minded direction and sense of purpose needed to move the business forward.

More Balls Than Most

Doing too much at once

The two founders of More Balls Than Most started up making a juggling kit consisting of a number of coloured balls. The product was sold into the executive toy market, with the aim of providing a challenging but enjoyable non-business activity for stressed business people. In its first two years the company opened a pub called The Jugglers Arms, considered opening a small chain of shops to sell its own and similar products, began to negotiate to open up in the US market and embarked on a major programme of new product development. Unsurprisingly, the two founders and their full-time staff of two quickly ran out of time and money. By the time they had put together a prospectus to raise £500,000 to finance their planned growth, they had crossed pubs, shops and the US venture off their list, and focused on expanding the domestic distribution channels for their existing product.

At this stage of growth, ideas the pioneer founder used to carry in his head have to be formalised. Policies need to be evolved, teams built up and key people appointed with specific roles to play and objectives to achieve. The personal management style of the founder becomes secondary to making the business efficient. Sometimes the founder is not the right person to lead the organisation through this phase and, either through lack of management skills or temperament, he or she may opt to give up or sell out.

Country Holidays

Knowing when the business needs a new leader

Philip Green, aged 37, an Ayrshire farmer's son, had already made himself a sizeable fortune from building up and selling a company called Country Holidays before launching into the training business.

Country Holidays is basically an agency which lets country cottages to holiday makers. He launched it in Skipton and sold it to his management for £14 million 12 years later, retaining a 10 per cent holding.

Businesses have phases, he says. Country Holidays reached the stage where it needed steady system management rather than the flat-out style of an entrepreneur. So Green went back to a two-roomed office in Skipton, putting his entrepreneurial talents to work in building a new business.

Green's selling tack is that most businesses need to improve their customer service and he can teach them how to do it. He also teaches improved telephone selling skills, which has immediately attracted some potential customers. Also, like so many others, from accountants to designers, Green will do a little management consultancy for anyone who wants it.

Green invested £80,000 of his capital in starting up Train and Motivate and budgeted to lose £100,000 in his first year and break even in the second.

If selling up is not for you then success at this stage of growth depends on finding, motivating and keeping key staff – no mean task. Research at Cranfield and elsewhere consistently shows this to be a key problem. As the company grows and matures, the directive top-down management style starts to become counter-productive. Others working in the organisation acquire more expertise about their particular sphere of operations than the boss. Not surprisingly, they want a greater say in the strategy of the business. Such subordinates either struggle for the power to be heard, or become demotivated and leave. This is the crisis of autonomy and if it is not recognised and managed, it will absorb so much energy and time that it will drag the company down. In one Cranfield study three out of five of the growth companies surveyed reported the loss of key employees. Two-thirds of them experienced this loss within a year of appointing the key employees.

Proprietors usually put defection of key employees down to better pay elsewhere. In this they are usually wrong. It is more likely that they just do not realise that what makes the staff 'tick' is more to do with having an interesting and worthwhile job than with pay alone.

Optiva

Motivating employees

Optiva produces a range of revolutionary sonic toothbrushes that clean teeth by vibrating water into a froth which erodes plaque and tartar. This high-tech product started out as a US$4,000 research project at the University of Washington. Several professors tried to sell the product to various Fortune 500 companies who just weren't interested.

Eventually, a direct approach to an entrepreneur, David Giuliani, paid off. He had just sold International Biomedics, his first company, to Abbott Laboratories. He raised US$427,000 from 25 local investors. When that money ran out he went back to the same people for more. Eventually, he raised US$9 million and within five years had built a business with US$130 million annual sales. With 31,057 per cent compound sales growth over the previous five years, Optiva at one point was the fastest growing company in the United States.

Giuliani attributes Optiva's success to adopting unusual ways to motivate his employees.

The company has a high reliance on people and is dedicated to seeing that they can achieve their full potential. Optiva offers interest-free loans so that people can buy their own home PC. It also runs a 24-hour personal problems helpline and educational courses in English as a second language for the immigrant workers at its Washington base. Generous stock options are on offer too.

Giuliani's rule is to have fun while you're growing the business. If you don't, people won't want to work for you.

Phase 3: growth through delegation

The solution to the crisis of autonomy is to recognise that more responsibility has to be delegated to more people in the company. The trouble is that most founders hang on to too many jobs in their firms, mostly out of a belief that nobody else can do the job as well as they can. The reasons for this argument are legion and include: 'It takes more time to explain the job than to do it myself', 'A mistake would be too costly', 'Others lack the experience'; and so on. There is probably an element of truth in all of these reasons, but until you learn how to delegate decisions rather than simply dumping tasks, your organisation will never reach full maturity.

Steljes

Relinquishing control

Nigel Steljes spent a decade building his business into the UK's leading multimedia presentation company with £25 million annual sales and a staff of 75. Steljes reckons expansion in the presentations business is second only to that in telecommunications. He sees presentation technology as the final link in the information revolution. His view is that all that data spinning round the globe is only usable if it can be seen, and the best place to view data is not on a computer screen.

This is a fast-moving business sector with technology leaping over technology at an ever increasing rate. 'My job is to see the wood for the trees', Steljes confirms. 'Once upon a time I was involved with everything to do with the company. My colleagues demanded that I relinquish some control. It was relatively easy to do it. I just had to be convinced. Now that they are under pressure they can't complain.'

Steljes is relaxed because his company has been successful for the past eight years. All the right things are in the right place: great people, a growing market and new technology. He has begun to indulge in three-week breaks, the last one in Portugal, something unheard of just a year or so ago.

Problems can arise at this stage. Firstly, a number of the managers you appointed earlier on will simply not be up to the task of accepting their new responsibilities. Not all people who can take direction can take part in a bottom-up planning process that is dependent on high-quality inputs. So this means you are back in the recruiting game. You may be wise at this stage to stop relying on personal contacts or direct press advertising as the majority of small firms do, and go for executive search through a consultancy using sound selection techniques. You probably thought this too expensive at Phase 1 and possibly at Phase 2, but by now you will have made enough mistakes in recruitment to know that it is a profession in its own right, and requires knowledge and skills you may not have. Furthermore, the indirect costs of getting the wrong people more than outweigh the cost of paying for an expert. One owner–manager was startled, to say the least, to discover that doing the recruitment himself cost him over six times as much as using an agency, allowing for the cost of his time and of productive time lost as he took six months to do a task an agency could do in three.

But even with good management teams in place further problems can occur. Once managers you can delegate to are in place, they will make their own decisions as well as the ones you delegate to them. In time the organisation will become increasingly fragmented and uncoordinated. This often becomes apparent in fairly dramatic ways, such as loss of profits, margin erosion, unplanned development and a lack of an overall strategy that everyone can commit to. Another crisis looms: the crisis of control.

Phase 4: growth through coordination

During this phase the crisis of control is overcome by achieving the best of both the delegation and the direction phases. Decision making (and power) is still delegated, but in a systematic and regulated way, with accountability becoming a byword for the first time. The organisation begins to put in place strategic planning of some sort, to combine bottom-up and top-down planning methods. Systems and policies are developed to regulate the behaviour of managers at all levels. Communication is vital and a corporate culture takes shape, giving new employees a feel for the way things are done in the company.

This growth phase usually ends in the crisis of red tape, where the clutter of rules and regulations that bind the company together results in missed opportunities. Bureaucracy rules and development and initiative are stifled. This crisis can be overcome, or even circumvented by introducing innovative, non-bureaucratic planning procedures, or by subdividing the business into manageable units with their own separate missions and management. This is fine as long as you do not return these units to Phase 1-type growth in a desperate bid to release creativity.

IBM, who successfully overcame the other crisis stages in its growth, nearly foundered at this stage. After growing to dominate the computer world in much the same way as Microsoft has and facing similar accusing voices, the company stumbled and nearly fell. The outside view of the company was encapsulated in the phrase used at that time to describe their staff: 'Button down shirt, button down mind'.

Nicola Becket, founder and chief executive of NSB and winner of the Veuve Clicquot 2000 Business Woman of the Year Award, worked in IBM just before its profits slide began. She claims that IBM was incredibly arrogant in the 1970s: 'We believed we were the best'. The trouble with having that belief is that change is difficult to implement from within, with an 'it ain't broke so why fix it' mentality.

Phase 5: growth through collaboration

The way to circumvent red tape is to inculcate an attitude of collaboration throughout the organisation. This calls for much-simplified and integrated information systems and an emphasis on team-orientated activity.

Many successful Japanese and European firms now organise their workforces into teams where there used to be production lines. Volvo, for example, has a team responsible for making and assembling a complete car. This has the effect of making a group of people responsible for the whole of one major portion of a task, rather than having individuals responsible for small and sometimes seemingly meaningless parts of the process. In this way people can be encouraged to generate solutions rather than just pass problems on down the line.

A further emphasis at this stage of growth is on management education and personal development, an activity viewed as a luxury in a new venture, and as a good investment in a mature venture.

Most independent businesses will lie somewhere between the crisis of leadership and the fourth stage of growth using Greiner's model. If this applies to your business, keep the some points in mind as you try to move through phases.

Firstly, tempting though it will be, do not try to skip phases. Each phase results in certain strengths and learning experiences that are essential for success in subsequent phases. When one owner–manager was introduced to this way of looking at growth, the scales fell from his eyes. He had tried to delegate authority and involve his key managers in developing strategy almost from the time he launched the business. As a result, there was not a clear enough set of goals for them to aim for and they left one after another. The organisation nearly failed too. This was as a direct result of trying to move too quickly from Phase 1 to Phase 3, skipping Phase 2.

Chapter 5 includes a checklist that will help pinpoint where your company is now, in terms of the phases of growth.

1 *Your mission*

Mission statements

Mission statements and prime objectives need examining at the beginning and at the end of the strategic review. If you already have or have had a mission and key objectives, you can find out how they should be changed and measure performance through analysis of strengths and weaknesses, threats and opportunities. If you have no mission or key objectives, that too will tell you something important.

Mission statements and objectives are 'what' statements; tasks and action plans are 'how to' statements. Without these your business will not have suffi-

Figure 1.1.1   The pyramid of goals

cient direction to pull you through the crisis in Phase 1 growth and into a more advanced growth phase.

Let's take mission statements and objectives first, as they are inevitably intertwined. These are direction statements, intended to focus your attention on the essentials that encapsulate your specific competence(s) in relation to the market and customers you plan to serve.

First, the mission should be narrow enough to give direction and guidance to everyone in the business. This concentration is the key to business success because it is only by focusing on specific needs that a small business can differentiate itself from its larger competitors. Nothing kills off a new business faster than trying to do too many different things at the outset. Second, the mission should open up a large enough market to allow the business to grow and realise its potential.

One of the highest incidences of failure in small business is in the building trade. The very nature of this field seems to militate against being able to concentrate on any specific type of work, or on customer need. One successful new small builder defined his mission in the following sentence: 'We will concentrate on domestic house repair and renovation work, and as well as doing a good job we will meet the customers' two key needs: a quotation that is accurate, and starting and completion dates that are met'. When told this, most small builders laugh; they say it cannot be done – but then most go broke.

Ultimately, there has to be something unique about your business that makes people want to buy from you. That uniqueness may be contained in the product, but it is more likely to be woven into the fabric of the way you do business. Try telephoning any three car hire firms, hotels, plumbers, or walking into three restaurants, print shops or exhaust-fitting centres. The chances are that it will not be their 'products', but their people and systems that differentiate them.

In summary, the mission statement should explain what business you are in or plan to enter. It should include some or all of the following:

- Market and customer needs – who are we 'satisfying'?
- With what product or service will we meet market and customer needs?
- What are our capabilities, both particular skills and knowledge, and resources?
- What market opportunities are there for our product or service, and what threats are there from competitors (and others)?
- What do we enjoy doing most?
- What do we want to achieve both now and in the future?

Above all, a mission statement should be realistic, achievable – and brief. Like McKinsey's: 'As management consultants we aim to help our clients make positive lasting and substantial improvements in their performance and to build a great firm that is able to attract, develop, excite and retain exceptional people' – and like that of Blooming Marvellous:

Blooming Marvellous

Having a realistic and durable mission

Blooming Marvellous is a company formed by two young mothers in and is now a £2 million business. Both founders were interested in fashion and clothing, although neither had great first-hand experience in the field. They started making clothes for children, mothers such as themselves, and some general fashion garments. This kept the money rolling in for the first few years but, despite recruiting some good staff, the company failed to grow significantly.

After a brainstorming session the founders decided to concentrate their resources on the market that seemed to offer the greatest potential commensurate with both their skills and personal desires. This led them to this mission statement, which provided the focal point for a burst of strong growth.

> Arising out of our experiences we intend to design, make and market a range of clothes for mothers-to-be that will make them feel they can still be fashionably dressed. We aim to serve a niche missed out by Mothercare, Marks & Spencer, etc, and so be a significant force in the mail order 'fashion for the mother-to-be' market.

The Blooming Marvellous mission has stood the company well. Today, a glance at the company's Web site would lead you to believe that this is an Internet business, and indeed it does generate much of its income from this route. But the founders' mission statement remains the same and in clear and plain English, unlike the jargon so prevalent in the rest of their sector. They have only added a line to that statement since 1980, to incorporate their entry into the baby-wear and nursery-products sectors. The heart of their proposition is the same.

Martin Sorrel at WPP set out in 1985 to establish 'A large multinational marketing services company and to be one of the best, by adding value and imagination to clients' products and services'. By the 1990s the mission statement had altered to be 'The largest multinational marketing company and THE best'. This will probably be modified again as Sorrel continues to add value from the centre.

Barrie Haigh, the founder of Innovex, revisited his mission statement with his top team for each of the six years after attending the Cranfield Business Growth Programme. Over that six-year period he took his business from £8 million a year turnover to a value of £550 million in a trade sale, netting himself some £350 million in the process.

More on missions

A manager with a small hosiery firm both impressed and irritated other participants at a training seminar by continually bubbling with enthusiasm about the
company he worked for. Although it seemed, in the words of one course
member, 'naïve verging on the obnoxious', no one questioned his commitment.
He clearly identified himself closely with the firm's aspirations. This manager
was not suffering from an acute case of business indoctrination. His dedication
stemmed from a sense of mission; a rational and emotional belief in his
company's products, services and business strategy.

Andrew Campbell, director of the London-based Ashridge Strategic Management Centre (ASMC), said in an article in the *Independent* (6 February 1994,
p 15), 'Many of the world's outstanding companies have employees with what
we call "a sense of mission". These people believe that their company is special;
they are proud of being part of it all'.

Campbell heads a research project into how managers can better understand
and create a sense of mission in their organisations. He is convinced that firms
increasingly need 'passionate' employees, and says, 'Many organisations have
become depersonalised to the point where energy levels are low, cynicism is
high and work failed to excite or fulfil employees. We find that committed staff
perform many times more efficiently than apathetic ones'.

ASMC's work on mission has grown out of research over two years into the
use and misuse of mission statements. These statements are used by business
leaders to share issues such as the company's philosophy, commercial rationale
and strategy with employees. Research from the United States suggests that
nearly half of the country's large companies have mission statements. ASMC's
work suggests a similar figure in Britain.

After an exhaustive study of more than 100 statements from US, Japanese and
European companies, the ASMC concluded that these statements in themselves
had little impact on business success. Much more important is whether a sense of
mission already exists in the hearts and minds of employees. Employees not only
need to have a clear understanding of what their company is trying to achieve but
have to be emotionally committed to its aims before a meaningful statement can
be written. If commitment is lacking, a mission statement is at best likely to be
ignored and at worst treated with cynicism. From these findings, ASMC has set
out five principles to help managers trying to create a sense of mission:

- Pick a theme around which to develop the new mission. It should capture
  the company's future strategy and values, and should be easy to translate
  into behaviours and standards.
- Focus on action rather than words.
- Make sure that key standards and behaviours clearly affirm the company's
  new direction.

- Be patient. Developing a new mission takes years.
- Build and sustain trust. This is often achieved by senior management being visible and open about the changes taking place.

'Leaders should not forget that although a sense of mission is an emotional force, it can be managed,' Campbell says, 'It is an aspect of business which cannot be ignored. An organisation with a sense of mission has a strong advantage.'

Prime objectives

Objectives give some idea of how big you want the business to be: your share of the market, in other words. It certainly is not easy to forecast sales, especially before you have even started on a new strategy, but if you do not set a goal at the start, but simply wait to see how things will develop, one of two problems will occur. Either you will not sell enough to cover your fixed costs and so lose money and perhaps go out of business; or you will sell too much and run out of cash: you will overtrade. Obviously, before you can set a specific market share and sales objective you need to know the size and trends in your market.

The 'size' you want your business to be is more a matter of judgment than forecast – a judgment tempered by the resources you have available to achieve those objectives and, of course, some idea of what is and what is not reasonable and achievable.

Baltimore Technology

Having challenging objectives

Fran Rooney bought a tiny Irish software company from an academic at Trinity College, Dublin, for less than £400,000 and built it into a FTSE 100 company in under four years. The company is losing money, employs fewer than 800 people across the world, and is valued at £2.5 billion.

Rooney has always gone in for goals. At 29 he decided that by the time he was 40 he wanted to be heading a company. At 45 he wanted to pay off his mortgage and at 50 he wanted to be in a position to retire. He is running a bit ahead of himself as at 43 he is worth about £68 million.

From day one, he wanted Baltimore to be a global company, even when the company only employed six people. He only employs dynamic self-starters who share his ambitious targets for the company.

Edwin Trisk

Being clear about where you are going

Edwin Trisk, manufacturer of paint curing equipment, under the stewardship of MD Robert Kilsby, has beaten off all international competition from Canada, Sweden and Italy to become the world leader in this niche market – and it is still growing at 20 per cent a year. Last year, Trisk, based in Sunderland, won the Queen's Award for Export Achievement.

The company has secured a presence in 58 countries by strong branding and a determined relationship with its importers. 'We set out on day 1 both in terms of products and customers to have a world market', says Robert Kilsby, who bought out the company five years earlier. Since then Trisk has made its presence felt in every country in which it has a market. The strategy is to grant an importer exclusive rights to the company's range of drying equipment. The productivity advantages of Trisk's equipment means that the time a body shop takes to dry a car can be cut from four hours to ten minutes.

In return for Trisk's exclusivity, the importers have to adhere to stringent criteria. They have to agree to exhibit at local exhibitions, provide Trisk with market information, sales and stock reports and use Trisk's own marketing strategy. The company is so hands-on that should the importer wish to advertise in any local media, Trisk supplies the fonts and transparencies to be used.

The policies might sound severe, but they work because Trisk has always been clear about where it was going, as a company, and how it was going to get there.

Trisk's success is helped by the fact that local competitors produce products of such poor quality. 'The Japanese are great with volume products, but in niche products it is a different world. There, they admire European technology'.

Kilsby and his team place huge importance on what he calls 'worldwide brand-building'. As he says, 'we wanted to give the image of a bigger company'. The brochures are glossy, the products are glossy, all in a 'dayglo' yellow much like the headquarters. And the philosophy has stood the company in good stead. Turnover is up to £6 million.

You may find the range of discretion over a size objective seriously constrained by the financial resources at your disposal – or realistically available from investors and lenders – and the scope of the market opportunity. But building the right management team is much more likely to be the limiting factor.

It will be useful to set near-term objectives covering the next 18 months or so, and a longer-term objective covering up to three or so years. Your objectives may also include profit levels and margins and return on investment (see ratio analysis, Chapter 4).

You will also have a personal objective for the business which may include selling it on, taking it to the stock market, or going on the acquisition trail yourself. All three of these objectives have important implications for the business, but unless you intend to involve all your staff in these tasks, and by implication provide them with an appropriate motivation and reward system, it's best to keep these visions to yourself and your co-owners. However, the way to achieve maximum value in all such objectives is to move your business through to the third and fourth phases of growth as speedily as possible.

If you are still the whole business, as most proprietors in Phases 1 and 2 of growth are, then you probably don't have the depth of management to get much value out of an acquisition (especially if it's a diversification). Anyone interested in buying your business would put in such a large 'earn-out' figure that it would hardly be worth selling; and the stock market would either not be interested, or place too low a valuation on your business.

An example of a mission statement and statement of key objectives follows.

Adventure Works Travel

Mission and objectives

At Adventure Works Travel our mission is 'to be the leading provider of hassle-free European adventure holidays to the 25- to 35-year-old young professionals market'. Initially operating within a 25-mile catchment area, we quickly started to sell our services worldwide via the Internet. Sales of travel services is the fastest growing category of business-to-consumer activity on the Internet. In 2000 the value of this market is an estimated £2,700 million.

At Adventure Works Travel we aim to put emphasis on providing a complete specialist service based on having a detailed knowledge of the holiday destination and adventure activities being offered. Our market research shows that the major criticism our type of client has of existing travel agencies is that they 'know nothing about their products, but just open the catalogue and read', to quote one of the many disappointed adventure holiday takers.

Also, by using our experience in the Adventure Works clothing shop, we will be able to both advise and signpost our clients to sources of the type of travel equipment they will need to get the very best out of their holiday experience.

Objectives
Our financial objectives are to earn at least £180,000 post tax profit in the next year, up from £80,000 last year. We intend to make £300,000 in two years' time. Our profit margin on sales by year 3 will be a respectable 10 per cent, up from the present 7 per cent. We also intend that the business should be fun. The present staff are passionate about adventure holidays, and we intend to maintain their enthusiasm by constant product and skill training. We will only recruit new people who share our vision.

Assignment 1

Write your mission statement and principal objectives

1. Write your current mission statement if you have one, linking your product(s) or service to the customer/market needs it is aimed at.
2. What were your principal objectives when you started or took over your business? How well have you succeeded in achieving them?
3. What do you think the mission statement of the most successful company in your market is?

We will return to missions and key objectives in more detail at the third stage of the strategic review, when we put together business plans (see Chapter 17).

2 *Opportunities and threats*

Having looked again at the reasons why you started the business (your first mission statement) and the objectives you set yourself, the next step in clearly understanding 'where are we now' is to look in some detail at:

- your marketing environment;
- your customers and markets;
- your competitors.

The purpose of each exercise, spelt out in checklists for you to complete in Assignments 2–4 at the end of this chapter, is to understand what has changed since you started and is likely to continue to change. What are the new opportunities and possible threats posed in this changing environment and what conclusions do you draw from them in terms of how you should respond?

The elements of the marketing process we will be following in Chapters 2, 3, 7, 8 and 13 are summarised in Figure 1.2.1. To illustrate each step a simple example is shown, taken from a study by academics Wong, Saunders and Doyle (1989), contrasting 15 matched pairs of leading Japanese companies in the UK and their major British competitors.

Your marketing environment

Keeping yourself appraised of the marketing environment that created your business, and of subsequent developments in this environment, is of primary importance for you as leader of the business.

Connectair

Robert Wright, a former British Airways pilot, in founding the Connectair air taxi business, saw a clear opportunity in the scaling down of activities by major airlines in the early 1980s. Economic recession caused cutbacks in staff and routes served. This opened the possibility for small feeder airlines to assist major airlines to maintain route coverage. Within two years the business was established, now benefiting from the improving economic climate. With the improved economy, however, threats developed from expansion plans of new entrants and major airlines, as well as the substantial sums of capital needed to develop a sizeable airline business. Survival was assured but by the late 1980s the question was whether to invest more or to realise a considerable capital gain by selling out to a major competitor.

Robert sold Connectair to Air Europe in 1989 for £7 million, spent two years flying for British Airways again, then amazingly was able to re-purchase Connectair from the receiver when Air Europe liquidated during the early 1990s recession. Renaming the company City Flier Express, Robert and his team quickly built the business during the prosperous 1990s and was able to sell to British Airways as the UK economy slowed in 1999 for 10 times his earlier price!

The Connectair example demonstrates that all businesses operate within definite economic cycles, often of around five to seven years' duration, requiring responsive business strategies of alternate growth and retrenchment. Monitoring such cycles and being prepared to alter course is a sign of strength, not weakness, and comes from a thorough reading of the usually well publicised economic signals. (For example, the second issue of *The Economist* each month summarises UK and European GDP forecasts for the next 18 months.)

Marks & Spencer, for example, responded to the prospect of recession in late 1998 by cutting its proposed European expansion plans by one third. Andrew Purves, on the other hand, as founder of furniture retailer Purves & Purves, and at an early stage of growth, took advantage of the slowdown to double his Tottenham Court Road retail floor space, as rents cooled and six-month rent-free offers reappeared.

Robert Wright also benefited from the deregulation measures favoured by the earlier Conservative government, measures that flowed also from the United States, which encouraged the development of second-line competitive airlines. This emphasises how important it is for you to keep abreast of legislation that can affect your market areas and of the longer-term implications of such changes (witness the extraordinary development in the US airline industry in recent years, 10 years on from deregulation).

Changes in technology clearly have the profoundest effects on both the creators of the change and on players in their industry.

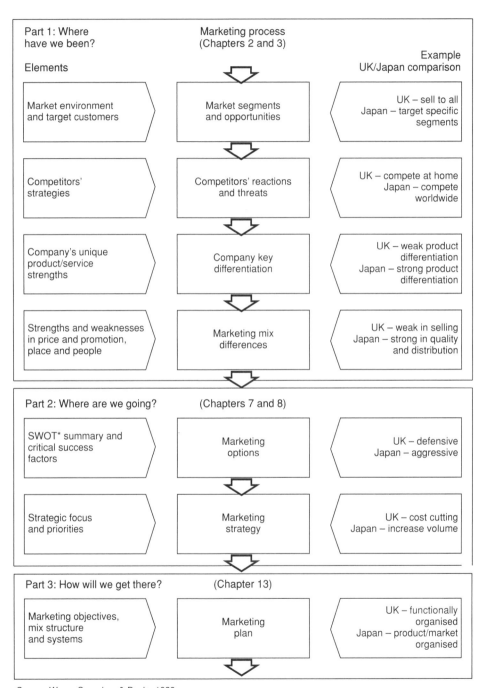

Figure 1.2.1 Marketing strategy

Pilkington Glass

Pilkington Glass, after years and millions of pounds of expenditure, revolutionised the flat glass industry in the 1960s with its production of float glass; the issue became whether the company should seek to dominate its industry by monopolising the invention. For competitors, the issue was whether their own research and development efforts should be redoubled. The imaginative solution by Pilkington (contrasting strongly with EMI's efforts to monopolise its medical scanner breakthrough) was to license the process to competitors, ensuring 25 years' revenue and growth stream for the inventor, and directing competitors to improve and add value (coatings, treatments) to the new process, rather than seeking to supplant it.

Technology changes not just the product and its cost structure, but also its presentation (for example, plastic versus glass bottles), its distribution (for example, the 747 airplane bringing Third-World competitors or markets within reach) and even the way we promote the product (for example, the Internet and promotional Web sites as well as computerised databases of customers providing one of the most useful direct marketing tools). Monitoring and adapting new technology in its many guises can clearly affect growth in your business.

Internet Bookshop

In the mid-1990s, two entrepreneurs, on two continents separated by over 3,000 miles, recognised the same opportunity brought about by new technology. For hundreds of years books had been sold in shops, and those shops were always too small to hold all the books that readers could possibly want. But the advent of the Internet and sophisticated database marketing tools gave Darryl Mattocks in Oxford, England, and Jeff Bezos in Seattle, USA, the opportunity to launch Internet 'book shops'. The 'book shops' had no theoretical limit to the number of books available for 'browsing'. And even the books they held were kept in low-cost, out-of-town warehouses rather than premium-cost high street shopping centres.

Within four years Mattocks had sold his Internet Bookshop to W H Smith for £10 million. Today, Amazon.com, Bezos' brainchild, is valued on the stock market at over US$5 billion. Not a bad four years' work.

Indeed, Internet-based e-commerce is now, according to many surveys, the greatest single business opportunity for most existing and growing businesses, even if this applies less to start-up dot.com businesses. The surveys are occasionally contradictory, but for the computer industry their most significant finding is one on which they agree, the rapid development of e-commerce.

Widely voiced fears over the security of online transactions are being conquered and the wider choice and convenience of Web shopping is making itself felt.

An online survey of more than 6,000 Internet users for Lycos, the Internet hub company, found that 53 per cent had shopped online. The internetTrak survey believes 1.6 million Britons had made an online purchase within the last three months. More than three million people said they used the Web to gather information before making a purchase either on- or offline. While shopping remains a comparatively small part of overall Web use – with most individual purchases for less than £100 – those who take the plunge into e-commerce quickly get the habit. The internetTrak survey found that Web buyers had spent an average of £1,356 each in the past six months.

Computer goods, software and hardware are the main Web purchases, bought by 43 per cent and 37 per cent of users respectively, says internetTrak. Books (23 per cent) and CDs (17 per cent) are rapidly gaining ground, as the Lycos survey also found.

It does not take users long to realise that they can find a book or a CD much quicker by clicking on a few search boxes on a retail site than they can by scouring the shelves in shops. What's more, the search is quite likely to give them a result even if they can only half remember the title or the author's name.

Another great growth area for e-commerce is the travel business. Lycos found that 43 per cent of users had booked airline tickets through the Net, while 35 per cent had made travel-related transactions such as hiring cars or booking hotels.

Surprisingly, about 20 per cent of respondents to both polls had either bought or looked at clothes on the Net. It's hardly the place to try things on, so this must be a tribute to the virtual-reality models used on some retail sites. Another unexpected result in the Lycos poll was that 43 per cent of users had sought information about cars on the Net, one way of getting round the legendary distrust of the car salesman.

Microsoft's *Computer Age Report* has extraordinary statistics about families and computers. The over-60s spend most time at the keyboard, about ten hours a week rather than the average seven hours; these 'silver surfers' are more likely to regard the computer as a main topic of conversation.

But the more you earn, the more time you are likely to spend at the PC, 11 hours a week for those who earn £30,000 plus, possibly because they bring work home. The UK has 7 million Internet users – a figure that is growing at a rate of 1 million every six months. Europe has nearly 100 million Internet users and the United States has the same number again.

The surveys quoted were carried out as follows:

● For the internetTrak report, NOP held telephone interviews with 9,026 people in France, Germany and the UK on behalf of Yahoo!, the Internet media company, Dell computers and Ziff-Davis, the publishers.

- The Lycos survey was carried out through online and e-mail questionnaires by Milward Brown International, the market researchers, and is based on 6,000 responses.
- The Microsoft *Computer Age Report* is based on telephone interviews by Opinion Research International as part of a two-year study into 500 computer-owning households in London, Manchester, Glasgow, Newcastle and Birmingham.

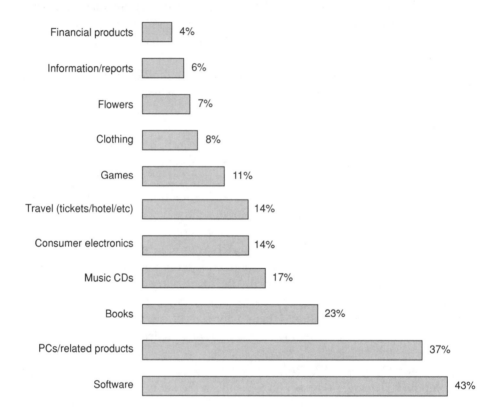

Figure 1.2.2 Products purchased online

There are the quite well-known demographic and social changes going on that are neglected by business. Examples are the 'greying' of the population and reduction in school-leavers; the growing concern about protecting the environment – how are these issues likely to affect your business? (See also Chapter 5.) More importantly, how can they be seen as major opportunities to grow your business?

Body Shop

Body Shop grew not just by providing, 'supplied to measure' quantities of natural beauty products, in returnable containers, but increasingly by the identification of the public with founder Anita Roddick's care for 'green' issues. Visits to the Amazon, that were well publicised but made through genuine concern, emphasised the group's claim to be protective of the environment and supported its affirmation that its products are natural. In-store promotions, emphasising protection of endangered animals, clearly appealed to Body Shop customers.

Companies ignore such concerns at their peril. But the response must be genuine and of practical value. One car wash company promoted its environmental concern by stating it used 'recycled water'. As all water is 'recycled' in our closed planetary system, this might not appear a genuine advance. As Mr Clean publicly explained in ads, however, 'Drought notices enforced by a number of local water companies have excluded car washes that use "recycled" water!'. Environmental concern and efficiency clearly work hand in hand in this case.

You should now be ready to answer the questions in Checklist 1 of Assignment 2.

Assignment 2

Checklist 1: the business environment (opportunities and threats)

1. In what ways will forecast changes in the general levels of national economic activity affect your business over the next one to three years?
2. Will changes in your local economy affect your business?
3. Will changes brought about in the European Common Market (for example, the Euro, or social changes) have implications for your business?
4. Have British Standards, European law and any other legal requirements which could relate either to your existing or planned product range been considered?
5. Are there any other changes in legislation that will affect your business, such as consumer law, health and safety or employee protection regulations?
6. Are there any significant changes in technology in your industry that could affect the way you or your competitors will do business in the future?
7. How will demographic changes affect your business?
8. Are there any social trends, such as growing environmental awareness or animal rights issues, that have implications for your business?

9. How are you taking advantage of falling prices in communication and computing to use the Internet to improve your business?

Businesses develop by painstaking attention to the needs of their customers. Seeing your business through the customers' eyes means realising that, say, customers want good pictures not good cameras; benefits to the customer must dictate the features of the product. Kenichi Ohmae of McKinsey provides a good example of this thinking:

> A Japanese home appliance company was developing a new coffee percolator. Should it be redesigned to match General Electric's or Philips'? The question changed to why do people drink coffee? Good taste was the answer. Lots of things affect taste: the beans, the temperature, the water. Of all factors, water quality made the greatest difference. The engineer's attention was redirected to providing features of a built-in dechlorinating function and a built-in coffee grinder. All the customer needed to do was to pour in water and beans; the machine did the rest. (Ohmae, 1988)

In this example, the product engineers were not responding to competitive products, but to the essential customer needs. You must, therefore, regularly step back and ask what the customers' inherent needs are, to determine what the product is really about. Personal attention to clients' needs is always rated number one in any survey of key competitive advantage (ie considered even more important than quality and price). Perrier saw its US customers adding lemon and orange squeezes to its mineral water; so the company introduced a new product with built-in flavours – and increased price! Reckitt and Colman saw customers making their own mustard by adding vinegar to dry mustard powder; the company mastered the process and the market by providing customers with what they really wanted, ready-mixed mustard. McDonalds decided that its core customer value was to never let customers wait in line for more than a couple of minutes and organised its service accordingly.

Constantly asking the question 'Why do people buy from us?' as your company develops is essential. You need to know whether the purchase decision is rational or emotional, planned or made on impulse. It helps to know how your performance compares with competitors' in order to decide and prioritise features of your products and services. With this customer focus, you will be making what you can *sell*, rather than selling what you can *make*.

One useful distinction to make in customer analysis is the difference between customers and consumers. Children may be the ultimate consumers for toys, but the buying decision may be made by the parent whose 'needs' might include product features such as 'safety' – quite different from the ultimate consumer's view! Close attention to the 'buying decision' will help focus much of your marketing effort.

Autoglass

Autoglass started in the early 1970s to provide a nationwide windscreen replacement service. Reaching thousands of customers who had to make quick decisions following an accident seemed an impossible marketing task, however strong the company's depot coverage. Payment for the broken windscreen, however, was in most cases covered by comprehensive insurance policies. By approaching individual insurance companies and meeting their needs (with guaranteed prices for guaranteed work) a manageable process of assisting drivers (needing instant replacement, on credit) could be developed, with recommendation slips included with annual insurance reminders suggesting drivers contact Autoglass in emergencies.

The needs of the ultimate consumer and of customers linked in the buying process (including retailers, and wholesalers in the distribution chain) have, therefore, all to be regularly reviewed. Finally, and self-evidently, remember that customers change! Alan Melkman (1979) has provided a useful framework for classifying your existing customers (see Table 1.2.1). It may be a stimulus to action to broadly categorise your major customers by these stages. Clearly, relaunching the relationship by revisiting and re-analysing customer needs in the wedlock and deadlock stages, before the otherwise inevitable loss of business to competitive suppliers, may be the quickest way to rekindle sales. Checking on why customers have not re-ordered, against the frequency of your visits and personal contacts is probably the other side of the same coin. Tracking and retaining customers acquired expensively on the Internet is even more vital for long-term profitability and should be easier to do as the Internet can provide rich data on customer behaviour.

Table 1.2.1 Customer dynamics

Stage / Objective	Courtship	Engagement	Honeymoon	Wedlock	Deadlock
Customer attitude	Suspicious	Moderately suspicious	Trusting	Bored	Disenchanted
Supplier objective	Get first order	Get repeat order	Increase sales volume	Maintain sales	Sell in new products

Building on your customer analysis, by grouping customers who exhibit the same broad characteristics, you can construct market segments which, when combined, will make up your total market. Market segments can be constructed principally from:

Who buys: customers can be grouped by age, sex and education, by income and occupation (for example a company might state '20 per cent of female office workers in the Victoria area now buy our bagels').

What is sold; analysis of physical product sales by volume, price, outlet (for example the company might state 'hot-melt bagels represent 30 per cent of our Victoria depot sales, compared with 15 per cent in City depot sales').

The purpose of market segmentation is to provide a means of measuring your sales achievement, as well as a stimulus to further marketing thought and action to improve performance. By knowing, for example, that you have only achieved a 20 per cent penetration of office workers in the Victoria area, your marketing promotion activities can be fruitfully focused to improve this rate. Segments, therefore, have to be measurable (through desk research on published information, or field research amongst suppliers and customers) and reachable (to help you decide where to locate and how to advertise). Most importantly, regular information can be gathered to monitor whether your market segments are growing or declining.

Autoglass found it difficult at the outset to calculate the size of the UK replacement windscreen market; figures on the total UK car population were, however, regularly published, showing a steady 3 per cent per annum growth. Windscreen manufacturers agreed that the replacement rate on toughened windscreens was approximately 3.5 per cent per annum, slightly higher on laminated windscreens. Combining the replacement rate and car population gave a replacement market of half a million windscreens, growing at above 3 per cent per annum as laminated windscreens were introduced. The market could be segmented by product (laminated and toughened windscreens) and geography (Department of Transport figures on motor mileage by standard region), as well as by customer grouping (commercial fleet owners, company cars, insurance companies for private cars) giving Autoglass definable market groups and measurable market shares for focused marketing activity.

Having achieved targeted market shares in windscreen product and customer groupings over 10 years, by a programme of new depots, building relations with commercial fleet owners, insurance groups and so on, Autoglass was subsequently able to expand its market by opening new segments (replacement sun-roofs and side windows) and geographical expansion (European acquisitions).

Estimating the size of your markets, through contact with manufacturers, industry associations, published government statistics on the economy and industry sectors, and being aware of the trends in market segments, provide an indispensable framework for your major business decisions. Your products and services can then be planned properly.

AccorGroup

The French AccorGroup saw growth in four key sectors and designed its hotels and prices accordingly:

Sofitel Hotels, for city centre luxury and business-conference market.

Novotel, 3-star hotels close to airports and stations for travelling businessmen.

Ibis, 2-star hotels in city centres for families and package tourists.

Formula One, basic accommodation with shared facilities and low prices, close to motorways, for travelling families.

Keeping in touch with your customers and markets, and enlisting the help of your customers to run your business, requires careful thought and systems. Restaurants that invite customer suggestions through contact addresses on the menus and deal quickly with complaints; invoices that require sales personnel to ask customers how they heard of the service; retailers who organise customer discussion panels – all of these are practical methods to ensure that customer satisfaction is at the centre of your business.

Choc Express (www.chocexpress.com)

Choc Express, offering luxury chocolate gifts via direct mail order and the Web, boosted sales by creating a 'Chocolate Tasting Club' amongst its mainly AB1 female buyers. Club members received a monthly box of different chocolate mixes, which they were asked to score. Mixes could then be varied to respond to individual taste and preference, and Choc Express saw its average order size increase from £12 to £40, helped by extending the practice and inviting all customers to select their preferred chocolates online and vote for them.

Assignment 3

Checklist 2: customers/markets (opportunities and threats)

1. What proportion of your sales do your five largest customers take up?
2. Do you know why your customers buy from you?
3. Can you distinguish between consumers and customers for your business and identify their individual needs? List the needs of consumers and customers separately.
4. Can you classify your major customers under the following categories? – courtship; engagement; honeymoon; wedlock; deadlock.
5. List your major customers by how often you speak and visit them – daily; once a week; once a month; less often than once a month.
6. Have you been able to use the Internet to gain further information on your customers' buying behaviour?
7. How many customers did you lose last year? Name them and state why they stopped buying from you.
8. Have you segmented the market for your products and services? Do you know the size of each segment and your percentage share?
9. Which segment of the market did you enter first?
10. What market segments are still open to you to exploit?
11. What are the growth prospects for each of these segments and what is the size and annual average growth rate of your total market?
12. What methods and systems do you use to measure and keep in contact with your customers and markets?

The starting point for competitor analysis is simply to identify those major competitors you admire or fear the most and which you intend to monitor on a regular basis.

Coldshield Windows

Coldshield Windows identified Everest and Anglian Windows as the likely long-term leaders in the double-glazing market. Although limited companies, their individual published accounts could not be separated from their controlling groups; their colour supplement advertisements and promotional activities, however, could be studied regularly. The Coldshield salesmen were asked to compare pricing and selling terms, particularly when attending trade exhibitions. Coldshield's advertising agency subscribed to MEAL data analysis giving monthly estimates of competitive advertising expenditures.

The objective of competitive analysis is to try to understand in detail how your competitors' products and services satisfy customer needs. A developer of private residential nursing homes, for example, knew that customers' confidence in choosing a home was built on: the number of qualified nursing staff provided; the availability of separate single rooms; having purpose-built accommodation; offering value for money. Therefore, before each new nursing home was developed, a thorough survey of competitors in each area was undertaken, to help determine the features to be built into the new development (see Table 1.2.2 for the results of one such survey: Cranfield Working Papers, 1992). Learning in the process of the survey that each nursing home had a lengthy waiting list of customers for rooms encouraged the developer to go ahead and match some of the better facilities available.

The thoroughness with which Japanese companies have bought, broken down and analysed Western competitive products and subsequently built matching and, in terms of customer needs, superior products is well documented. The automotive industry, where product reliability was diagnosed as being needed more than chrome attachments, is a prime example. In the same way, by purchasing and analysing competitors' products and services, visiting exhibitions and studying advertisements, you should regularly compare your product offerings with those of competitors. Not all competitors are obvious: reduced market share may be the result, not of the activities of a direct brand rival, but of substitute product offerings.

Table 1.2.2 Competitor analysis: example comparing nursing homes

Name of Home	Mngt	Nurses	Beds	Single	Time	Building	Price per week	Prom
The Laurels	Owner	22	32	Y	1	PB	£370	N/A
Aldbourne Nursing Home	Mnger	29	N/A	Y	1	PB	£450	10
Ashbury Lodge	Mnger	26	18	Y	2	C	£390	7
Ashgrove House	Owner	23	N/A	N/A	2	N/A	N/A	N/A
Bethany House Nursing Home	Owner	16	N/A	N/A	4	N/A	N/A	N/A
Park View	Mnger	15	15	Y	1	PB	£360	6
Station Court	Mnger	32	N/A	Y	2	PB	£400	10
Weymuss Lodge	Mnger	9	27	Y	2	PB	£375	6
Southdown	Mnger	10	14	N	1	C	£360	%
Total		**182**	**106**					

KEY: Mngr = Manager or owner manager
Mngt = Type of management
Single = Single rooms (yes or no)
Time = How long since registration (years)

Building = Type of building (purpose built or conversion)
PB = Purpose built
C = Conversion
Prom = Promotion (rating of quality)

The purpose behind the analysis is to understand thoroughly the key factors for success in your industry. Are competitors successful as a result of features of their product or their after-sales service? Is company image more important than payment terms? Professor Michael Porter sees competitive analysis as the way to make yourself different from your competitors (Porter, 1981). By identifying a competitor's strengths and weaknesses, understanding its position in your industry (as price-leader or price-cutter), what its goals are and how it might retaliate to your offerings, you gain knowledge of what you are competing with – making an important contribution to the marketing strategy you pursue.

Perrier

Perrier had built a 50 per cent market share in the UK bottled mineral water market over a period of 10 years, using a humorous poster campaign (featuring the slogan 'Eau-la-la!') to change a sleepy market sector into a vibrant one. Realising the importance of image to its health-conscious customers, Perrier had no hesitation in withdrawing all supplies from the market following a benzene scare at its bottling plant, prior to relaunching with new factory production. Realising also the difficulty of building further market share in the face of numerous new competitive British bottled waters, Perrier widened its competitive strategy by purchasing Buxton Mineral Waters. Through this purchase Perrier challenged domestic producers and reached parts of the market previously denied to it on chauvinistic grounds.

As the above example shows, competitors, like customers, also change all the time; hence the need for constant review. So how do you regularly keep track of your present and potential competitors? As noted in some of the examples above, buy and analyse their products and services, study their Web sites, visit trade exhibitions, work with them, in trade associations, in pursuit of higher trade standards. This may not only serve the customers' needs better, but, by raising standards, build barriers to entry to new competitors in your market. The Glass and Glazing Trade Association, for instance, in addition to serving customers' needs by requiring members to adhere to strict British standards in terms of materials, workmanship and insurance, only allows new members to join and use the GGF symbol after two years' successful trading – quite a long time for some double-glazing companies! Stew Leonard, of the famous In Search of Excellence store in New England actually organises staff visits, by specially ordered buses, to major competitor openings! Food for thought for you?

Please remember, as you complete these checks, never to knowingly underestimate your competitors. General Motors underestimated the Japanese motor industry's ability to produce quality cars. Make new mistakes in finding out about your customers and competitors, but do not repeat old mistakes like this!

Assignment 4

Checklist 3: competitors (opportunities and threats)

1. Who are your principal direct and indirect competitors?
2. What do you know about their sales growth, profitability, selling methods and so on? Could you rank them in order of success?
3. How do your major competitor's products and services satisfy customer needs?
4. Write down how your product or service compares with the competition with respect to:
   - price;
   - performance;
   - packaging;
   - safety;
   - reliability;
   - durability;
   - quality;
   - delivery;
   - after-sales service/maintenance;
   - guarantees;
   - promotion/advertising;
   - image;
   - interactive Web site;
   - payment terms.
5. So what exactly do you think makes your successful competitors successful?
6. What do you see as your main competitor's principal weaknesses?
7. Do you anticipate any new competitors coming into your market in the near future?
8. What barriers to entry exist, or could be erected, to prevent competitors entering your markets?
9. What changes have your major competitors made in the last 12 months in their competitive approaches?
10. How are you regularly tracking major competitors' activities?

3   *Strengths and weaknesses*

Analysis of the external market should have provided a summary of the constantly changing opportunities and threats facing your business; analysis of your own company's internal strengths and weaknesses should summarise your ability to take advantage of, or at least to cope with, this environment. This analysis should be made under four headings:

- products and services;
- pricing and distribution;
- advertising and promotion;
- sales and sales management.

Through analysis of each of these you should take stock of how your business originally matched up to, and how it currently matches up to, the marketing environment.

Products and services

There are no such things as pure products or pure services; each product has a service element and each service a product element. In an increasingly competitive world the way in which some products are differentiated from each other, which is how your company initially succeeded, may be in their service terms.

Philips

Philips' Whirlpool white goods are strictly comparable to competitors' products. Philips, however, provide distinctive service terms for customers and retailers. Customers, therefore, are allowed to replace any machine in the first 12 months which cannot be repaired; all parts are guaranteed for 10 years. Additionally, Philips provide a 24-hour call care line for customers and will pay £12.50 if its repair engineers do not arrive within 2 days of a call. All retailers are provided with dealer support for advertising and finance for display stock and inventory, together with extended payment terms.

Service businesses can be more difficult to differentiate, because services, being intangible, are often seen as a commodity and are certainly difficult to taste or test in advance! The customers even play a role in determining the quality and delivery of a service: in an English restaurant a complaint can lead at best to an improvement or, at worst, a complete withdrawal of service! Marketing a service, therefore, requires strong, consistent branding. The company name is frequently the brand (for example, 'I'm with the Woolwich'); making the company name synonymous with good quality is making the service more tangible. Your company name and reputation may be the only difference between you and your competitors.

Being able to protect your company name and brand names and to communicate properly are, therefore, important aspects in marketing your product or service. Wally Olins of Wolff Olins, the corporate design specialists, has described the three main ways companies communicate their identity:

> Many small as well as major companies have a monolithic identity; IBM uses its company name on all its products, so that if it opened a supermarket it would be called IBM Stores. General Motors, on the other hand, use an endorsed identity, whereby the group company name is used to reinforce local brand names: Vauxhall in England is promoted as being 'part of General Motors'. Finally, with branded identity, the name of the owning company is invisible, so that, eg until recently, Pearson's name was not used in the marketplace to add support to *The Financial Times* or *The Economist*. Brand names as strong as these may not need extra support. (Olins, 1989)

The early growth company probably follows the IBM example, so it is important to ensure that not only are your products patented, if this can be achieved (for example as Pilkington did with float glass) but also that your company name, brand names, and Web site domain names are given trademark protection. (Trademarks protect 'what something's called'.) Common law can then be used to prevent competitors from passing off similar goods and services trading on your product's reputation. Imitation may be the sincerest form of flattery, but it can be harmful to growth, particularly for a single product or service company. By protecting your product or name, you may be able to effectively prolong the natural life cycle of your product or service.

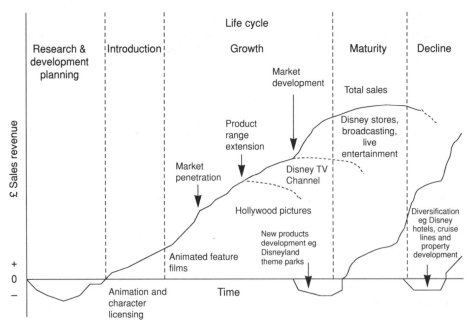

Figure 1.3.1 Product market strategy and the product life cycle

Knowing approximately in which stage of the life cycle your product or service is located is important, both in terms of your promotional plans (which may be to sustain launch in early growth stages by making people aware; or to prolong life in a mature, competitive market) and your strategic need to develop or acquire new, replacement products, as Figure 1.3.1 illustrates in Disney's evolution.

As the dotted curves in Figure 1.3.1 indicate, sales would naturally mature or decline without the new product or market segment initiatives. The more your company name or reputation is known, the longer it may take to carefully test the market and research each new line addition, although acquisition can probably speed sales results.

For many products and services, product life cycles have been shortening under the impact of technology and speedier communications: it took 25 years for sales of mechanical typewriters to fall below sales of electromechanical ones; then 15 years for electromechanical models to give way to electric ones. Within 7 years electric models had been overtaken by micro-processor controlled machines. In turn, home computers with printers now dominate the role once filled by typewriters.

Yet some products with good brand names and promotional support seem to last forever; witness the ongoing success of Oxo cubes and the 'Oxo family'.

Keeping your products and services fresh and alive, where technology permits and points the way, requires regular assessment on your part of the *features* built into your offerings (often inspired by your customer and competitor analysis) and the corresponding *benefits* derived by the customers from these elements. The process is outlined in Table 1.3.1.

Table 1.3.1 Product features and corresponding customer benefits

Your product **features**	What **benefits** do these **features** bring to customers	Customer **benefits**	Benefits become product/service **promises** to promote to **customers**
Size Colour Weight Taste Feel Smell Other	Ask the question: 'What does it mean to me?'	Saves me time, money. Keeps me warm. Makes me feel better, etc.	Save money, buy now! Sleep easier. Pay less taxes

In the double-glazing industry, for example, manufacturers have worked hard to introduce Low-E coated glass, giving two pieces of glass the power of triple glazing. This permits salespeople to promote extra customer benefits in terms of saving money via lower heating bills and noise reduction by better sound insulation. Building in extra features (which for services might include staff training, or accurate recording of complaints) may well, like identifying new market segments, enable you to prolong your product or service life cycle by helping to keep your company different from the competition.

Declining product or service profitability is probably one of the tell-tale signs of life cycle maturity, as increasing competition or shrinking markets puts pressure on margins. Monitoring product profitability can be an important life cycle guide; yet market maturity may not be the problem if product or service quality has deteriorated after the early pioneering launch days. Visible and measurable signs of poor quality are easy to detect; they include errors, missed deadlines and warranty costs. Not so visible, but equally important signs include customer dissatisfaction, complaints and poor employee morale. Developing systems to monitor these less measurable indicators is important to enable you to spend more time on prevention (education and training) than the more costly problems of dealing with product or service failure (such as rework, repeat calls).

Carphone Warehouse

Charles Dunstone started the Carphone Warehouse from his flat in Harley Street with savings of £6,000. Current sales are £700 million with profits of £40 million, with 800 outlets in 14 countries. Carphone's success owes much to Dunstone's first rule for the company 'If we don't look after our customer, someone else will'. Carphone sends a questionnaire to every new purchaser about services received. It receives 4,000 replies a month; 96 per cent of customers agree that they would recommend Carphone Warehouse to a friend. Mystery shoppers visit every store, every month, with the store manager's salary tied to a satisfactory result. 95 per cent of all incoming telephone calls are answered instantly; all e-mails are replied to within one hour. Carphone's Web site only accounts for 2 per cent of sales direct, but has reduced queuing time in store through pre-education of customers with its catalogue browsing facility.

Monitoring and measuring company performance, therefore, can help you keep your offerings better and different. A McKinsey survey has shown that 'companies lose two-thirds of their customers not because of product or price dissatisfaction, but simply through indifference to customer complaints. Well over 80 per cent of customers would repurchase if their complaints were quickly resolved' (McKinsey, 1990).

As recent Harvard Business School research has shown, retaining and satisfying existing customers, by dealing quickly and efficiently with customer complaints, just as retaining and satisfying existing employees, by measuring and rewarding reliability, are the keys to achieving 'breakthrough service and profits' (Jones and Sasser, 1995).

Assignment 5

Checklist 4: products and services (strengths and weaknesses)

1. Is your business still dependent on one product or service for over 80 per cent of profits?
2. Are your products and brand names protected (or able to be protected) through patents, copyright and the like?
3. Do you have a strong company name, brand name and slogan which works for your company and your customers?
4. How easy are your products or services to copy?
5. What proportion of your product or service range is in each phase of the life cycle?

6. When did you last launch a new product? Is developing and launching new products one of your business strengths?
7. How long did it take to succeed from 'concept to test market' and from 'test market to final customer'?
8. Do your product or service benefits match customers' needs or are there gaps? List your product features and benefits and compare them to customer needs.
9. How accurately can you assess the *profitability* of individual products (or groups of products as well as groups of customers)?
10. How do you measure customer satisfaction with the quality of your products and services?

Pricing and distribution

The product, promotion and distribution aspects of your business can all be justified as creating value for the customer. But pricing, as Tom Nagle of Boston University has observed, is the time 'when you grab a chunk of that value and put it in your own pocket. It's a company's moment of self-interest and it cannot be portrayed as service to the customer'. It is also the biggest decision your company has to make and to keep constantly under review – and the one that has the biggest impact on company profitability.

In a new, or existing business, undertake the favourite consultant's exercise of computing and comparing the impact on profits of a 5 per cent cut in your overheads, a 5 per cent increase in volume sales, a 5 per cent cut in materials purchased and a 5 per cent price increase. All these actions are usually considered to be within a manager's normal reach. Almost invariably, the 5 per cent price increase scores highest, as it passes straight to the net profit, bottom line. Even if volume falls, because of the effect price has on gross margin, it is usually more profitable to sell fewer items at a higher price; for example, at a constant gross margin of 30 per cent, with a 5 per cent increase, profits would be unchanged even if sales declined 14 per cent. Yet if prices were cut 5 per cent, an extra 20 per cent increase in sales would be needed to stand still.

Deciding what is a fair price is a problem that has taxed economic humankind ever since money was invented in the 5th century BC. It has been difficult because most useful items have a low value in exchange, such as water (before the advent of designer mineral water), while the least useful items, such as silk, have a high value in exchange. Value, like beauty, is often in the eye of the beholder; but this degree of subjectivity means that companies have a great deal of discretion in the area of pricing. A good quality product, priced too low, often does not have its quality recognised. There is a strong belief in the link between price and quality – you get what you pay for – with the Japanese probably equating price with quality more than any other national group. When Brown-Forman, the distillers, tried to boost Jack Daniel's sales in Japan by reducing the price of its premium brand, sales fell. On the other hand, how do you justify £50 for an ordinary bottle of champagne in a nightclub?

Economists offer conflicting advice, from charging what the market will bear (hence the price of nightclub champagne) through marginal cost (what you pay for the last or least wanted item), to where your supply and demand curves intersect. Few growing companies are able to accurately draw their supply and demand curves, so, according to business magazines, over 80 per cent of UK companies price by reference to their costs, either using cost plus (which is materials plus a percentage, perhaps 50 per cent) or a cost multiplier (eg 3 times material costs).

While it is important to know your product or service costs, and to be seeking through supply chain management to control or even reduce them, perhaps using the Internet to compare and reduce supplier costs, thereby boosting margins, this is only one element in the pricing decision. You have clearly, in addition, to take into account the marketplace (particularly your competitors); the way you are positioning the product (for example as a luxury item, with strong branding for wealthy customers); and the life cycle stage of your product or market.

Mark Sanders, in designing and launching his innovative folding bicycle, the Strida, into the 100-year-old bicycle market recognised that: his manufacturer's capacity was strictly limited; and his target was well-to-do city commuters or lifestyle weekenders.

An initial price of nearly £200 per model was well above established competitive models, but gave good margins to dealers in taking up the product and left room for manoeuvre later in the product life cycle when competition would react to the Strida's unusual features. Mark's initial skimming price strategy could then be replaced by a penetration strategy, aimed at building market share.

Frequently, resistance to increasing prices, even in the face of inflationary cost rises, can come from your own team members, eager to blame price for performance lapses. In these instances it is important to make detailed price comparisons with competitors, using a scoring scheme such as the one in Table 1.3.2. Such an analysis should help you either to improve your product or service, or to justify your pricing stance, or at least to calm 'in-house' nerves to show that your prices are justified.

In Autoglass Ltd, the sternest critics of improved prices were a number of front-line depot managers, who feared their own bonus-related sales targets would be made impossible to achieve. Competitive analysis showed the company to be providing a unique 24-hour call-out service, on a nationwide basis, and gave the initially reluctant managers arguments to justify the increases to fleet customers.

Table 1.3.2   Pricing comparison with competitors

	Worse −3 −2 −1	Same 0	Better +1 +2 +3
Product attributes			
Design			
Performance			
Packaging			
Presentation/appearance			
After-sales service			
Availability			
Delivery			
Colour/flavour/odour/touch			
Image			
Specification			
Payment terms			
Others, eg Web site			

Pricing and distribution channels you operate are clearly closely related, particularly in terms of the trade or quantity discount structure you will need to ensure your products or services are adequately represented in the marketplace. Managers all too readily blame prices for poor performance when in fact poor distribution may be the reason for low market share.

When Saturday Comes

Dan Duncan, MD of the fast-growing football magazine *When Saturday Comes* had been delighted when a specialist distributor had agreed to deliver the magazine to newsagents throughout the South-East UK. Previously sales had been organised by an army of volunteers on Saturday afternoons outside football grounds. As sales climbed, however, and as major retail outlets such as John Menzies agreed to handle the magazine, Dan reluctantly realised the excellent regional distributor would have to be replaced by a major national distributor.

If your product could potentially achieve a 50 per cent market share, but it only reaches 25 per cent of the market where only 50 per cent of the public will buy it, it is not surprising that your maximum market share is only 6 per cent. No amount of extra promotional expenditure or price changes can alter the result.

Bridgewater

Compared to setting up a retail or distribution deal with a third party, the Internet provides an easy way for a company to gain new distribution channels both in the home market and abroad. For Bridgewater, an exclusive pottery firm employing over 80 people in three UK locations, it is the ultimate form of direct selling.

On Bridgewater's Web site customers can push a virtual shopping trolley around a virtual china shop, picking the pieces they want and paying for them at a virtual checkout.

The main benefits of the Internet distribution channel is that it is worldwide and is 24 hour. In that way the company is reaching customers they could never reach any other way. Emma Bridgewater, the 34-year-old mother of three who founded the company, is open about her goals: 'World domination, without moving from Stoke-on-Trent'. But she confesses personally to have little time for computers. They drive her mad, but she does see how they can help her achieve her goal.

Equally, the way in which you distribute your products may be as significant as the products themselves.

Telford-based TWS, a window systems manufacturer, faced with static sales, commissioned a customer survey on the merits of its German window profile system. The major surprise of the survey was to discover that 80 per cent of actual and potential TWS customers did not have fork-lift trucks, the result being all deliveries had to be handled off, depriving the fabricating customer of 'window-making' time. The solution was to commission the production of a new delivery vehicle, complete with its own fork lift. 'Now it just takes 15 minutes instead of two hours to unload two stillages and we don't use the fabricator's manpower', explained the MD of TWS.

The beneficial impact on TWS sales by this improved delivery service is easily imagined! Even *how* you collect may also be a way of differentiating your business; Glen Fayolle, MD of Paper Safe, a security paper-shredding company, grew his customer base by supplying them with special plastic containers, designed to take valuable grade (to paper merchants) computer print-out paper.

Whether or not to invest in property, rather than in the working assets of your business, is often a painful decision for businesses in securing adequate distribution for products and services. The situation is aggravated in the UK where long leaseholds on property are common (20–25 years), compared with very short but renewable leases, for example, in Asia-Pacific (where 2-year leases are normal). The apparently low UK annual lease rent disguises the unbreakable capital commitment to payments over 25 years. Increasingly, prudent businessmen baulk at investment in 'safe' property, when money can be better invested in stock, which can perhaps be guaranteed to be turned over say five times per annum and earn 20 per cent each time. Businesses 'protected' by freehold property from the market environment may, in turn, not adapt in time to the challenges of that changing market place.

The arrival of e-tailing further aggravates this situation; one US textbook forecasts that 'European retailing is digging its own grave by constantly increasing selling space. Physical infrastructure can be deadweight. You can make the shopping experience much more interesting on the Internet than in shops' (Birch, Gorbert and Schneider, 2000). As the cost of developing and maintaining interactive Web sites often runs to six figures, many growing businesses are now facing this dilemma.

Finally, monitoring your own company's (and competitors') product or service availability, clearly requires frequent visits, inspection and interrogation of distributors and customers alike. Sometimes the results, as for TWS above, can be surprising.

Andrew Purves was offered the opportunity to double his floorspace to 20,000 sq ft by relocating to a newly developed site, opposite his store in Tottenham Court Road. He estimated he would need an extra £1 million finance loan to equip, stock and finance the extra sales from the larger display areas. The Purves & Purves Web site was not 'interactive' and would require significant extra investment as well, as he realised that even furniture was now being widely sold over the Net in the United States. Andrew decided to relocate, but also planned to control future space need by developing his Web presence accordingly.

Assignment 6

Checklist 5: pricing and distribution (strengths and weaknesses)

1. What would be the effect on your profits of a 5 per cent increase or 5 per cent decrease in your major product/service price?
2. What formula do you use to decide your prices?
3. Do you use different prices for a product/service depending on its life cycle? Give examples.
4. How do your prices compare with your major competitors'?
5. When did you last increase your prices and by what percentage?
6. How do you monitor your own and competitors' prices?
7. What discount structure do you offer to volume customers or middlemen?
8. Describe the distribution chain between you and the customer.
9. What property investment have you made to ensure easy availability to the customer of your goods and services?
10. Do your customers and target market segments have easy access to your goods and services? How do you monitor this?

Advertising and promotion

Advertising

The economist J K Galbraith has commented on the power of advertising: 'In great measure, wants are now shaped by advertising... the individual product or service has little consequence' (Galbraith, 1975). Good advertising and promotion is a powerful way to differentiate products and services; advertising, frequently known as *above the line* expenditure, is, as Saatchi and Saatchi's Tim Bell has noted 'an expensive way for one person to talk to another'. It is about communicating effectively with your target customers. Promotions, be they press releases, exhibition brochures or discount items, are frequently called *below the line* expenditure, as they are often not so visible as press and TV advertising. Both are expensive and aim to create a favourable image for your company.

Doing business without advertising, it has been said, 'is like winking at a person in the dark. You know what you are doing but no one else does!' The most cost-effective advertising for your company is probably related to your main selling methods.

In the UK double-glazing market there are more than 2,000 separate companies aiming to secure business. In principle, the product installation and services offered by each of the companies are basically very similar; yet Everest gradually emerged as 'fitting the best' because this is what their TV commercials told us for a number of years. The commercials, frequently costing some 10–15 per cent of sales revenue, supported a large army of self-employed salespeople, many using cold-calling, door-to-door selling techniques, where recognition of company name and slogan facilitated their sales conversion efforts.

Yet major TV and newspaper expenditure of this sort is rarely within the financial capacity of most growing businesses and the benefits of such expenditure are frequently hard to quantify. The benefits of the huge advertising expenditure of companies recently privatised, such as BT and the gas and electricity suppliers, are difficult to assess considering their monopoly or near-monopoly positions.

Promotion

The growing business has to focus more precisely on how to reach target customers at lowest cost; working for the most part with relatively small, fixed sums of money rather than elastic 'percentage of sales' type allocations. Frequently, below the line promotional expenditure may be larger than above-the-line items, as personal calling efforts require brochures in the hand, or relatively expensive exhibition stands, and since informing and persuading customers for relatively young life cycle products takes precedence over reinforcing advertising which may be necessary for more mature products. Whatever is the situation for the company, delivering the most cost-effective advertising or promotional activity is vital.

Autoglass asked each customer, when paying bills in Autoglass depots, how they had heard of the company's service. A form beside each till recorded each of the company's promotional activities: depot sign, *Yellow Pages* advertisement, insurance company recommendation, press adverts etc. In early years, *Yellow Pages* reference was by far the highest, so the company sought representation in all regional *Yellow Pages*. Later, when insurance company recommendations increased, expenditure on *Yellow Pages* coverage could be dramatically reduced. Equally, later experimentation with local radio, TV and even its Web site could be monitored within days and weeks to judge its effectiveness.

In this way, Autoglass could not only judge the effectiveness of budgeted advertising expenditure, but could also ensure that specific planned increases would be likely to increase sales. Working with an advertising agency may also be easier, for both parties, if the mechanism is in place to judge the results of their efforts and recommendations. Agencies paid by media rebate (10–15 per cent discounts on advertising spend) will, not surprisingly, rarely recommend reductions in media expenditure, hence the need for accurate information on response rates (costs per lead, conversion rate per lead) to judge advertising and agency effectiveness. Nonetheless the achievements of an agency like Leo Burnett in turning a commodity (water) into a desirable designer product (Perrier), shows how the support of such agencies should not be underestimated.

Determining the most effective below-the-line promotional expenditure is just as important, given the higher expenditure most early growth companies are likely to have in this area. More money is actually spent on sales promotion techniques than on agency advertising. Yet both must work in harmony, as the objectives are the same: advertising campaigns are aimed at building long-term custom, while sales promotions are typically short-term activities to keep your company going. So, effective sales promotion can speed up stock movement, encourage repeat purchases, get bills paid on time, induce trial purchases. For example, your target customers may be the trade or even customers within your own organisation and you may be offering money (prizes, bonuses), goods (gifts, vouchers) or even services (free training, free services).

However, for the growing business, promotional opportunities that stimulate interest and awareness among new and existing purchasers, at lowest cost, are the most important. While discounting to move slow-moving lines may be necessary from time to time, the main positive promotional activities should include:

- ensuring all company small items are coordinated and effective (from business cards to Christmas cards);
- issuing regular press releases (public relations);
- participating in exhibitions (with new leaflets and brochures);
- experimenting with direct mail (databases) and telemarketing (direct response).

Business cards that are memorable (with perhaps a map on the back, for a hard-to-find restaurant) and commercial Christmas cards that are not blasphemous and help sales, may perhaps not seem worthy of a chief executive's attention, but they cost thousands of pounds and are perhaps the tip of the iceberg for your corporate identity programme. If they don't excite attention, perhaps your corporate communication package as a whole is unappealing.

What makes a good corporate Christmas card is highly subjective. The Midland Bank (now HSBC) spent more than £50,000 each year sending such cards; one year a new chief executive decided to suspend this activity and to donate a similar sum to a number of charities. A press release describing this decision, and the joy of recipients, was widely reported in all major newspapers, achieving much greater sympathetic visibility for the bank.

Recent research has also shown that 94 per cent of all press releases issued by companies are not printed. With UK editors receiving an average of 80–90 press releases per week, the rules that they must be newsworthy, topical, relevant, factual and informative, as well as free of 'puffy' jargon are not always being closely followed. The benefits of free publicity, however, should encourage companies to persevere and improve in this activity.

Paper-Safe, having been unsuccessful with press releases, approached Jamieson Farmer PR Ltd, who proposed that, as a large number of confidential waste disposal contracts are reviewed at year end, a product press release on the Paper-Safe disposal bins should be sent to 100 magazines for their November issue. The article was published in seven magazines, producing 41 sales leads.

Exhibitions

Exhibitions are not free. A tiny stand for four days in the Spring Gift Exhibition at Birmingham NEC will cost at least £1,500; for the Ideal Home Exhibition in Earls Court, you are looking at 10 times this amount. Lighting, display stands and manning costs will then more than double these costs. Yet similar outlays on newspaper advertisements are visible by customers for a few seconds on one day only, whereas with exhibitions you are at least guaranteed eye-to-eye contact with committed trade and retail buyers for as long as you can stimulate their interest. Because each exhibition is specific, both costs and sales benefits arising from it can be easily determined; each time you exhibit you have an opportunity to refocus your company by being forced to produce new exhibition leaflets, to rethink your personal selling messages and to re-listen to what your key customer groups tell you about your company!

Direct marketing

Finally, there are the exciting (or alarming) marketing media channels. Alarming for Europeans, who already believe we are deluged with junk mail, to discover that in the United States, 65 per cent of advertising expenditure is direct mailing (against 20 per cent in the UK) and, while UK citizens receive 29 direct mail items per annum, in the United States each person receives 300 items per annum. Is it worth it? Well, for the Post Office it is (representing a £7 billion market) and 62 per cent of UK recipients claimed to read their direct mail! Telemarketing is also growing rapidly, taking advantage of customer database lists provided by list brokers; so much so that 60 per cent of company purchasing managers receive a minimum of five calls a week. Again, is this effective?

Paper-Safe early sought the help of a telephone marketing company (UK Connect) to help launch their shredding service. In a Cranfield Working Paper, MD Glen Fayolle comments:

> We could have done the work ourselves, but they did it faster, contacting 270 companies in two weeks, where we could only contact a maximum of 10 companies per week. They encouraged two companies which were interested in our services immediately, and the cost was easily offset by the number of positive leads fed immediately to our salesmen.

Remember also that your Web site, which can give you international exposure, needs to be regularly promoted in all your promotional literature and efforts.

Choc Express gained 20 per cent of its turnover from Internet sales over a period of two years. The company's site address is included in all its mail-order catalogues, nine of which are issued per year, as well as in all company literature, mail and sample boxes. Potential customer databases are bought from other mail order firms similar to Choc Express. Postcards, featuring the company's products, Web site and e-mail address are then mailed to the new target audience. The purchasing decisions of this group, particularly those made by e-mail, are then recorded and monitored.

Assignment 7

Checklist 6: advertising and promotion (strengths and weaknesses)

1. Have you determined the most cost effective advertising media for your business?
2. Do you work with an advertising agency to plan your advertising/promotion activities? How is the agency remunerated? (Fixed fee or percentage media rebate?)
3. Do you budget annual sums or a percentage of sales for advertising and promotion? How much (£) per annum for advertising and how much (£) for below-the-line promotion?

4. What increase in sales spend do you expect to achieve for every extra pound spent on advertising?
5. What is your average cost per sales lead from advertising?
6. Which below-the-line promotional items create most business for you? Please describe.
7. Have you market-tested a new promotional method recently, internally (using your own staff) or externally?
8. When did you last issue a press release and with what effect?
9. Do you take part in exhibitions each year? If so, which and why?
10. Is direct mail, telemarketing or your Web site effective in securing new customers for you?

Sales and sales management

Personal selling is the vital link in the communications process between company and customer; every growing organisation has to have someone responsible for this important first or last step, depending on your point of view, activity. Traditionally, the sales manager and the salespeople are the personable, likeable, smiling faces of the organisation, the Mr Nice Guy in comparison with Mr Mean in Accounts! Mr Mean, being not very likeable, is usually efficient in order to survive; Mr Nice, on the other hand, being well liked, has to be motivated and very well directed if his efforts are not to be totally diffused. Professor McDonald of Cranfield University has noted:

> Among European salesforces, there is an alarming lack of planning and professionalism. Salespeople frequently have little idea of which products and which groups of customers to concentrate on, have too little knowledge about competitive activity, do not plan presentations well, rarely talk to customers in terms of benefits, make too little effort to close the sale and make many calls without any clear objective. Even worse, marketing management is rarely aware that this important and expensive element of the marketing mix is not being managed effectively. (McDonald, 1990)

Many studies have shown that if the average salesperson's salary is £18,000 per annum, the real cost to the company after travel, expenses and fringe benefits, is frequently double or even treble that, if sales support is added. At the same time, however, less than a third of the salesperson's working time is actually spent in front of the customer. Hence the need for responsible sales management able to:

● set and monitor sales target achievement;

- motivate, train and support the sales staff;
- recruit and organise competent staff.

Sales target setting, at the simplest level, may simply be in terms of ensuring minimum sales to recover the new salesperson's costs; for example, a minimum £75,000 extra sales, at 50 per cent gross margin, to recover the average salesperson's real cost. It may also be in terms of unit sales volume, mix of products or even numbers of target customers to convert. Monitoring of sales achievement may not be simply in terms of these quantitative targets (to which may be added number of sales calls per day, letters written, exhibitions organised etc), but also in terms of qualitative achievement in terms of work planning and time spent in front of customers (as shown in Figure 1.3.2).

Given such precise targets, the task of sales management in motivating and training sales personnel is made easier. Under-achievement may point to the need to evaluate salesforce call frequency and utilisation.

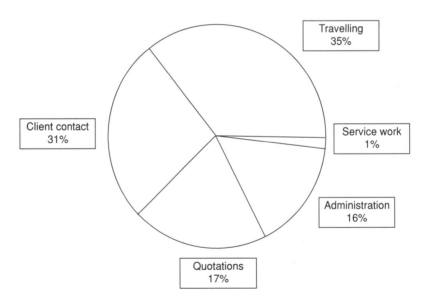

Figure 1.3.2   Analysis of salesforce time

JTM Business Consultants, in a customer survey, found that customers wanted the sales representative to call monthly, while their existing call pattern was fortnightly. This meant that salesforce time could be released to handle other work, such as new product introductions. Equally, another review found that the salesforce was calling on accounts too small to justify a call; it was decided to transfer small customers to the sales office and to use the telephone to make regular calls.

Sales targets should be mutually agreed between sales personnel and sales management, and motivation can be improved by judicious use of incentives. Analysts like David McClelland have shown that all individuals have goals and aspirations and, if their needs are met, they will work harder (McClelland, 1992). A remuneration plan, with bonus or commission related to performance, remains pre-eminent, however, and often needs to encourage teamwork as well as accomplishment of specific sales targets.

At specialist hi-fi chain Richer Sounds, branch managers get a cash bonus of 1 per cent of total profits and sales personnel get half of this. Employees are rewarded not just on the basis of sales but, as the quality of service is important, branches are also assessed monthly on numbers of customer complaints, how swiftly staff answered phones, punctuality and efficiency in maintaining stocks of popular lines. Richer's package of staff incentives also includes the use of a country house near York and the loan of the boss's Rolls-Royce for a month.

Excessively complicated bonus schemes should, however, be avoided. Quite often, providing the salesforce with information (eg sales by customer) and tools to make the selling task easier (from sales brochures to route planning) are as important as any incentives that can be created. Sales and product training need to be repeated regularly. In particular, businesses which pay a bonus of less than 10 per cent of basic salary might do better to spend their money on these aspects of salesforce relations.

Good and motivating compensation packages will clearly assist companies in recruiting and staffing the sales function. Consider carefully the number of sales staff required for: opening new accounts, showing new products, servicing existing customers for orders and chasing up debts. Many of these functions can be handled by mail or telephone (such as repeat orders and debts); the number of personal sales personnel will depend on workload involved in visiting, selling to and administering (eg using record cards) your customers. Increasingly, information technology can help to reduce this workload, such as customer ordering terminals, and switching in to supplier stocking displays. Supplying customer database information to sales personnel can also reduce their administrative tasks. These developments are important for the growing business, where competing with major companies for good salespeople is always difficult.

Finally, recruitment by the small growing business has traditionally been among family and friends, if for no other reason than these are likely to have been cheaper and keener than the all-too-expensive professional! Yet the informality of this process has to be generally replaced by more formal procedures (as we will see in Chapter 14 – with job descriptions, formal interviews, telephone checking on referees etc), particularly when one realises that one misfit could destroy a small business while doing relatively little harm to ICI. At the same time it is important to remember that technical skills are usually less important than the fit of new sales personnel in your organisation. It is no sin *not* to employ people you do not like, however expert. Remember, however, that there is a role, even in a sales team, for a Mr or Ms Nasty. Don't let your customers, however, always be referred to as debtors! You may need to ensure this is not happening by regularly visiting customers with your sales staff.

Assignment 8

Checklist 7: sales and sales management (strengths and weaknesses)

1. *Who* is responsible for achieving the company's sales targets?
2. What *targets* is each salesperson set and how are these arrived at? List the targets under two headings: quantitative targets; and qualitative targets.
3. What *incentive* is there for salespeople to achieve these targets?
4. What *support* does the salesforce have in terms of sales presentation, technical literature, back up?
5. What *information* on results does each salesperson receive?
6. Have salespeople undergone specific sales *training* – and if so, when?
7. *How many* sales staff, agents, etc, do you have and how are they organised? (By area? By products?)
8. How do you *recruit* your sales staff? Please describe the process.
9. What would happen to your sales if *either* you added an extra salesperson, *or* you lost one of your sales personnel?
10. When did you last go out with a salesperson (or wait on customers for a day)?

4

The financial position

There is a story told about a farmer in the Australian outback who entered a famous three day race. All the other runners were 'professionals' with coaches and support teams. He was alone. He won the race in just over two days, coming in almost 24 hours ahead of the second-fastest runner.

When questioned as to his success, it transpired that all the other runners had made a number of two-hour stops. These stops were generally accepted by the experts as being essential if the runners were to last the course. As no one had told the farmer about the stops he just kept running.

The next year when the race was run again, all the runners came in with times closer to two days than the three days that had been the norm until the farmer showed the way.

This story has a message about 'benchmarking,' which itself can be seen as the art of analysing your own performance and comparing it with best practice.

The benchmarking centrepiece of nearly all position audits on business organisations is an appraisal of the profit-and-loss account, the balance sheet and the derived ratios. The case for it is simple. Typically, the figures are readily available and they are comparatively easy to handle. Identical questions can be put to a variety of firms and the precision conveyed by a numerical answer assists interpretation and comparison. Here, if anywhere, management could become a science.

By contrast the non-quantitative information gathered using the checklists provided in earlier chapters is much more difficult and time-consuming to obtain. The questions are less obvious, many may or may not apply to a particular organisation, they are liable to be misunderstood and they rely on at least a measure of subjective interpretation. As a result there is a tendency to concentrate on statistics and ratios, and to assume that these alone are the position audit. But ratios, while providing a good backdrop, are by no means the whole picture, as the example below illustrates.

Virgin

Financial figures are not always easy to come by

The first thing that strikes anyone interested in Sir Richard Branson's empire is its sheer complexity. It is hard to get up-to-date financial information about his businesses. They are not neatly held in a consolidated group, but are in a clutch of offshore trusts in the Channel Islands and Virgin holding companies in the British Virgin Islands, where there is no obligation to publish accounts.

Over the past few years Branson has converted the equity capital of several of the British holding companies into 'bearer shares,' an unusual form in which there are no registered shareholders. One consequence is that it is impossible for outsiders to know if the firm has minority shareholders, or who they are.

Virgin explains that there is nothing sinister in these arrangements. Its directors give different explanations for their purpose. Branson admits that 'indirectly' its structure was set up to reduce the tax bill. The finance director, Stephen Murphy, says it is not tax-driven. He says that Branson originally chose to situate companies in the British Virgin Islands because he wanted to keep information from British Airways during a commercial dispute in the early 1990s. Since then Virgin has used the islands for companies that might one day be listed outside Britain. And bearer shares enable Branson to restructure the various companies without some of the costly bureaucracy that is normally associated with registered shares.

Because individual companies have different year-ends, it is also hard to follow the movement of assets between companies. For instance, when Virgin's property firm was making a loss, it was sold by its British parent company for some £50 million, only to reappear in Britain a year later, purged of its losses, bought back by another Branson company for only £11 million. In effect, the losses were taken on to the books of an offshore holding company (which does not have to publish accounts) rather than a British company (which does).

Source: 'Behind Branson', *The Economist*, 21 February 1998

However, not all companies arrange their affairs in such a creative manner as does Virgin. And with any luck your own accounts, at least, will not have been constructed to confuse you and your team.

Business objectives

There are universal methods of measuring what is happening in a business, but before we can measure anything we need some idea of what level or type of performance a business is wanting to achieve. All growing businesses have three fundamental objectives in common which allow us to see how well (or otherwise) they are doing.

Making a satisfactory return on investment

The first of these objectives is to make a satisfactory return (profit) on the money invested in the business. It is hard to think of a sound argument against this aim. To be satisfactory the return must meet four criteria:

- It must give a fair return to shareholders, bearing in mind the risk they are taking. If the venture is highly speculative and the profits are less than bank interest rates, your shareholders (yourself included) will not be happy.
- You must make enough profit to allow the company to grow. If a business wants to expand sales it will need more working capital and eventually more space or equipment. The safest and surest source of new money for this is internally generated profits, retained in the business: reserves. (A business has three sources of new money: share capital or the owner's money; loan capital put up by banks etc; retained profits generated by the business).
- The return must be good enough to attract new investors or lenders. If investors can get a greater return on their money in some other comparable business, they will invest there, not in your business.
- The return must provide enough reserves to keep the real capital intact. This means that you must recognise the impact inflation has on the business. A business retaining enough profits each year to meet a 3 per cent growth is actually contracting by 1 per cent if inflation is running at 4 per cent.

To control the business we have to examine carefully the various factors that affect return on investment. Shareholders' and other lenders' funds are invested in the capital, both fixed and working, of the business, so this must be the area we relate to profitability. The example in Table 1.4.1 shows the factors that directly influence the return on capital employed – ROCE – (capital employed = investment: remember the balance sheet must balance).

You can see that Table 1.4.1 is nothing more than a profit-and-loss account on the left and the capital employed section of the balance sheet on the right. Any change that increases net profit (more sales, lower expenses, less tax etc), but does not increase the amount of capital employed (lower stocks, fewer debtors etc), will increase ROCE. Conversely, any change that increases capital employed without increasing profits in proportion will reduce ROCE.

We shall look in detail at all the important factors that affect ROCE later.

Table 1.4.1 Factors that affect the return on capital employed (ROCE)

	£		£	£
Sales	100.000	Fixed assets	12,500	
– Cost of sales	50,000			
= Gross profit	50,000	Working capital		
– Expenses	33,000	Current assets	23,100	
		– Current liabilities	6,690	16,410
= Operating profit	17,000			
– Finance charges				
and tax	8,090			
Net profit	8,910	Capital employed		28,910
		= % return on capital		30.82%

Maintaining a sound financial position

As well as making a satisfactory return, investors, creditors and employees expect the business to be protected from unnecessary risks. Clearly, all businesses are exposed to market risks: competitors, new products and price changes are all part of a healthy commercial environment. The sorts of unnecessary risk that investors and lenders are particularly concerned about are high financial risks, such as overtrading.

Cash-flow problems are not the only threat to a business's financial position. Heavy borrowing can bring a big interest burden to a small business, especially when interest rates rise unexpectedly. This may be acceptable when sales and profits are good; however, when times are bad, bankers, unlike shareholders, cannot be asked to tighten their belts – they expect to be paid all the time. So the position audit is not just about profitability, but about survival capabilities and the practice of sound financial disciplines.

Achieving growth

Making profit and surviving are insufficient achievements in themselves to satisfy ambitious entrepreneurs, who want the business to grow too. But entrepreneurs do not just want the number of people they employ to get larger, or the sales turnover to rise, for example. They want the firm to become more efficient, to gain economies of scale and to improve the quality of profits.

Ratios – the tools of analysis

All analysis of financial information requires comparisons. We have already seen that certain objectives are fundamental to all types of business. It is also true that there are three aspects of business performance you might want to measure:

- You can see how well you are meeting a personal goal. For example, you may want to double sales or add 25 per cent to profits. In a more formalised business this activity would be called 'budgeting', then comparisons would be made between actual results and the budget.
- You might want to see how well you are doing this year compared with last, comparing performance against a historical standard. This is the way in which growth in sales or profits is often measured. There are two main limitations to this sort of comparison. One rarely affects a small business and one affects all sizes of business.

   If accounting methods change from year to year, perhaps in the way depreciation is dealt with, then you are not comparing like with like. Also the pounds in one year are not worth the same as the pounds in another, simply because inflation has changed their buying power, so a 10 per cent growth in sales when inflation is running at 15 per cent represents a real drop in sales volume.
- You may want to see how well you are doing compared with someone else's business, perhaps a competitor, someone in a similar line of business elsewhere (see Table 1.4.2), or an industry norm. This may provide useful pointers to areas for improvement, or to new and more profitable business opportunities. For this type of analysis you need external information. Fortunately, most developed countries with stock market activity have a wealth of readily available financial data on companies and industries.

The main way in which all these business yardsticks are established is through the use of ratios. A ratio is simply something expressed as a proportion of something else, and it is intended to give an appreciation of what has happened. For example, a percentage is a particular type of ratio, where events are always compared with a base of 100.

We have already seen the ROCE ratio, which was expressed as a percentage. In our everyday lives we apply ratios to tell us how well, or otherwise, something is performing. One measure of a car's performance is in miles per gallon (petrol consumption). If the mpg rate drops, say, from 35 to 1 to 20 to 1, it tells us the car is long overdue for a service – or worse.

In the financial field the opportunity for calculating ratios is great, for computing useful ratios not quite so great. Here we will concentrate on

Table 1.4.2 The best performing small, quoted companies: four-year growth performance

Company	Sector	Four-year average turnover growth (%)	Four-year average profit growth (%)	Four-year average profit margin (%)	Four-year average EPS growth (%)	Current market capitalisation (£m)
Colleagues Group	Media agencies	56	119	6	230	63
Dawson Group	Transport	143	129	198	12	106
Dickie (James)	Engineering	27	126	5	71	18
European Colour	Chemicals speciality	10	469	7	151	33
Filofax Group	Printing, paper	46	165	15	77	83
Finelist	Distributors	124	143	7	122	88
Flying Flowers	Retail	58	105	12	14	25
GWR Group	Media broadcasting	50	127	10	94	127
Lynx Holdings	Support services	64	230	7	24	72
Persona	Distributors	46	255	5	224	68
PizzaExpress	Restaurants	66	470	16	72	143
Sharpe*Fisher	Building merchants and materials	14	124	4	487	34
Sheriff Holdings	Building and construction	32	126	12	88	35
Spargo Consulting	Support services	59	1,601	13	1,452	22
Tinsley Robor	Printing	14	815	2	231	35

explaining the key ratios for a small business. Most you can calculate yourself, some you may need your bookkeeper or accountant to organise for you. All take a little time and may cost a little money, but they do tell you a lot about what is going on. One business school president summed this field up nicely in the following quotation: 'If you think knowledge is expensive, try ignorance'.

One main value of the position audit is that it points to questions that need answers. A large difference between what actually happened and what standard was set suggests that something may be wrong. The tools of analysis (the ratios) allow managers to choose, from the hundred of questions that might be asked, the handful that are really worth answering. In a small or expanding business where time is at a premium, this quick pre-selection of key questions is vital.

Measures of growth

Growth can be measured in many ways. Three important measures that are in general use are explained below. (The numbers in parentheses that follow each ratio title show their position in the summary of ratio tables on page 94).

Sales growth (1)

This is the increase in sales year on year, in percentage terms. The accounts for a company called High Note (on page 64) which follow (see Table 1.4.3) reveal a 30 per cent growth in sales (£100,000 rising to £130,000). Sales growth is a measure of increase in market power and gives you a feel for how fast an organisation is growing.

Table 1.4.4 shows how the fastest-growing companies in the healthcare sector performed in this respect. Notice they are all small firms – no Glaxo SmithKline equivalents here!

Profit growth (2)

This is the increase in net profit after tax year on year, in percentage terms. For High Note the profit growth is 48 per cent (£8,910 rising to £13,200). Profit growth shows how much more money the business is generating for shareholders, which in turn could be ploughed back to finance further growth.

Table 1.4.3 High Note's profit-and-loss account for years 1 and 2

	£	£	%	£	£	%
Sales		100,000	100		130,000	100
Cost of sales						
Materials	30,000		30	43,000		33
Labour	20,000	50,000	20	25,000	68,000	19
Gross profit		50,000	50		62,000	48
Expenses						
Rent, rates etc	18,000			20,000		
Wages	12,000			13,000		
Advertising	3,000			3,000		
Expenses		33,000		2,000	38,000	
Operating or trading Profit		17,000	17		24,000	18.5
Deduct interest on:						
Overdraft	900					
Loan	1,250	2,150		1,250	2,050	
Net profit before tax		14,850	14.9		21,950	16.9
Tax paid		5,940			8,750	
Net profit after tax		8,910	8.9	13,200		10.2

Table 1.4.4 Greatest increases in turnover

Company name	Turnover this year £000	Turnover last year £000	Increase %
1. Rorer Pharmaceuticals Ltd	40,239	8,490	373.95
2. Regent Laboratories Ltd	8,620	3,146	173.99
3. Knoll Ltd	1,441	571	152.36
4. Cortecs Ltd	4,767	1,973	141.61
5. Lorex Pharmaceuticals Ltd	4,951	2,298	115.44
6. Consolidated Chemicals Ltd	1,140	575	98.26
7. Pharmacia Ltd	33,471	17,221	94.36
8. Fine Organics Ltd	17,448	9,700	79.87
9. Letap Pharmaceuticals Ltd	18,975	11,339	67.34
10. Immuno Ltd	5,540	3,401	62.89

Headcount growth (3) and employee efficiency measures (4–6)

Headcount growth is the percentage increase in the number of full-time or full-time equivalent employees, year on year. It needs to be accompanied by three further ratios to show whether or not you are getting good value from the extra people and not just a bigger overhead bill (see Table 1.4.5):

- sales per employee (4) (sales in £ ÷ number of employees);
- profit per employee (5) (net profit after tax ÷ number of employees);
- value added per employee (6) (sales – (materials + bought in services in cost of sales) ÷ (number of employees).

A reasonable and probably more accessible approximation for value added is gross profit.

The wide variation in performance of the companies shown in Table 1.4.4, whose turnover ranged between £1.1 million and £40.2 million, give food for thought. As Table 1.4.5 shows, Regent Labs only generated half the sales per employee that Serona did in the year in question, and their return on capital employed was less than a fifth of the better performing company.

Table 1.4.5   Headcount growth

Company	Sales per employee £	Profit per employee £	Value added per employee £	ROCE
Regent Labs	51,928	1,644	9,590	6%
Swartz Pharma	95,567	820	12,432	14%
Serona Labs	101,509	2,578	15,684	33%
Servier Labs	96,310	1,264	17,480	27%

Measures of profitability

There are two main ways to measure a business's profitability. They are both important, but they reveal different things about the performance and perhaps even the strategy of the business. To know and understand what is happening you need information in both areas: ROCE and profit margins.

ROCE (7)

The financial resources employed in a business are called capital. We have already seen that capital can come into a business from a number of different sources. These sources have one thing in common: they all want a return – a percentage interest – on the money they invest. There are a number of ways in which return on capital can be measured, but for a small business two are particularly important.

The ROCE ratio is calculated by expressing the profit before long-term interest and tax as a proportion of the total capital employed. So if you look at the High Note profit-and-loss account (as shown in Table 1.4.3) you can see that for year 1, the profit before tax is £14,850. To this we had to add the loan interest of £1,250. If we did not do this we would be double counting our cost of loan capital by expecting a return on a loan which had already paid interest. This makes the profit figure £16,100. We also ignore tax charges, not because they are unimportant or insignificant, but simply because the level of tax is largely outside the control of the business, and it is the business's performance we are trying to measure.

Now look at the balance sheet (Table 1.4.1). The capital employed is the sum of the owner's capital, the profit retained and the long-term loan, in this case £28,910 (£10,000 + £8,910 + £10,000). So the ROCE ratio for the first year is:

$$\frac{£16,100}{£28,910} = 0.56 \text{ which expressed as a percentage} = 56\%$$

The great strength of this ratio lies in the overall view it takes of the financial health of the whole business. If you look at the same ratio for the second year, you will see a small change. The ratio gives no clue as to why this has happened, it simply provides the starting point for an analysis of business performance, and an overall yardstick against which to compare absolute performance. A banker might look to this ratio to see if the business could support more long-term borrowing (though not in isolation, of course).

Return on shareholders' capital (ROSC) (8)

The second way a small business would calculate a return on capital is by looking at the profit available for shareholders. This is not the money actually paid out as dividends and so on, but is a measure of the increase in worth of the funds invested by shareholders.

In the case of High Note, the net profit after tax is divided by the owner's capital plus the retained profits (these, although not distributed, belong to the shareholders). So in our example this would be the sum:

$$\frac{£\,8,910}{£18,910} = 0.47 \text{ which expressed as a percentage } = 47\%$$

And for the second year this ratio would be 41 per cent.

If someone was considering investing in shares in this business, this ratio would be of particular interest to them.

Once again, the difference in the ratios is clear, but the reasons are not. This is only the starting point for a more detailed analysis.

Gearing (9)

All businesses have access to two fundamentally different sorts of money. Equity, or owner's capital, including retained earnings, is money that is not a risk to the business. If no profits are made then the owner and other shareholders simply do not get dividends. They may not be pleased, but they cannot usually sue.

Debt capital is money borrowed by the business from outside sources; it puts the business at financial risk and is also risky for the lenders. In return for taking that risk they expect an interest payment every year, irrespective of the performance of the business.

In our example this would be:

$$\frac{\text{Share capital}}{\text{All long-term capital}} = \frac{18,910}{28,910} \quad \begin{array}{l} 0.65 \text{ which expressed as a percentage} \\ = 65\% \end{array}$$

Finlay and Co

The dangers of having too much debt

Arundbhai Patel, former Chairman, Finlay and Co:

> The capitalist system is one where you take risks, but only a few people in the world are prepared to take them. We bought Finlay's, a chain of newsagents and tobacconists, for £21.5 million at the height of a retail boom. At one point we had a turnover of £50 million a year and we were offered £60 million for the chain of 282 shops. But we were heavily geared – and no business can generate more money just because the interest burden is rising. We could not pay them, and so the banks sent in the receiver. We lost everything. It hurts to lose millions of pounds, you miss the cash, but one learns from the experience. I am a Hindu, and my religion is about a sense of duty to others. I believe if one does one's duty correctly, then one will go to Heaven. One is thankful to God even for failures.

Heathcote Home for the Elderly

Business debts put intense pressure on business owners

Clem Rogers of Heathcote Care Home for the Elderly:

> The whole thing has given me a partial nervous breakdown – everybody seems to think you are guilty if you try to run your own business. I had a home for very dependent elderly people, with a staff of 15 and 18 residents who paid £275 a week. I had a lot of borrowing, and last summer was difficult, because it was so warm and a number of residents died. We filled up again by the autumn, but I got £13,000 behind in interest payments to the bank with a business worth around £1 million. It was a cash-flow situation, and the bank decided to foreclose. The home has carried on since the receiver took it over, with my impetus – my former matron runs it – but the debts were around £700,000. I have lost my house and will also be in court, because my former wife is suing me for unpaid maintenance. My long-term partner has broken up with me over it all – I can see why people top themselves.

As well as looking at the gearing, lenders will study the business's capacity to pay interest. They do this by using another ratio called 'times interest earned'(10).

This is calculated by dividing the operating profit by the loan interest. It shows how many times the loan interest is covered, and gives the lender some idea of the safety margin. Once again rules are hard to make, but much less than 3 x interest earned is unlikely to give lenders confidence. The x is shorthand for 'times,' a convention when using this and other ratios.

Gearing levels can also have strategic implications that affect a company's competitive stance.

Profit margins

Any analysis of a business must consider the current level of sales activity. If you look at High Note's profit-and-loss accounts which follow (Table 1.4.6), you will see that materials consumed in sales have jumped from £30,000 to £43,000, a rise of 43 per cent. However, a quick look at the change in sales activity will show that the situation is nothing like so dramatic. Materials as a proportion of sales have risen from 30 to 33 per cent (30,000/100,000 = 30% and 43,000/130,000 = 33%). Obviously, the more you sell the more you must make. To understand why there have been changes in the level of return on capital employed, we have to relate both profit and capital to sales activity. The ROCE equation can be expanded to look like this:

$$\frac{\text{Profit}}{\text{Capital}} = \frac{\text{Profit}}{\text{Sales}} \times \frac{\text{Sales}}{\text{Capital}}$$

That gives us two separate strands to examine, the profit strand and the capital strand. The first of these is usually called profit margins. The capital strand will be looked at later.

When we examine profit margins, all costs, expenses and the different types of profit are expressed as a percentage of sales. This ratio makes comparisons both possible and realistic.

An analysis of High Note's profit-and-loss account (Table 1.4.6) will show the following changes:

Table 1.4.6 High Note's profit-and-loss account results

Area	Change	Some possible causes
Material cost of sales	Up from 30% to 33%	(a) Higher price paid (b) Change in product mix (c) Increased waste
Labour cost of sales	Down from 20% to 19%	(a) Reduction in wage rates (b) Increase in work rate (c) Change in product mix
Gross profit	Down from 50% to 48%	(a) 3% increase in materials (b) 1% decrease in labour = net 2% decline in gross margin
Operating or trading profit	Up from 17% to 18.5%	A 3.5% improvement in expense ratios offset by a 2% decline in gross margin = net 1.5% improvement in trading profit
Net profit before tax	Up from 14.9% to 16.9%	Interest charges down from 2.1% of sales to 1.6%. Means another 0.5% increase in net profit + 1.5% net increase in trading profit = 2%

Had we simply looked at the net profit margin, we would have seen a satisfactory increase, from 8.9 to 10.1 per cent. It is only by looking at each area in turn, the components of gross profit, operating or trading profit and net profit, that a useful analysis can be made. High Note's owner now has a small number of specific questions to ask in the search for reasons for changes in performance.

To summarise, the ratios of profitability that allow attention to be focused on specific areas are as follows.

Gross profit percentage (11)

This is deducting the cost of sales from the sales, and expressing the result as a percentage of sales.

In the High Note example, for year 1 this is:

£100,000 (Sales) – £50,000 (Cost of sales) = £50,000 (Gross profit)

then

£50,000 (Gross profit) ÷ £100,000 (Sales) = 50%

This ratio gives an indication of relative manufacturing efficiency.

Operating or trading profit percentage (12)

This is calculated by deducting expenses from the gross profit, to arrive at the operating profit. This figure is then divided by sales and expressed as a percentage. For High Note, in year 1 this is:

£50,000 (Gross profit) – £33,000 (Expenses) = £17,000 (Operating profit)

then

£17,000 (Operating profit) ÷ £100,000 (Sales) = 17%

Net profit before tax percentage (13)

In this case finance charges are deducted from operating profits to arrive at net profit before tax. This is then expressed as a percentage of sales.

For High Note, in year 1 this is:

£17,000 (Trading profit) – £2,150 (Interest charge) = £14,850 (Net profit before tax)

£14,850 (Net profit before tax) ÷ £100,000 (Sales) = 14.85%

This ratio can also be calculated after tax. See Table 1.4.3.

High profit margins are not always the passport to riches if their strategic implications are not clearly understood; Filofax is a classic example of a company failing to recognise the relationship between profit and market attractiveness.

Filofax

Few companies rode the yuppie boom higher than Britain's Filofax, maker of the fashionable leather-encased personal organisers beloved of media trendies and financial whizzes. Filofaxes, invented for engineers, had been sold to British army officers, clergymen and the like since 1910, but only when they became a fashion fad did sales soar; from £681,000 to £14.7 million in just six years, and all without a single line of advertising. The formula was, however, flawed. While some customers were prepared to pay extra for the Filofax name, many simply wanted a good-quality ring-binder with diary, address book and information sheets. Because Filofax's profit margins were so high, and its products so costly, imitators could easily match the company's quality while beating its prices.

Losing market share is tolerable when your market is booming, but being a one-product company with a narrow customer base is a precarious way to live. Filofax's market stalled as soaring British interests rates (over half its sales are in Britain) made yuppies downwardly mobile. Worse, those who could still afford fads splashed out on new ones like electronic organisers and portable telephones. In the first half of the year after Filofax's record performance sales fell by a fifth, while its sparkling profits were transformed into a £554,000 pre-tax loss. In 1998 Filofax was taken over by Dayrunner to reappear as filofax.com and was restored to its former glory.

Working capital ratios (or liquidity)

The capital strand of the return on capital employed (ROCE) calculations has two main branches of its own.

$$\frac{\text{Profit}}{\text{Capital}} = \frac{\text{Profit}}{\text{Fixed assets} + \text{working capital}}$$

The more dynamic of these is working capital – the day-to-day money used to finance the working of the business. It is important to monitor the relationship between sales and the various elements of working capital to see how effectively that capital is being used. But as the working capital is the difference between current assets and current liabilities, it is also important to monitor their relationship, both in total and in their component parts.

Table 1.4.7 High Note's balance sheet for year-ends 1 and 2

Fixed assets	£	£	£	£	£	£
Furniture and fixtures			12,500			28,110
Working capital						
Current assets						
Stock	10,000			12,000		
Debtors	13,000			13,000		
Cash	100	23,100		500	25,500	
Less current liabilities						
Overdraft	5,000			6,000		
Creditors	1,690	6,690		5,500	11,500	
Net current assets			16,410			14,000
Capital employed			28,910			42,110
Financed by owners						
capital	10,000			18,910		
Profit retained	8,910		18,910	13,200		32,100
Long-term loan			10,000			10,000
Total capital			28,910			42,110
employed						

This is very often referred to as liquidity, or the business's ability to meet its current liabilities as they fall due. The most important ratios in this area are the current ratio and the quick ration or acid test.

The current ratio (14)

A business's ability to meet its immediate liabilities can be estimated by relating its current assets to current liabilities. If for any reason current liabilities cannot be met, then the business is being exposed to an unnecessary level of financial risk. Suppliers may stop supplying or could even petition for bankruptcy if they are kept waiting too long for payment.

In the financial statements given for High Note, the first year's picture on the balance sheet shows £23,100 current assets to £6,690 current liabilities (see Table 1.4.7).

$$\text{Current ratio} = \frac{\text{Current assets}}{\text{Current liabilities}}$$

Therefore High Note's

$$\text{Current ratio} \quad = \quad \frac{23,100}{6,690} \quad = \quad 3.5$$

This shows current liabilities to be covered 3.5 times, and the ratio is usually expressed in the form 3.5:1. In the second year this has come down to 2.2:1. At first glance this figure may look worse than the first year's position. Certainly, current liabilities have grown faster than current assets, but up to a point this is a desirable state of affairs, because it means that the business is having to find less money to finance working capital.

There is really only one rule about how high (or low) the current ratio should be. It should be as close to 1:1 as the safe conduct of the business will allow. This will not be the same for every type of business. A shop buying in finished goods on credit and selling them for cash could run safely at 1.3:1. A manufacturer, with raw material to store and customers to finance, may need over 2:1. This is because the period between paying cash out for raw materials and receiving cash in from customers is longer in a manufacturing business than in a retail business. It is a bit like the oil dipstick on a car. There is a band within which the oil level should be. Levels above or below that band pose different problems. So for most businesses, less than 1.2:1 would probably be cutting things a bit fine. Over 1.8:1 would mean too much cash was being tied up in such items as stocks and debtors.

An unnecessarily high amount of working capital makes it harder for a business to make a good ROCE because it makes the bottom half of the sum bigger. Too low a working capital, below 1:1 for example, exposes the business to unacceptable financial risks, such as foreclosure by banks or creditors.

The quick ratio or acid test (15)

The quick ratio is really a belt and braces figure. In this, only assets that can be realised quickly, such as debtors and cash in hand, are related to current liabilities.

$$\text{Quick ratio} \quad = \quad \frac{\text{Debtors} + \text{Cash}}{\text{Current liabilities}}$$

In the High Note example, looking at year 1 only, we would exclude the £10,000 stock because, before it can be realised, we would need to find customers to sell to and collect in the cash. All this might take several months. High Note's quick ratio would be £13,100 (debtors + cash) + £6,690 (current liabilities): a perhaps too respectable 1.9:1. In the second year this has dropped to 1.2:1 (£13,500 + £11,500).

Once again, general rules are very difficult to make, but a ratio of 0.8:1 would be acceptable for most types of business.

Credit control

Any small business selling on credit knows how quickly customers can eat into their cash. This is particularly true if the customers are big companies. Customers going bust can have a domino effect on their suppliers.

It remains to be seen whether or not legislation introduced in 1998 to allow SMEs to charge interest on late payment will have any effect on collection periods. In European countries such as France, that have had such legislation for a number of years, the evidence is not particularly inspiring. (See Table 1.4.8.)

There are two techniques for monitoring debtors. The first is to prepare a schedule by age of debtor. Table 1.4.9 gives some idea of how this might be done.

This method has the great merit of focusing attention clearly on specific problem accounts. It may seem like hard work, but once you have got the system going it will pay dividends.

Table 1.4.8   Payment period in Europe – Percentage of enterprises with average payment periods over 60 days

Country	%
Italy	90
France	58
Ireland	50
Luxembourg	50
Portugal	47
Belgium	28
UK	28
Netherlands	23
Germany	10
Sweden	3
Denmark	3

Source: Observatory for SME Research, 1997

Table 1.4.9   High Note's debtors schedule: end of year 1

	2 months (or less) £	3 months £	4 months £	Over 4 months £	Total £
Brown & Co	1,000				
Jenkins & Son	1,000				
Andersons		3,000			
Smithers		2,500			
Thomkinsons			500		
Henry's			2,500		
Smart Inc				2,500	
Total	2,000	5,500	3,000	2,500	13,000

The second technique for monitoring debts is using the ratio average collection period (16). This ratio is calculated by expressing debtors as a proportion of credit sales, and then relating that to the days in the period in question.

$$\text{Average collection period} = \frac{\text{Debtors}}{\text{Sales}} \times 365$$

Let us suppose that all High Note's sales are on credit and the periods in question are both 365-day years (no leap years). Then in year 1 the average collection period would be:

$$\frac{£13,000\ \text{Debtors}}{£100,000\ \text{Sales}} \times 365\ (\text{days in period}) = 47\ \text{days}$$

In year 2 the collection period is:

$$\frac{£13,000\ \text{Debtors}}{£130,000\ \text{Sales}} \times 365\ (\text{days in period}) = 36\ \text{days}$$

So in the second year High Note is collecting its cash from debtors 11 days sooner than in the first year. This is obviously a better position to be in, making its relative number of debtors lower than in year 1. It is not making the absolute number of debtors lower, and this illustrates another great strength of using ratios to monitor performance. High Note's sales have grown by 30 per cent from £100,000 to £130,000, and its debtors have remained at £13,000. At first glance then, its debtors are the same, neither better nor worse. But when you relate those debtors to the increased levels of sales, as this ratio does, then you can see that the position has improved.

This is a good position audit ratio, which has the great merit of being quickly translatable into a figure any businessperson can understand, showing how much it is costing to give credit. If, for example, High Note is paying 12 per cent for an overdraft, giving £13,000 credit for 37 days will cost:

$$\frac{(12\% \times £13,000 \times 36)}{365} = £153.86$$

Average days' credit taken (17)

Of course the credit world is not all one-sided. Once a small business has established itself, it too will be taking credit. You can usually rely on your suppliers to keep you informed on your indebtedness, but only on an individual basis. It would be prudent to calculate how many days' credit, on average, are being taken from suppliers: a very similar sum to that for average collection period. The ratio is as follows:

$$\text{Average days' credit} = \frac{\text{Creditors}}{\text{Purchases}} \times 365$$

For High Note, in year 1, this sum would be (assuming all materials purchased this period):

$$\frac{£1,690 \text{ Creditors}}{£30,000 \text{ Purchases}} \times \quad 365 \text{ (days in period)} = 21 \text{ days}$$

In year 2 this ratio would be:

$$\frac{£5,500 \text{ Creditors}}{£43,000 \text{ Purchases}} \times \quad 365 \text{ (days in period)} = 47 \text{ days}$$

The difference in these ratios probably reflects High Note's greater creditworthiness in year 2. The longer the credit period you can take from your suppliers the better, provided that you still meet their terms of trade. They may, however, put you at the bottom of the list when supplies get scarce, or give you up altogether when they find a better customer.

Resource Administration

Looking professional can get you better terms

Resource Administration Group, a £4 million turnover recruitment and property maintenance company with 22 employees, tightened up the terms and conditions of its purchase agreements as part of a general review of its sales and purchasing systems. It then went along to its larger suppliers to explain what it was doing.

'We had operated a very loose system before,' explains Liam Forde, MD, 'now we set out formally that we will not take delivery unless the goods are of a suitable quality and delivered in a timely fashion.' A surprising outcome of this tightening-up was that some suppliers offered improved discount terms. 'Because we looked more professional, suppliers felt much safer in dealing with us and were prepared to offer us discounts.'

Resource Administration has also introduced a system of purchase order pads, one copy of which goes to accounts, so that tighter control can be kept of orders for items such as stationery. This system means that small orders can be combined to gain discounts or avoid paying delivery charges. It was possible to achieve savings of £4,000 from a single supplier within three months of introducing this system and savings of 5 per cent on an annual purchasing bill of £50,000 are expected.

There are two other useful techniques to help the owner/manager keep track of these events. One is simply to relate days credit given to days credit taken. If they balance out then you are about even in the credit game.

In year 1, High Note gave 47 days credit to its customers and took only 21 days from its suppliers, so it was a loser. In the second year it got ahead, giving only 36 days while taking 47.

The other technique is to age your creditors in exactly the same way as we did with the debtors. In this way it is possible to see at a glance which suppliers have been owed what sums of money, and for how long.

Stock control (18)

Any manufacturing, subcontracting or assembling business will have to buy in raw materials and work on them to produce finished goods. It will have to keep track of three sorts of stock: raw materials, work-in-progress and finished goods. A retailing business will probably only be concerned with finished goods, and a service business may have no stocks at all.

If we assume that all High Note's stock is in finished goods, then the control ratio we can use is as follows:

Days finished goods stock (18) =

$$\frac{\text{Finished goods stock}}{\text{Cost of sales*}} \times \text{Days in period}^1$$

For High Note, in year 1 this would be:

$$\frac{10,000}{50,000} \times 365 = 73 \text{ days}$$

In year 2 the ratio would be 64 days.

It is impossible to make any general rule about stock levels. Obviously, a business has to carry enough stock to meet customers' demand, and a retail business must have it on display or on hand. However, if High Note's supplier can always deliver within 14 days it will be unnecessary to carry 73 days' stock. The same basic equation can be applied to both raw material and work-in-progress stock, but to reach raw material stock you should substitute raw materials consumed for cost of sales. Once again the strength of this ratio is that a business can quickly calculate how much it is costing to carry a given level of stock, in just the same way as customer credit costs were calculated earlier.

CJ's Stores

Keeping stock levels down saves cash

Trevor Millett, MD of CJ's, a chain of 42 stores selling jeans and casual clothing, responded swiftly when he realised the next year was going to be difficult. Budgets were tightened, optimum staff levels reassessed and capital spending cut. But one area which Millett refused to trim involved the tills and computer systems which told him how quickly individual lines were selling and what his stock levels were. One of the main tasks of the sales manager Millett appointed at the beginning of the year is to keep an eye on stock levels.

'When a stock line is clearly not turning into money at sufficient speed we cut the price until it does', says Millett. Hooded tops, all the rage in April, were going out of fashion in June. Prices were cut and by late August, when other retailers also started discounting, Millett had almost cleared his stocks. When expensive items such as jackets sell better in certain stores than in others, Millett has no hesitation in switching stocks to the stores where demand is highest. Tight stock control ensures that the busi-

---

* Cost of sales is used because it accurately reflects the amount of stock. The sales figure includes other items such as profit margin. If you are looking at an external company it is possible that the only figure available will be that for sales. In this case it can be used as an approximation.

ness has a positive cash flow and keeps its bank overdraft to a minimum. CJ's is the trading name of Peter Millett and Sons, a Hayes, Middlesex-based company with a turnover of £12 million and a workforce of 230.

Retailers should be able to see fairly quickly where stocks are building up because the evidence is on the shelves and the racks in the shop window. Excess stock levels are not always so obvious in businesses which involve a long manufacturing process but controlling levels of inventory is of vital importance to any business which wants to weather the recession. 'I have spent a good part of the past six months telling people to get their stocks down', comments Jon Moulton, managing partner of Schroder Ventures, a venture capital company (VC). 'We closed a warehouse at one of our companies so they had nowhere to stock things. Companies must drive inventory out of their systems.' 'We have managed to save businesses by getting them to reduce stocks', says Allan Griffiths, head of the insolvency division of accountants Grant Thornton. 'If you can get rid of £250,000 from stocks of £500,000 you can relieve your cash flow problems. If you have cash in the bank you will survive the recession. If you do not you are in trouble.'

A common failing of large as well as small companies is to plan production levels to get the most out of their plant and equipment without taking into account the costs involved in holding stocks. There will be a direct cost in terms of borrowings to finance stocks while obsolete items may have to be sold at a discount and possibly even at below cost, warns Ivor Cohen, electronics industry advisor to the APA, a VC.

In a recession many small business owners attempt to keep their workforce busy, producing for stock even if demand has fallen. 'If your output levels are too high you must start cutting back straight away' advises Allan Griffiths. 'If you go on building up stocks you will face a bigger cash drain. If you have to take the nasty medicine and reduce your workforce, the sooner you do it the better.'

Waterstone's

Tim Waterstone started his eponymous book retail chain after he had been sacked by W H Smith. He read English at St Catherine's College, Cambridge, before becoming a marketing manager at Allied Breweries. He then worked for W H Smith, finally becoming chairman of the group's US subsidiary. With Waterstone's he proved that a good bookseller could be successful. Within 10 years he had struck a deal whereby W H Smith bought Waterstone's for £40 million. In 1998, Waterstone was part of a syndicate trying to buy Waterstone's back out of W H Smith's control.

When Waterstone's got under way the average value of stock per square foot across all booksellers was under £40, and sales per square foot were under £140. One fed upon the other, with the trade becoming used to a stock presentation that was simply inadequate to satisfy the public. Waterstone reckoned then, and does still, that a decent general bookseller cannot do a proper job with fewer than 40,000 individual titles in stock at any one time. He told his backers that he would be stocking his shops at at least twice the industry average. With stock at double the industry average at £80 per square foot (more than £120 per square foot now), Waterstone felt that sales of £300 per square foot were easily achievable, and it is at this level that selling books (with controlled occupancy costs) becomes very profitable.

Tim Waterstone, reflecting on the time when he set the business up, commented:

It really is strange that the situation had been allowed to degenerate to the level it had. In France particularly, but certainly in Germany as well, really good stockholding bookshops were trading all over the land ever since the post-war recovery. But when an industry starts to talk itself into a cycle of defeat, the momentum becomes irresistible. The myth of inevitable failure hung over everything the bookselling trade did and said. The perceived wisdom was that only W H Smith, operating very much in the middle and popular area, was viable. Nobody spent any money, and nobody opened any bookshops of any size. Even Dillons, purchased by Pentos later, remained quiescent and dormant for 10 years or so. The French and Germans could make money from bookselling, and the Americans – through B Dalton and Walden, and a number of lively regional chains – could move into a period of vigorous development, but here in Britain failure was the certainty, and the total dominance of the publisher over the retailer accepted as the natural course of events.

Cash control

The residual element in the control of working capital is cash or, if there is no cash left, the size of overdraft needed in a particular period.

Usually the amount of cash available to a small business is finite and specific, as is the size of the overdraft it can take, so stock levels, creditor and debtor policies, and other working capital elements are decided with these limits in mind.

Mulberry's clothes

Different growth strategies consume different amounts of cash

On his 21st birthday, Roger Saul's parents gave him £500. Instead of spending the money, their fashion-conscious son used it to convert an old shed in the back garden of his parents' Somerset home into a small workshop producing leather belts and bags. The Mulberry Company was born. Within 18 years, Mulberry had a large, purpose-built factory, 300 employees and worldwide sales of £30 million. Mulberry's clothes and accessories are sold in its own shops, franchises and 'shops within shops' in department stores. Last September, in a move that smacked of 'taking coals to Newcastle', Saul opened his first shop in Milan.

But financing Mulberry's growth has not been easy. Saul has changed bankers many times over the years. 'Each time we found we got a good service for the first two or three years but when we asked for more money the bankers suddenly said "No". They said they couldn't see the firm continuing to grow. In other words, they got cold feet.' Saul's reaction was simple: he went to a different bank.

Recessions can hit companies like Mulberry hard. During the last recession, sales, particularly in the United States, plummeted and, for the first time ever, the company made a loss. 'Our problem was that we had opened shops without realising the cash flow implications', says Saul. 'We were selling most retail, not wholesale, with the result that our money was tied up until the goods were sold.' Saul went wholesale and started a franchise operation. 'We could open franchise shops without spending a penny of our own money', he says.

Not all fast growing businesses control their cash as effectively as Mulberry.

Footprints

You need good and timely financial information to grow safely

When Sue Clark joined Footprints she was the oldest person in the company. Even at her interview for a low-level design job she could see the potential. The two people behind the company, Roger Hamilton, an art graduate, and Mike Ross, a mathematician, were very dynamic individuals, operating from a large studio and office in London's Covent Garden.

The Footprints idea arose out of a project Roger did, while working for his degree at Cambridge University. Basically the concept was town guides, with shop fronts drawn onto the map. Clients would advertise to have their business promoted on the maps, and the maps themselves were distributed widely in each city area.

Each map had a three-month life cycle from design to delivery. Despite being paid upfront, the company was spending all its cash in week 1. By week 12 they had run out of money to pay the printers. So they had to expand further, and make more cash to pay their bills.

After only 18 months, Footprints' turnover reached £2.5 million, but as the company's accounting records were stolen, along with its computers and back up files, the owners had no idea if it was profitable.

The company produced its first set of management accounts two years after it set up. By then they realised that, in Clark's words, 'Whilst we thought we were pushing up the sales figure, in reality we were pushing up the daisies'. Footprints had a £500,000 cash hole, and had to be 'sold' to their printers that year.

Circulation of working capital (19)

The primary ratio for controlling working capital is usually considered to be the current ratio. This, however, is of more interest to outside bodies, such as bankers and suppliers wanting to see how safe their money is. The manager of a business is more interested in how well the money tied up in working capital is being used.

Look at High Note's balance sheets for the last two years (Table 1.4.7). You can see that net current assets, another name for working capital, have shrunk from £16,410 to £14,000 – not too dramatic. Now let us look at these figures in relation to the level of business activity in each year.

$$\text{Circulation of working capital (19)} = \frac{\text{Sales}}{\text{Working capital}}$$

For year 1 this is:

$$\frac{1,000,000}{16,410} = 6\times \text{ and year 2 } \frac{130,000}{14,000} = 9\times$$

The $\times$ is shorthand for 'times' – a convention when using this ratio.

So we can see that not only has High Note got less money tied up in working capital in the second year, it has also used it more efficiently. In other words, it has circulated it faster. Each pound of working capital now produces £9 of sales, as opposed to only £6 last year and, as each pound of sales makes profits, the higher the sales the higher the profit.

Controlling fixed assets

A major problem that all new or expanding businesses face is exactly how much to have of such items as equipment, storage capacity and work space. New fixed assets tend to be acquired in large chunks and are sometimes more opportunistic than market-related in nature.

In any event, however, and for whatever reason acquired, once in the business it is important to make sure the asset is being used effectively. Controlling fixed assets breaks down into two areas: looking at how effectively fixed assets are being used, and how to plan for new capital investments.

The fixed-asset pyramid

Generally, the best way to measure how well existing fixed assets are being used is to see how many pounds' worth of sales each pound of fixed assets is generating.

Use of fixed assets (20)

The overall ratio is that of Sales ÷ Fixed assets, which gives a measure of this use of the fixed assets. Look back to the High Note accounts in Table 1.4.7. The use of fixed-asset ratio in that example is:

$$\text{Year 1 } \frac{100,000}{12,500} = 8\times \qquad \text{Year 2 } \frac{130,000}{28,110} = 4.6\times$$

This means that each pound invested in fixed assets has generated £8 worth of sales in year 1 and only £4.60 in year 2.

This inefficient use of fixed assets has consumed all the benefit High Note gained from its improved use of working capital – and a little more. In fact, this is the main reason why the ROCE has declined in year 2. This may be a short-term problem which will be cured when expected new sales levels are reached: not at all unusual if, for example, a new piece of machinery was bought late in the second year.

Looking at the overall fixed asset picture is rather like looking at the circulation of working-capital ratio only as a means of monitoring working capital. There we looked at stock control, debtors and creditors as well. Fixed assets use is looked at both in total and in its component parts. A pyramid of ratios stretches out below this prime ratio.

The fixed-asset pyramid will look something like Figure 1.4.1, although the nature of the assets of a particular business may suggest others be included. For example, a shop will also be interested in sales per square foot of selling price.

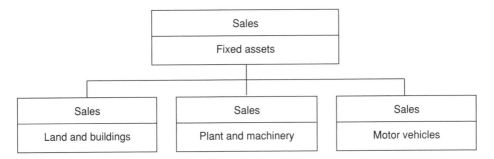

Figure 1.4.1 The fixed-asset pyramid

More sophisticated businesses also monitor the output of individual pieces of equipment. They look at down time (how long the equipment is out of commission), repair and maintenance costs, and the value of the equipment's output. If your business warrants it, you can do this by simply expanding the pyramid, as shown in Figure 1.4.2.

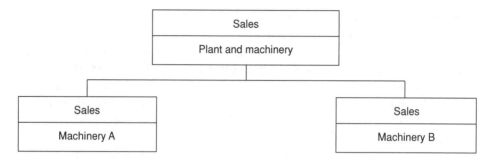

Figure 1.4.2 Extension of fixed-asset pyramid

Averaging ratios

Ratios that involve the use of stock, debtors or creditors can be more accurately calculated by using the average of the opening and closing position. Seasonal factors or sales growth (contraction) will almost always make a single figure unrepresentative.

Look back to the High Note accounts (page 64). Here you can see an example where sales have grown by 30 per cent, from £100,000 in the first year to £130,000 in the second. Obviously, neither the opening stock figure of £10,000 nor the closing stock of £12,000 is truly representative of what has happened in the intervening year. It seems much more likely that the average of the opening and closing stock figures is the best figure to use in calculating the stock control ratios shown earlier. So in this example, the figure to use would be calculated as follows:

$$\frac{(£10,000 + £12,000)}{2} = £11,000$$

Other ratios

The ratios covered here are by no means the only ratios that can be usefully calculated. Each industry and trade will have special areas of its own. For example, advertising is a relatively large proportion of the cost of some cars, so that industry monitors comparative advertising expenditure. The ratio they use is 'pounds spent on advertising per car sold'. The figures for the UK car market are given in Table 1.4.10.

Table 1.4.10 Advertising expenditure per car sold in UK

Make	£
Saab	401
Seat	321
Fiat	319
Citröen	294
Mazda	251
Renault	239
Audi-VW	197
Lada	183
Honda	167
Mercedes-Benz	165
Rover	112
Vauxhall	70
Ford	62

Market tests

This is the name given to stock market measures of performance. Four key ratios here are: earnings per share, price earnings ratio, yield and dividend cover.

$$\text{Earnings per share} = \frac{\text{Net profit}}{\text{Shares outstanding}}$$

> The after-tax profit made by a company divided by the number of ordinary shares it has issued.

$$\text{Price earnings ratio} = \frac{\text{Market price per share}}{\text{Earnings per share}}$$

> The market price of an ordinary share divided by the earnings per share. The price earnings (PE) ratio expresses the market value placed on the expectation of future earnings, ie the number of years required to earn the price paid for the shares out of profits at the current rate.

$$\text{Yield} = \frac{\text{Dividends per share}}{\text{Price per share}}$$

> The percentage return a shareholder gets on the 'opportunity' value of their investment.

$$\text{Dividend cover} = \frac{\text{Net income}}{\text{Dividend}}$$

> The number of times the profit exceeds the dividend, the higher the ratio, the more retained profit to finance future growth.

Some problems in using ratios

Finding the information to calculate business ratios is often not the major problem. Being sure of what the ratios are really telling you almost always is. The most common problems lie in the four following areas.

Which way is right?

There is natural feeling with financial ratios to think that high figures are good ones, and an upward trend represents the right direction. This theory is, to some extent, encouraged by the personal feeling of wealth that having a lot of cash engenders.

Unfortunately, there is no general rule on which way is right for financial ratios. In some cases a high figure is good, in others a low figure is best. Indeed, there are even circumstances in which ratios of the same value are not as good as each other. Look at the two working capital statements in Table 1.4.11.

The amount of working capital in each example is the same, £16,410, as are the current assets and current liabilities, at £23,100 and £6,690 respectively. It follows that any ratio using these factors would also be the same. For example, the current ratios in these two examples are both identical, 3.4:1, but in the first case there is a reasonable chance that some cash will come in from debtors, certainly enough to meet the modest creditor position. In the second example there is no possibility of useful amounts of cash coming in from trading, with debtors at only £100, while creditors at the relatively substantial figure of £6,600 will pose a real threat to financial stability. So in this case the current ratios are identical, but the situations being compared are not. In fact, as a general rule, a higher working capital ratio is regarded as a move in the wrong direction. The more money a business has tied up in working capital the more difficult it is to make a satisfactory return on capital employed, simply because the larger the denominator the lower the return on capital employed.

Table 1.4.11   Difficult comparisons

	1		2	
Current assets	£	£	£	£
Stock	10,000		22,990	
Debtors	13,000		100	
Cash	100	23,100	10	23,100
Less current liabilities				
Overdraft	5,000		90	
Creditors	1,690	6,690	6,600	6,690
Working capital		16,410		16,410
Current ratio		3.4:1		3.4:1

In some cases the right direction is more obvious. A high return on capital employed is usually better than a low one, but even this situation can be a danger signal, warning that higher risks are being taken. And not all high profit ratios are good: sometimes a higher profit margin can lead to reduced sales volume and so lead to a lower ROCE.

In general, business performance as measured by ratios is best thought of as lying within a range, liquidity (current ratio), for example, staying between 1.2:1 and 1.8:1. A change in either direction represents a cause for concern.

Accounting for inflation

Financial ratios all use pounds as the basis for comparison: historical pounds at that. That would not be so bad if all these pounds were from the same date in the past, but that is not so. Comparing one year with another may not be very meaningful unless we account for the change in value of the pound.

One way of overcoming this problem is to adjust for inflation, perhaps using an index, such as that for consumer prices. Such indices usually take 100 as their base at some time in the past, for example, 1975. Then an index value for each subsequent year is produced showing the relative movement in the item being indexed. Tables 1.4.12 and 1.4.13 show how this could be done for High Note.

These unadjusted figures show a substantial growth in sales in each of the past two years. Now if High Note's owner used a consumer price index for the appropriate period to adjust the figures, the years could be properly compared.

Let us assume that the indices for years 1, 2 and 3 were 104, 120 and 135 respectively. Year 3 is the most recent set of figures, and therefore the one we

Table 1.4.12 Comparing unadjusted ratios

Year	Sales	Sales growth	Percentage growth (ie the ratio year on year)
	£	£	
1	100,000	–	–
2	130,000	30,000	30.0
3	145,000	15,000	11.5

want to use as the base for comparison. So to convert the pounds from years 1 and 2 to current pounds, we use this sum:

$$\text{Current pounds} = \frac{\text{Index for current year}}{\text{Index for historic year}} \times \text{Historic pounds}$$

For year 1 sales now become: 135/104 × £100,000 = £129,808
For year 2 sales now become: 135/120 × £130.000 = £146,250
For year 3* sales now become: 135/135 × £145,000 = £145,000

We can now construct an adjusted table, showing the real sales growth over the past three years (see Table 1.4.13).

The real situation is nothing like as rosy as we first thought. The sales growth in year 2 is barely a third of the original estimate. In year 3, High Note did not grow at all – in fact it contracted slightly.

The principle of this technique can be applied to any financial ratio. The appropriate index will, to some extent, depend on the nature of the business in question. Information on current British indices is published regularly by the Statistics Office.

Apples and pears

There are particular problems in trying to compare one business's ratios with another. You would not expect a Mini to be able to cover a mile as quickly as a Jaguar. A small new business can achieve quite startling sales growth ratios in the early months and years.

Expanding from £10,000 sales in the first six months to £50,000 in the second would not be unusual. To expect a mature business to achieve the same growth

---

* In other words, year 3 is virtually 'now'

Table 1.4.13 Comparing adjusted ratios

Year	Adjusted sales £	Adjusted sales growth £	Adjusted growth ratios £
1	129,808	–	–
2	146,250	16,442	12.7
3	145,000	–1,250	–0.9

would be unrealistic. For ICI to grow from sales of £5 billion to £25 billion would imply wiping out every chemical company in the world. So some care must be taken to make sure that like is being compared with like, and allowances made for differing circumstances in the businesses being compared (or if the same business is examined, the trading/economic environment of the years should be compared).

It is also important to check that one business's idea of an account category, say current assets, is the same as the one you want to compare it with. The concepts and principles used to prepare accounts leave some scope for differences.

Seasonal factors

Many of the ratios that we have looked at make use of information in the balance sheet. Balance sheets are prepared at one moment in time, and reflect the position at that moment; they may not represent the average situation. For example, seasonal factors can cause a business's sales to be particularly high once or twice a year. A balance sheet prepared just before one of these seasonal upturns might show very high stocks, bought in specially to meet this demand. Conversely, a look at the balance just after the upturn might show very high cash and low stocks. If either of those stock figures were to be treated as an average it would give a false picture.

Ratios in forecasting

Ratios have another valuable use – they can be an aid to making future financial projections. For example, if you believe it prudent to hold the equivalent of a month's sales in stock, once you have made the sales forecast for future years, the projections for stock in the balance sheet follow automatically.

Sources of financial information

All the ratios described derive their base information from the business's balance sheet and profit-and-loss accounts. For your own business you will no doubt have these to hand. For your competitors you will have to use an outside agency, such as the one described below.

One Source UK gives financial details of 360,000 UK companies, five years of accounts plus key ratios and basic company history and director information. It can search by company name, geographical location, SIC code, turnover, number of employees.

One Source Europa is similar in content to One Source UK but covers European companies. It provides accounts details in local currency, sterling and US dollars.

One Source provides summarised profit-and-loss accounts, and balance sheet data, a four-year trend and some key ratios. See Tables 1.4.14 and 1.4.15 below, which are an example of the information provided, in this case for a fictitious business.

Table 1.4.14   Global Travel profit-and-loss account

Date of accounts	1/31/2000	1/31/99	1/31/98	1/31/97	1/31/96
Consolidated	No	No	No	No	No
No of weeks	52	52	52	52	52
Subsidiary status	No	No	No	No	No
All GBO (000s)					
Turnover	14,071	4,920	3,500	3,906	342
Cost of goods sold	13,250	4,517	–	–	–
Gross profit	821	403	–	–	–
Employees remuneration	248	153	176	71	–
Directors remuneration	132	74	122	59	2
Audit fees	4	3	2	2	2
Trading profit	269	103	–	–	–
Depreciation	33	24	16	5	0
Operating profit	236	79	–	–	–
Non trading income	0	0	0	0	0
Interest	0	0	–	–	–
Pre-tax profit	236	79	59	50	2
Taxation	63	26	17	14	1
Profit after tax	173	53	42	36	1
Dividends payable	106	43	45	15	0
Retained profits	67	10	–3	21	1

Table 1.4.15 Global Travel business ratios

Date of accounts	1/31/2000	1/31/99	1/31/98	1/31/97	1/31/96
Consolidated	No	No	No	No	No
No of weeks	52	52	52	52	52
Subsidiary status	No	No	No	No	No
Profitability ratios					
ROCE (%)	245.83	179.55	310.53	227.27	200.00
Return on total assets (%)	66.48	9.92	25.11	48.54	0.84
Pre-tax profit margin (%)	1.68	1.61	1.69	1.28	0.58
Revenue ratios					
Turnover/Total assets	39.64	6.18	14.89	37.92	1.44
Turnover/Fixed assets	158.10	129.47	64.81	114.88	342.00
Working capital/Turnover (%)	0.05	0.12	−1.00	−0.31	–
Credit and liquidity ratios					
Current ratio	1.03	1.01	0.84	0.85	1.00
Quick ratio	1.03	1.01	0.84	0.85	1.00
Debtor days (days)	3.3	37.6	16.8	0.1	148.3
Creditor days (days)	0.9	5.6	15.6	4.4	108.9
Gearing ratios					
Total debt/Net worth (%)	0.00	51.72	0.00	0.00	0.00
Share funds/Total liabs (%)	37.07	3.78	23.46	9.32	–
LT debt/Net worth (%)	0.00	0.52	0.00	0.00	0.00
Interest/Pre-interest profit (%)	0.00	0.00	–	–	–

Benchmarking

Developed by the Department of Trade and Industry and Business Link the benchmarking index is dedicated to following SMEs. Some 80 per cent of the 1,200 firms that have undertaken benchmarking employ between 11 and 250 staff and almost 100 new service and manufacturing companies are being added to the index each month.

The first half of the benchmarking exercise measures quantitative performance data against other firms within a given sector. Participants are compared in terms of sales, costs, product and service innovation, return on capital and other factors.

The second half is based on the Business Excellence Model developed by the European Quality Foundation. The information is largely qualitative and is gathered from staff from all levels within a company. Its performance is then rated in nine areas, which include leadership, people management, customer and staff satisfaction and results.

Alfas Industries

Using benchmarking to find out how you are doing

Alfas Industries, with profits of £550,000 on sales of £5 million, has used benchmarking to good effect. Whilst senior managers were pleased to discover that the company's profit margins were in the top quartile for the chemical, plastics and ceramics sectors in which it operates, they were less pleased with the results of the qualitative benchmarking.

MD Mike Hamilton says: 'I was absolutely devastated to discover we ranked so low for customer satisfaction. I had a gut feeling it was an area where we could do better. But I was taken aback to discover how low our scores were'.

The statistics showed Alfas was poorly rated by its customers for failure to deliver on time. They also showed that the number of customers making complaints was far higher than the average for its sector.

George Thompson, the sales director, says: 'We thought we were quite good for customer satisfaction, but actually we were rubbish'.

Not only were the delivery contractors failing to achieve their targets, there were a number of internal problems within the company's 35,000 sq ft premises in Washington, Tyne and Wear, where Alfas produces tape products and silicone sealants for glaziers and other construction businesses.

Errors were being made when telephone or written orders were transcribed on to production documents. Special discounts agreed between sales staff and customers were not being reflected quickly enough in the invoices sent with each delivery.

'Customer satisfaction went shooting up the agenda when the benchmarking results came through', says Hamilton. 'Our priorities had to be adjusted double-quick sharp.'

Despite the shock, Hamilton, 49, is an enthusiastic advocate of benchmarking. 'What we need to know is not what we are doing right but what we are doing wrong. That information is far more valuable', he says.

Assignment 9

The financial audit

Carry out the financial audit, using ratios. Figure 1.4.3 is included to enable you to summarise the financial elements of the position audit, identify trends, and throw up differences between your firm and your competitors' firms (or the industry norm if you know it).

You should also start to make some notes on the likely action required, or targets to set, for later in the strategic planning process. For example, you may need some specific goals for the business plan, such as to improve your average collection period by X per cent.

You may find it more manageable if you first do the ratios on your firm and look at historic changes, and then do ratios for your competitors. Then compare and contrast your performance with that of competitors.

Figure 1.4.3 Financial audit: summary of ratios

Ratio	3 years ago	2 years ago	Last year	This year	Average % growth	Main competitors	% Difference from our performance	Action required*
1. Percentage sales growth								
2. Percentage profit growth								
3. Headcounter growth								
4. $\dfrac{\text{Sales}}{\text{No of employees}}$								
5. $\dfrac{\text{Profit}}{\text{No of employees}}$								
6. Value added per employee								
7. ROCE $\dfrac{\text{Profit before interest and tax}}{\text{Capital employed}}$								
8. ROSC $\dfrac{\text{Profit after tax}}{\text{Share capital and reserves}}$								

Figure 1.4.3 Financial audit: summary of ratios (*continued*)

Ratio	3 years ago	2 years ago	Last year	This year	Average % growth	Main competitors	% Difference from our performance	Action required*
9. Gearing: $\dfrac{\text{Share capital and reserves}}{\text{All long-term capital}}$								
10. $\dfrac{\text{Operating profit}}{\text{Loan interest}}$								
11. $\dfrac{\text{Gross profit}}{\text{Sales}}$								
12. $\dfrac{\text{Operating profit}}{\text{Sales}}$								
13. $\dfrac{\text{Net profit}}{\text{Sales}}$								
14. Current ratio: $\dfrac{\text{Current assets}}{\text{Current liabilities}}$								
15. Quick ratio: $\dfrac{\text{Debtors and cash}}{\text{Current liabilities}}$								
16. Average collection period $\dfrac{\text{Debtors}}{\text{Sales}} \times 365$								

Figure 1.4.3 Financial audit: summary of ratios (*concluded*)

Ratio	3 years ago	2 years ago	Last year	This year	Average % growth	Main competitors	% Difference from our performance	Action required*
17. $\dfrac{\text{Creditors}}{\text{Purchases}} \times 365$								
18. $\dfrac{\text{Stock}}{\text{Cost of sales}} \times 365$								
19. $\dfrac{\text{Sales}}{\text{Working capital}}$								
20. $\dfrac{\text{Sales}}{\text{Fixed assets}}$								
21. Other key ratios								
22.								
23.								
24.								

* You do not have to wait to the bitter end to take steps to improve performance. So if, for example, you see your sales per employee is way out of line with the norm in your industry, jot down any ideas for improvement as you go along.

5 *How to diagnose your organisation*

In answering the question 'Where are we now?' any growing business will want to look not only at its market position and its financial status but also at the viability of its organisation. The windows of opportunity don't stay open for long in the e-world; the business needs the capacity to make rapid, cross-functional changes to deliver an effective market strategy.

The purpose of this chapter, which is spelt out in the checklists of Assignment 10, is to help you take a fresh look at your organisation in the light of:

● organisation 'fit' with your changing business environment (identified in Assignment 2);
● your organisational phase of growth (Greiner, 1972);
● benchmarking against best practice.

Assignment 10 also asks you to suspend for a minute your logical left-brain thought processes and engage the creative right brain in drawing a picture of how you perceive your organisation as it is now. There is a saying that 'a picture is worth a thousand words' and, like all the assignments in this workbook, this exercise can also provide a fun way of involving your team in the thinking that will eventually come together in your business plan. So far a rich cache of organisation pictures has produced: islands without bridges; castaways in a stormy sea of shark competitors; ships with crews asleep and drunk downstairs; even a cosy, comfortable country cottage. The messages can be strong!

Organisation 'fit' with the environment

In trying to diagnose whether you've got the right organisation in place there are unfortunately no clear rules about numbers of people, or management style or reporting relationships. It all depends on the business environment in which you operate. For example, if you're selling marketing services to the pharmaceutical industry and you rely on a professional, flexible salesforce, the last thing you want is a heavy, central organisation, which stops the local salesperson taking initiative with the customer. Then again, if you're selling battleships perhaps you do!

In fact there is no such thing as the right organisation, there is only one which is appropriate to what you're trying to do with your business. Even then, as Greiner tells us, it won't stay right for long. The concept of 'fit' says that your organisation is right if it fits the business environment in which you are operating and if it helps you achieve your strategy. Indeed, without an effective organisation, you won't have a strategy!

Here are some typical examples of fit and misfit between organisations and their changing environments:

- When ICL was selling large 'boxes' and the customer wanted user-friendly desktop systems, there was an almost fatal misfit between strategy and environment.
- When ICL moved its strategy to selling solutions it found that the financial processes necessary for monitoring the sale of a few large boxes were no longer adequate for measuring many small sales – there was an organisation misfit to do with internal systems.
- When Robb Wilmot, then-MD of ICL, tried to move the organisation of 20,000 people towards his strategy for survival, he found an immensely frustrating misfit of resistance from his management team who hoped change would go away. Subsequently, ICL was first acquired by STC, a take-over that totally failed to realise synergistic benefit, and then became part of Fujitsu, when it moved out of manufacturing totally.
- When George Davies was removed from the board of Next, there was a very public management style misfit.

● When Sears Holdings tried to diversify into new markets it encountered a major structure misfit as its then highly centralised 'supertanker' shape failed to allow a fast response to customers.

The sheer pace of environmental change, driven by an unbelievable acceleration of information, is so fast that many businesses are being boiled alive. As Professor Charles Handy tells us, 'if you put a frog in a pan of cold water and gently bring it to the boil, it will sit there until it is boiled alive. The frog (and many organisations!) can't sense that the temperature of the water is changing' (Handy, 1989).

Sock Shop

Sophie Mirman, explaining the demise of Sock Shop, said:

> Of course we made mistakes. The biggest was our expansion into the United States. But we had an awful lot of bad luck at home: two hot summers, which depressed hosiery sales, combined with a series of train and tube strikes, which kept so many of our shops closed one day each week over several months. And on top of that, interest rates doubled to 15 per cent. Any one of these factors we could have coped with but not all of them together. And there was absolutely nothing we could do about any of them. I felt like a rabbit caught in headlights.

The moral of the story is never get complacent, always have your antennae out to spot unpleasant signals and don't go into denial when you see something you don't like!

Like nostalgia, business 'ain't what it used to be'. Every era has fads – in the 1960s it was mergers and acquisitions, in the 1970s product and market diversification, and by the 1990s strongly back to mergers and acquisitions on a grand scale. During the years, however, as an article in *The Economist* ('Change then Change Again', March 1991) has suggested, 'several business trends have started to emerge which look decidedly less faddish, some of them appear to be transforming the management map for good'.

The status quo will no longer be a feasible way forward. The economics of the market place are changing drastically. As markets change, so must managers. The odds are that tomorrow's bosses will have to be capable of managing highly decentralised businesses in a global market place. There are exponential changes in product technology, life cycles are shrinking, and e-commerce is transforming the way we do business.

To keep pace, Western businesses are tossing their old assumptions aside. Change is, after all, only another word for growth, but growth will no longer be achieved by doing 'more of the same'. Today's competitors are as likely to be partners as they are rivals. Suppliers are being brought in to help design products. Every aspect of organisation – people, systems and structure – is changing. Companies are sweeping away sprawling headquarters and drastically cutting layers of management. The skyscraper shape of business is going for good. As it grows flatter the company of the future may well resemble the shamrock organisation envisaged by Charles Handy, its three leaves representing a central band of core workers, a secondary band of sub-contractors and a loose network of part-time and temporary workers. Vertical career paths are disappearing – managers will have to take the horizontal path to gaining experience. Firms will become 'greener' and more interested in their business philosophy and ethics. A cross-disciplinary approach will be the key to business success in the future.

Your organisational phase of growth

Having identified in Assignment 2 the major external pressures on your business, you are in a good position to start diagnosing whether you have the right organisation for your present stage of growth. For example, one entrepreneurial company successfully providing marketing services discovered when carrying out an environmental scan just how volatile the market place had become. They found that a government White Paper could cause them to lose the lot, that some customers were dissatisfied with the service, and that new competition was a much bigger threat than had previously been realised: 'They're coming after us'. The conclusion was that 'we have been too inward looking and egocentric' and that the organisation had to become much more flexible and responsive, and much less complacent.

The Greiner model of the five phases of growth through which all businesses move is a very good basis for diagnosing where you are in the development cycle, and therefore what kind of organisation problems you can expect to meet. Most businesses will probably lie somewhere between the crisis of leadership and the fourth stage of growth. Each growth phase brings its own organisational challenge. Phase 2, for example, brings the challenge of putting in necessary systems and procedures whilst finding, motivating and keeping key staff. Phase 3, the challenge of letting go, replacing a top-down management style with delegation and team building. Phase 4, addressing an increasingly fragmented organisation through coordination, control and corporate culture.

Innovex (now part of the Quintiles Group)

In 1996, Barrie Haigh sold his £80 million turnover business to Quintiles, a US-based contract research group, for £550 million. He personally made in excess of £300 million from the deal. He had good reason to congratulate himself. He founded Innovex in 1979 to conduct clinical trials and to outsource sales resources needed by global pharmaceutical companies. The business, started in 1979 as a tiny group of people in a back room in Marlow, had become a global player that can talk on equal terms to the biggest pharmaceutical companies in the world. Let's see how he got there.

Innovex started as a typical Phase 1 owner/founder organisation. The founder was an enormously energetic entrepreneur whose physical and mental energies were absorbed with the customers. 'Success was down to a very few people, primarily the chairman.' Communication among employees was frequent and informal and usually around the billiard table. Employees worked every hour they could, and were rewarded by an involved, happy atmosphere. The approach to customers was action-orientated and the feedback instant. There was a passionate attempt to avoid politics and a disdain of internal management.

All this wonderful creative, exciting buzz was essential for the company to get off the ground. But therein lies the problem. As the company grew in size and age, more efficiency was needed in managing money and resources; new employees didn't always know what was going on, more people made informal communication more difficult to achieve. The company found itself burdened by unwanted management responsibilities that it reluctantly saw as necessary but didn't regard as fun. Instead of everyone being happy 'hunters' the business needed the 'farmers' of a Phase 2 organisation. Here is how people described their organisation as they approached the crisis of leadership:

'We're self-centred rather than customer centred.'
'We're happy amateurs.'
'We're not businesspeople, totally top-line, sales-driven.'
'We're unplanned and confused.'
'It's organised chaos, you sink or swim.'
'We let ourselves down on detail.'

In this case, the chairman weathered the crisis of leadership, survived the first phase and went on to install the functional organisation, accounting systems, and direction needed for Phase 2 growth. The business moved out of its quaint offices into a streamlined and prestigious building, the organisation grew enormously in number of employees and turnover, the customer reputation sparkled. The problems were over ... or were they? Just as every young business is permanently hungry for money, so it seems a fact of life that every past success leads to future problems. The list of once-lionised business heroes who haven't been able to move on from past successes is endless.

So the company's success in Phase 2 growth creates the seeds which made a second revolution and crisis inevitable. The chairman, as he saw his organisation become more diverse and complex, had less inclination to manage it all himself. After all, his skills were as the entrepreneurial/outward face of his organisation. He began to see the organisation as cumbersome and centralised, with the customers no longer understanding who did what. Even worse, because of the personal power and charisma of the chairman, the lower level managers were not accustomed to making decisions for themselves. Yet at the same time they were demanding more responsibility: 'If we are managers, then let us alone'. The crisis of autonomy had arrived.

The moral of the story is that as the owner/founder you may be getting in the way of growth. At the very least you need to recognise different stages of growth and constantly re-invent your role and leadership style accordingly.

Many, many companies founder during this stage. There is a desperate paradox. The man or woman at the top must let go; must move from meddler to strategist. Not only may this change in role make the owner/founder personally feel extremely uncomfortable as power is relinquished, but he or she frequently finds that there is no one to relinquish power to! There is a vacuum; lower levels of management want power but their history hasn't taught them how to use it. The top person must withdraw, delegate and build a management team but at the same time, as the owner/founder of the business, he or she may need to continue to reinforce the special vision and company culture that he or she, largely alone, has painfully built over the years. As Anita Roddick, founder of Body Shop, says in her autobiographical *Business as Unusual*, 'I have a founder's role, but does that mean that I may be impeding the direction of the company in some way?' A recent press announcement suggested that she has answered this question for herself and will, over the next few years, be leaving the business into which she put her heart and soul. Leaders of businesses who can recognise their own vulnerability and shortcomings are well on the way to success. For example:

Barrie Haigh took himself off on the Cranfield Business Growth Programme, restructured Innovex into profit centres with much greater responsibility, formalised communication and instituted both an innovative reward package and a programme of management development to start building the strength of his management team. The company was by then sailing the smoother waters of Phase 3, growth through delegation. However, the management team didn't fool themselves that the battle was won. They were anticipating the next crisis, and sure enough it materialised in the form of a crisis of control. For the first time in the company's history a chief executive was recruited from outside. The pull for control between the new CEO and his founder chairman started to become very apparent. Rifts began to emerge as new allegiances formed. Political behaviours counter to the company's founding culture were everywhere. Indeed the culture itself was in transition as new recruits from different background made their views felt. The business only served the UK market, but saw immense global opportunities if it could only get its act together. As it moved into

Greiner's fourth phase of growth, managed expansion through merger and acquisition brought great success, particularly because Innovex was so careful to assess cultural 'fit' with target partners. By the mid-1990s, Innovex employed more than 3,000 people, and had a significant presence in mainland Europe. By 1996, Innovex had joined forces with the North Carolina-based group Quintiles, to form the largest contract pharmaceutical business in the world, employing well in excess of 10,000 people globally.

However, the newly combined management team would be the first to say that the only certainty in their organisation is that whatever is right for them now will be wrong in the future. The managers are far from complacent. They recently surveyed every single member of staff, to benchmark their changing culture and to ensure that it stays appropriate in tomorrow's world. They are already anticipating the next challenge of growth and the next crisis, spelling both threat and opportunity for their business.

The moral of the tale is that businesses never stay the same, the bad news is that whatever you did well in the past will sow the seeds of your next crisis, and the good news is that recognising and overcoming crisis will fuel accelerated growth!

Benchmarking against best practice

In order to diagnose the organisational health of your business, we have so far suggested two approaches: firstly to assess how far your organisation 'fits' the external pressures from your business environment; secondly to identify your stage of development (measured against Greiner's five phases of growth).

There is a third approach: to look around for best practice in the corporate world, against which to benchmark your organisation. This, of course, is the approach sold in books such as Tom Peter and Robert Waterman's *In Search of Excellence* (1985) where case studies give a blueprint of what successful companies are doing. In combination with our earlier approaches, this can give you some clues, or at least reinforce that you're heading in the right direction!

There are probably as many blueprints as there are management bestsellers. You're free to pick out your own from any airport bookstall! However, there do seem to be common themes offering useful clues about the shape of things to come.

Characteristics of effective organisations

We have found the following to be useful and practical ways to help to grow businesses into effective organisations. In your company, you need to:

- tune in to your company's environment;
- create and communicate a clear vision;
- build a strong culture/pride in the organisation;
- empower people: make everyone a hero;
- establish flexible organisation structures;
- build coalitions and heighten teamwork;
- create reward systems that share credit and recognition.

Let's look briefly at each.

Tune in to your company's environment. This summarises the need to stay in touch with your customers, competitors and other external pressures for change and to try to design your organisation around changing business requirements.

Sometimes when you carry out a quick radar scan of your external environment you will find that the terrifying blip on the screen turns out to be a seagull rather than a super-tanker. But if it's the other way round, it's perhaps better anticipated!

It is amazing to what extent top teams of businesses are capable of deluding themselves that what they would like to happen is what is actually happening.

Create and communicate a clear vision. It is increasingly being said that the one job of the leader is to inspire others with a vision for the future.

'I have a dream' said Martin Luther King, and with this dream he changed the world forever. It is vision that puts the passion and the power into dry old businesses. It is vision that sells the business to its potential recruits, its employees and customers, and not least to the financial markets for capital. In our work at Cranfield we have repeatedly observed how vision magically transforms the most apparently mundane of businesses and the quietest of entrepreneurs. Indeed it is those people who are set alight by a passion for their business, bordering on obsession, who will succeed. That is, if they can communicate the vision to others as passionately as they live it in their heads. This vision creates momentum; it pulls people through the uncomfortable process of change by offering the picture of an exciting future. It gives people something to identify with, a meaning and purpose – just as the vision of a holiday, of marriage, or of retirement helps us to get through the daily routine! Many leaders have their own personal vision of their business, but it tends to stay in their heads as a kind of private daydream. Often the manager assumes that this vision will transmit itself into the skulls of his or her employees by some miraculous paranormal process. Nothing could be further from the truth! To have any value to the organisation, the vision must be owned and lived by *everyone in the organisation*, and for this to happen it has to be constantly stated, restated and reinforced. There is an archetypal story of the lift operator taking the chairman to his penthouse executive suite and chatting in the meantime about the business. The chairman mentions a possible diversification; the lift operator immediately presses the emergency button and stops the lift. 'Mr Chairman,' he says, 'this cannot happen: it is inconsistent with our business vision.' Just so! The vision should guide people's behaviour at all times. Don't be like the managers who said, 'We have a vision, but we don't tell anyone about it'. Make sure your passion is everyone else's passion too.

Body Shop has been driven by the passion and obsession of Anita Roddick. She has created a company with a strong values system, socially, ethically and environmentally. 'That's what sets us apart. If you took that away from us, we'd be a 'dime a dozen' cosmetics company' (Roddick, 1991). The challenge is for the business to reinterpret its vision as she disengages from the business.

Steve Jobs had a clear vision for Apple and gained enormous commitment from employees in working towards it. He went on to do the same thing at Next.

Build a strong culture of pride in the organisation. Culture provides a rule-making framework that enables everyone to cope with the unpredictable. Effective organisations develop shared values that reinforce their vision. For example, the shared values of an entrepreneurial Phase 1 organisation create an emphasis on fun, informality and customer responsiveness. It is shared values (or culture) which motivate managers to stay with a Phase 2 organisation as it puts on the straitjacket of structure and systems. It is a strong culture that grows the commitment of Phase 3's growth through delegation, and it is a strong culture that provides the control and coordination of Phase 4. These values sum up 'the way we do things around here' and define the unique personality, almost the fingerprint, of the organisation. The culture is the genetic code letting people know what is acceptable behaviour in terms of working practice, socialising, drinking habits and dress. Successful companies, big and small, tend to have strong cultures. The old command and control style of management doesn't work any more. Things happen too fast in the e-economy to wait for someone up on high to give the answer. The guiding principles need to be clear to everyone in the business; that way everyone knows what to do, and everyone is empowered to do their bit in giving excellent customer service. If the 'brand' represents the external image, then culture represents the internal values and practices which turn promotional 'puff' into solid reality:

> Culture not product. Increasingly, companies are having to market their culture or brand image, not simply their products, in order to beat their competitors. BMW and Sony sell an image called 'quality'; Britain's Body Shop sells 'environmental friendliness'. But this will convince consumers only if the appropriate culture

thrives throughout the company. Japanese managers have this driven home to them throughout their careers; Western business schools still find the idea hard to teach. But teach it they must.
Source: The Economist, 2 March 1991

- Jim Treybig, who founded Tandem Computers in 1974, had soon built a US$1.6 billion turnover business with 10,000 employees. His company is famous for his 'beer busts', for an informal style, for a president who attends every induction programme, and for a selection process which is a gruelling inquisition, even if the post is for a stock clerk! The message is clear – you have to be good to work at Tandem.
- Johnson & Johnson have long held a credo that passed the ultimate test: it guided the company's behaviour through the potentially devastating cyanide pollution of their product Tylenol.
- McDonalds strive to provide QSCV (Quality, Service, Convenience, Value).
- Toshiba have a self-selection video spelling out the commitment that gives the flavour of the factory – if you won't like it 'you might want to think twice'.
- ICL Fujitsu has had, since 1983, the 'ICL Way', a statement of seven core beliefs.

Empower people: make everyone a hero. The days of the leader as hero are gone. The world is too complex for any one person to manage. Too many case studies of dinosaur organisations in the UK show that needing change doesn't make it happen, nor, on its own, does a new CEO at the top of the organisation. In the grown-up world of e-business, transactions, both business-to-consumer and business-to-business, are fundamentally shifting power. As buyers leverage their purchasing power, power shifts away from seller to buyer. New intermediaries appear and old ones die out. The more you outsource the more you are managing empowered resources you don't own and control. If they don't like the way you manage them, your assets can walk. The consumer is far more informed and expectations are higher. The delivery times which would have been tolerated in the past are being smashed to pieces in a world where a book ordered in the United States can be delivered to the Cotswolds two days later.

Many of the recent business successes have been service providers, rather than old-style product businesses. In these businesses, every person in the organisation, from receptionist to order-taker, has a vital role in delivering customer satisfaction. Power shifts again, empowered individuals are more able to deliver a fast, responsive, personalised response to customers. More than this, the margin for error in such businesses is so small that the price of a wrong decision from a disempowered employee can be enormous. You need to mobilise the support of your people behind constant and unpredictable change. You need to help people focus their energies on the new ways. Growing businesses we see around are doing just this. They are doing it by:

- designing organisations around the needs of the customers and making the successes and failures visible;
- immersing all employees in a 'customer first' culture;
- tapping reserves of creativity and energy through brainstorming sessions to find better ways of doing things;
- pushing responsibility down as low as possible so that those at the front line of customer contact are empowered to solve problems;
- creating open communication and involvement through weekly 'happy hours', away days, training sessions;
- involving everyone in the vision and the future of the business.

Establish flexible organisation structures. The organisation structure of the past was like a New York skyscraper: very tall, lots of levels of hierarchy, a great distance between boss and subordinates, vertical rather than horizontal communication. The shape for the future is different; even the metaphors have changed! People are talking of organisations being like doughnuts or amoebas or shamrocks – the search is on for new and creative organisation shapes which provide flexibility, integration and customer focus. Around entrepreneurial business organisations we see the following clear trends:

- Smaller, flatter shapes. Organisations are doing away with levels of management so that there is as little hierarchy as possible between chairperson and newest recruit.
- Emphasis on teamworking within small business units (aligned to customer needs) but also teamworking across the organisation to enable a fast integrated response across different functions.
- Less emphasis on the old span of control rule as the job of the manager becomes more that of setting the rules and orchestrating the team rather than directing and controlling it. Less difference between the boss and subordinates, both are now very much part of the team.
- Less concern with keeping everything inside the organisation and a more flexible boundary with the outside world, which includes sub-contracting the transport fleet, outsourcing, collaboration with competitors, joint supplier agreements.
- More temporary forms of structure which run parallel to the formal organisation, ie multi-functional/cross boundary project teams, quality circles, business units which are spun off.

Build coalitions and heighten teamwork. The local business team will always provide the strongest identity, but increasingly businesses are making attempts to create a total corporate identity, for example sending production people out to meet customers, rotating job roles, holding regular problem-solving meetings across departments, meeting up regularly with customers and suppliers. This creates a more flexible and adaptive business.

It is worth remembering that in making the decision whether or not to invest in your business, venture capitalists will put as high a priority on the strength of your management team as they do on the business plan and financial stability. One of the greatest challenges of a growing business is to create under the original owner/founder a second tier management team that can run the day-to-day business, and free the founder up to create tomorrow's business.

Create reward systems that share credit and recognition. What gets measured gets produced. What gets rewarded gets produced again. As a small company moves through Greiner's phases of growth it will constantly need to change both what is rewarded and how rewards are made. For example, in Phase 1, growth, the need is for customers, the rewards are likely to be immediate, sales-related and perhaps commission-based. In Phase 2, growth through direction, control-based systems are introduced and managers measured against their control of costs. In Phase 3, the move towards profit centre responsibility necessitates rewarding not sales, not cost control, but profit performance and the rewards may more sensibly be linked to some measure of corporate profit sharing. There is room for continuous ingenuity in seeking out different rewards: individual or group incentives, free tickets and gift certificates, profit sharing, promotion, excellence awards, new work assignments.

The rule is expect it (and reward it) or forget it.

Assignment 10

Diagnostic checklists

1. Draw a picture of how you see your organisation now (warts and all). Your picture should not be an organisation chart and should not include words. (What picture would your managers draw and is their perception in line with yours?)
2. Complete the Organisation Development Diagnostic Questionnaire below to locate where your business appears to be in relation to the Greiner growth phases. What are the organisation issues you are likely to be facing?

Instructions for completing the organisational development diagnostic
The organisation development diagnostic consists of 60 descriptive statements. Your task is to work through this list and to identify those statements you believe to be accurate in describing your company.

Each time you come to an apt description you should tick it on the questionnaire. When you have looked through all 60 statements, please transfer the ticks to the score sheet, recording your choice on the score sheet by putting a tick in the box carrying the same number.

Add up your ticks and total them at the bottom. Around which vertical columns do your scores group? This would appear to be your diagnosis of your company's present stage of development. What are the inherent challenges you face?

Organisational development diagnostic questionnaire
(adapted from John Leppard, 1987)

1. ☐ The organisational structure is very informal.
2. ☐ Top management are finding themselves bombarded with many unwanted management responsibilities.
3. ☐ Management focus mainly on the efficiency of operations.
4. ☐ Staff lower down in the organisation possess more knowledge about, for example, markets, products, trends etc than do top management.
5. ☐ The main management focus is to expand markets.
6. ☐ Those in top management feel they are losing control of the business.
7. ☐ The main management focus is coordination and consolidation.
8. ☐ There is a lack of confidence between line managers and specialist staff/head office and the field.
9. ☐ The main focus of management is on problem solving and innovation.
10. ☐ There is an over-emphasis on teamwork.
11. ☐ The top management style is very individualistic and entrepreneurial.
12. ☐ Top management takes too long in responding to queries and requests.
13. ☐ The organisational structure is centralised and functional, ie based on specialists.
14. ☐ There is insufficient delegation to provide freedom for those who are capable of making decisions.
15. ☐ The organisational structure is decentralised and individual divisions or departments have a high level of autonomy.
16. ☐ Many people at lower levels have too much freedom to run their own show.
17. ☐ Decentralised units have been merged into product groups.
18. ☐ Line managers resent heavy staff direction.

19. ☐ The organisational structure is a matrix of task or project teams.
20. ☐ There is a dependency on group-think to the extent that some managers are losing the confidence to make individual decisions.
21. ☐ The main control system is whether or not the sales targets are met.
22. ☐ Top management does not provide enough direction.
23. ☐ Top management style tends to be directive.
24. ☐ Management tends to be over-directive and could easily delegate more.
25. ☐ The top management style is delegative.
26. ☐ The organisation has probably become too decentralised, breeding parochial attitudes.
27. ☐ The top management style is to be a watchdog.
28. ☐ We seem to have lost the ability to respond to new situations or solve problems quickly.
29. ☐ The top management style is highly consultative, meeting together frequently on problem issues.
30. ☐ We are directing too much energy into the functions of our internal teams and tending to overlook what is happening in the outside world.
31. ☐ Long hours are rewarded by modest salaries but with the promise of ownership benefits in the future.
32. ☐ Top management isn't as visible as it ought to be.
33. ☐ The main control systems seem to be concerned with standards and costs.
34. ☐ Flexibility suffers because those who could take decisions have to wait for management to agree.
35. ☐ The main control seems to be in the form of profit centre reporting.
36. ☐ Power seems to have shifted away from top management.
37. ☐ Each product group is an investment centre with extensive planning controls.
38. ☐ Everyone is criticising the bureaucratic paper system that has evolved.
39. ☐ The main control system is for work groups to evaluate their own performance through real-time information systems integrated into daily work.
40. ☐ There is almost too much personal feedback about behaviour at meetings etc.
41. ☐ The management focus is mainly on making and selling.
42. ☐ Top managers are very harassed; conflicts between them are growing.
43. ☐ The main way managers are rewarded is by salary and merit increases.
44. ☐ People are demotivated (even leaving) because they do not have enough personal autonomy in their jobs.
45. ☐ The way managers are rewarded is by individual bonuses.
46. ☐ More coordination of operations is needed if things are to improve.

47. ☐ The way managers are rewarded is through profit sharing and stock options.
48. ☐ Fun and excitement seem to be lacking in the company.
49. ☐ Rewards are geared more to team performance than to individual achievement.
50. ☐ The constant high expectation for creativity in the organisation is stressful.
51. ☐ Top managers are close to customers and have a good understanding of what the market requires.
52. ☐ Top managers do not seem able to introduce the new business techniques that are necessary.
53. ☐ To get on in this company, lower managers do not question decisions made by their seniors.
54. ☐ Staff have their performance appraisals from bosses who have little understanding about the subordinate's job and work problems.
55. ☐ People are told what is expected of them and then allowed to get on with their jobs as they see fit. It's management by exception.
56. ☐ Senior managers are continually checking up to make sure that jobs are completed – they tend to overdo this.
57. ☐ There are many head office personnel who initiate company work programmes to review and control line managers.
58. ☐ Too many people are working to the book.
59. ☐ Interpersonal conflicts are brought into the open and, on the whole, managed in a non-destructive way.
60. ☐ Trying to be always spontaneous and open in relationships at work is proving stressful.

3. Benchmark your organisation against best practice (the seven characteristics of an effective organisation) as shown in Figure 1.5.2.

Organisational Phases for Growth
The five phases of growth (after Greiner)

Phase 1 Growth through creativity	1 Crisis of leadership	Phase 2 Growth through direction	2 Crisis of autonomy	Phase 3 Growth through delegation	3 Crisis of control	Phase 4 Growth through coordination	4 Crisis of red tape	Phase 5 Growth through collaboration	5 Crisis of ?
1	2	3	4	5	6	7	8	9	10
11	12	13	14	15	16	17	18	19	20
21	22	23	24	25	26	27	28	29	30
31	32	33	34	35	36	37	38	39	40
41	42	43	44	45	46	47	48	49	50
51	52	53	54	55	56	57	58	59	60

Table 1.5.1 Organisational development diagnostic: score sheet

	Characteristics of effective organisations	Tick		
		Needs attention	OK	Good
1.	*Tune in to company's environment* How outward looking is your business in monitoring and understanding changing trends of customers, competitors, market place, technology, legislation?			
2.	*Create and communicate a clear vision* Do you have a vision of the kind of business you are trying to create? Does everyone in the organisation know about and feel committed to your company philosophy?			
3.	*Build a strong culture/pride* What's your internal brand image? What values is the business built around and how much do all employees feel a sense of pride in, and identification with, the organisation?			
4.	*Empower people* How far do your people feel a sense of ownership of problems? Do they take necessary action without being told to?			
5.	*Establish flexible organisation structures* How far beyond the formal organisation chart do you go? For example, in setting up project teams, quality circles, informal get-togethers?			
6.	*Build teamwork* To what extent do people identify with their immediate team rather than the total business?			
7.	*Appropriate reward systems* Are you measuring the really important performance criteria and rewarding people for the appropriate behaviour?			

Table 1.5.2 Benchmarking an organisation against best practice

6   *Assessing people, structure and systems*

Following picturing and benchmarking, you can now look at your organisation in more depth: examining its people, its structure and its systems. This exercise aims at enabling you, in Assignments 11 and 12, to carry out a comprehensive analysis of your current organisation capability as a way of assessing whether you have the resources in place to achieve your plans for business growth.

The model we will use for analysis purposes is given in Figure 1.6.1 and you will find a worked example, along with checklists of questions (Figure 1.6.7), at the end of this chapter.

So far we have been looking outward at the fit between the total organisation and the business environment in which you are trying to survive (see Figure 1.6.2).

It's now time to look inside, at your organisation's structure, systems and people organisation and at how they fit not only with the external challenges but also one with another.

In its construction a business organisation is similar to an individual human being. Just like us, the organisation has a skeleton, a nervous system and some blood and guts. The skeleton of the organisation is its structure or shape – the thing that gives it form and indicates its potential for growth. Just as the starfish doesn't have the skeleton to grow into an elephant, so a vertical skyscraper-type business cannot behave like a small informal network business.

Its processes and infrastructure represent the nervous system of your business, from the sales invoicing system to how people communicate with one another, from budgeting to appraisal. Systems form the connections between one bit of the business and another.

The blood and guts, the messy bits of your business, are provided, as you

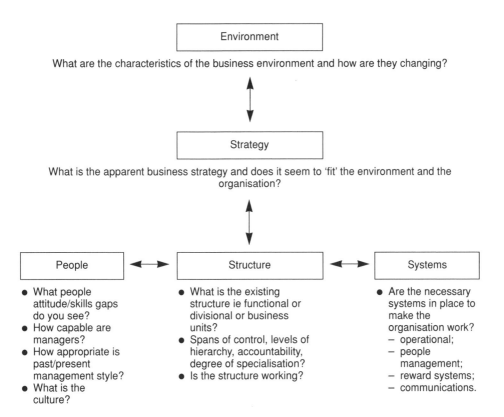

Figure 1.6.1 Organising for change

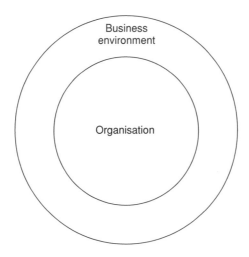

Figure 1.6.2 The fit between organisation and environment

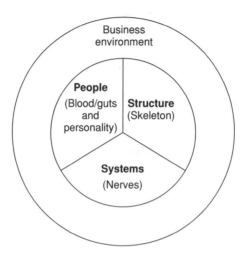

Figure 1.6.3 People, systems and structure fit

probably suspected, by the people in it who, as individuals and as teams, contribute to the unique personality of your business entity. If, for example, you are diversifying into new market niches, you may choose a business centre structure and profit-sharing-type systems. However, you will be in trouble if your people come from one function only, (such as sales or finance) and are incapable of knowing how to operate as general managers.

Our model suggests that as the environment changes so the organisation, in one bound, shifts to accommodate the new reality. Unfortunately, this is rarely the case. Even with enormous environmental changes (like the impact that Japanese competition had on the Swiss watch industry) it can take a very long time before the organisation is prepared to recognise the unpleasant writing on the wall. Even when it does, different bits of the organisation will respond at different speeds – and therefore get out of sync. For example, your structure is almost always a reflection of what you needed in the past rather than now. Even when you change the structure you will find you also need to revamp the appraisal system, your method of tracking performance, or your management training. Running your own business is very like the feat of the circus performer trying to keep a great many plates spinning on sticks at the same time – one plate is always in a state of terminal wobble and in need of an urgent 'tweak'!

We'll now examine what 'tweaking' you may need to do to keep your people, systems and structure plates spinning smoothly and safely.

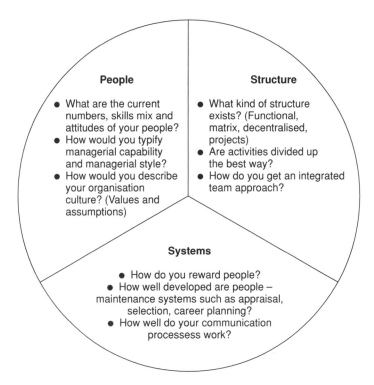

Figure 1.6.4   Assessing organisation capability

Assessing people capability

It is useful to look at people capability in terms of: skills and attitudes; management capability and style, and culture.

Skills and attitudes

In his book *Teaching the Elephant to Dance* (1990), Jim Belasco says: 'Regardless of the intentions expressed in the strategic plan, where you put your key people and money is the direction in which your organisation is going to move.' This means getting the right number of people with the right skills and attitudes in the right jobs. It means investing your resources in your new tomorrow. Even if you have the resources in place now, Greiner tells us that you won't for very long. Of course, when you do identify a misfit, for example the need for marketing skills, there will always be a time lag in acquiring those skills. Whether you train, recruit from outside, or even make people redundant, it all takes time and must be planned for.

Skills mix is the first place to start. Ask yourself the following question:

Will existing skills be adequate or do these need to be built up before the business can grow?

There are several ways you can slice the skills cake: one is to look at it function by function, another is to look at the different levels of your organisation and yet another is to assess how many square pegs you feel you have in round holes.

If you look at the functional mix of skills it is inevitable that you will find shortages as the business grows. For example, the typical business start up in Greiner's Phase 1 is rich in sales skills. However, as it moves into Phase 2, growth through direction, it will demand skills to do with accounting and setting up basic systems – very different from the entrepreneurial profile of the Phase 1 employee. As the business moves into Phase 3, growth through delegation, it is quite probable that there will be a need for some kind of personnel function, maybe professional marketing skills and, above all, management skills needed to run small parts of the business as autonomous units.

Bruce Elliot set up Elliot Brothers Audio Sounds Ltd, in a very interesting business sector, involving specialist engineers selling services to install radio stations and recording studios. Bruce was well aware of the skills mix issues of moving from Phase 1 through Phase 2. In Phase 1 tremendous commitment of time and energy was needed from all staff in setting up prestigious recording facilities for the pop star clients. Bruce, not unnaturally, tended to recruit in his own image. As he sat in his shorts one hot summer day puffing unashamedly on a cigar, he described his recruitment profile as being 'male, ex public school and rugby playing'. However, as he endeavoured to set up the initial systems for Phase 2, growth through direction, Bruce found that when it came to setting up a new filing system, he and most of his recruits had already left for the pub! Despite good year on year growth, the people issues continued to plague the business. Relocation issues became pressing, as it proved impossible to align individual and corporate agendas. Things reached a head in 1993, when Bruce fell out with his brother and co-founder and put the company into liquidation. He reinvented himself, starting up again on his own in the same business sector, eventually backing into a larger business. He recently managed the installation of all the sound and communications systems for the new Royal Opera House, and is thoroughly enjoying doing what he does well. Incidentally, his brother now works for the same company!

The moral is, recruit what the business needs, don't over recruit, don't be scared of recruiting people who will challenge you and, above all, don't recruit clones of yourself!

It was the same story for Marks & Spencer; its very success in recruiting partic-ular skills became an albatross around the neck of development. M & S recog-nised this and at one time actively sought to recruit rebels, people who wouldn't fit in with their previous stereotypes. Similarly, when Citibank in the United States moved for market share in an environment of very passive financial insti-tutions, it sought to employ a very different kind of animal as CEO – a guitar-playing PhD!

It's also worth taking a slice diagonally through your organisation in order to identify any skills vacuums or even blockages. When chairman and founder Mike Evans was on the Business Growth Programme, his business, then named Agrafax, specialised entirely in the agricultural sector, operating from offices outside London. As he diagnosed the key issues of growth, Mike saw that the business was in danger of 'major cardiac arrest' caused by blockages in the flow of people into and through the organisation. He explained to me:

> The people within are a high calibre, talented bunch but there are signs of stress, of blood pressure rising. Recruitment difficulties (in Shropshire) are restricting the flow of new blood into the organisation and the young blood, who are all very highly motivated, are putting pressure on for more autonomy, less restriction from above, more say in strategy, more initiative and greater reward.

Traditionally, in large hierarchic organisations, it has been those at supervisor/middle manager levels who have been blockages, like lumps of cotton wool draining away the life blood of the organisation. In a younger busi-ness it may be that the blockages are higher up. It's worth asking yourself whether it's even possible that you are the blockage and should remove yourself, or whether the board of directors you set up eight years ago now has the right characteristics and calibre for future growth. As the business grows, relation-ships inevitably change, sometimes painfully. As Mike Evans explained:

> I've identified some casualties of growth; for example, when I set up the business 'M' was my only co-director and we enjoyed a very immediate and special relation-ship. Now I have a board of directors and a young management team, 'M' is off to one side. He doesn't like it and I'm not sure he can cope.

Finally, as above, it may be better to face up to the square pegs in the round holes that are, after all, inevitable consequences of growth. Very often people left in such positions – marooned at high tide – are uncomfortable and quite well aware that they are not performing. Facing the problem may be a relief to both parties.

As well as assessing skills mix, you will find it valuable to take a barometer to the attitudes and morale of your employees. Asking yourself the following ques-tions may help pinpoint whether you have a problem:

What is my employee turnover rate? How does it compare with my competitors/last year?

Are levels of sickness/absenteeism high or low?

Do I know why people are leaving?

A useful diagnostic tool to use when trying to answer the last question is the exit interview. Anyone leaving the company is questioned by an impartial person who can establish the reasons why. For example, is that person leaving for more money, because of a better opportunity, or because he or she feels frustrated? Most people in these circumstances are quite happy to talk freely and you can learn a great deal. Attitude surveys, particularly if you carry them out year on year, will benchmark levels of employee morale and highlight problem areas.

Management capability and style

In looking at where your organisation is now, ask yourself the following questions:

Do I have enough managers to run my business well?

How much growth could they handle without becoming overstretched?

Is there anyone who can run the business in my absence?

How do I go about recruiting key managers?

How much can I delegate?

Example 1

When Mike Evans, Chairman of Agrafax (now part of the Mistral Group) asked himself the questions above he identified significant gaps. Until then the business had been small enough for most people to be working pretty much as loners. Where they managed, they managed accounts, rather than people. However, as the business grew in size there was a strong requirement for good man-management. Mike identified the management animal of the future as someone who was not only a technical specialist and a good communicator, but also a business person and motivator of people. As one of his directors explained at the time, 'We have come through gangling adolescence and reached our twenty-first birthday'. Since then, the adolescent has grown up. Mike entered a new phase of growth as he diversified out of a 95 per cent reliance on the troubled agricultural sector to build new business in other niche markets. He changed the name of the business from 'Agrafax' to 'Mistral', to reflect a more European approach. He envisages moving from two to four regional offices, but notes that in the 'virtual' world of the future remote working will become the norm.

At every stage of organisational growth, new challenges create the requirement for new managerial skills. It pays off to face painful management issues head on; they won't go away.

Example 2

As Barrie Haigh assessed the management team he had built up at Innovex (now part of the Quintiles Group), he saw people who were highly intelligent, young, lively, capable, articulate and best of all highly motivated. The level of job satisfaction was remarkable. Yet Barrie saw little reason for complacency. He saw that as Innovex continued its phenomenal rate of growth, lack of depth of management potential could easily become the major constraint on growth. One hundred per cent of managers felt that they had as much as they could cope with at that moment and would be quite happy to stay in their present jobs for a further one to three years. Lack of obvious successors, both to himself and to his MD, had 'become a major issue'. His conclusion was 'we needed more depth of management throughout – and quickly'.

Taking up the challenge of building a strong second tier management team is a prerequisite of continued growth.

Take a look not only at the management capability of yourself and your team but also at your management style. As the old saying goes, 'It's not what you do but the way that you do it'. Ask yourself:

What typifies your management style and that of your managers?

One Yorkshireman described his immediate boss as 'having the charisma of a slug'. Or do you lean towards the Attila the Hun style typified by Harold Geneen of ITT in his philosophy: 'Express criticism, withhold praise and instil job insecurity'. The management style of the founder can sometimes be a major block on growth in Phase 2 and beyond. Nor should you believe that you are frozen into one way of behaving. With a conscious effort even management leopards can change their spots.

John Hornsey, a young and abrasive technical director, moved south from Yorkshire to attempt the turnaround of a threatened engineering factory. He succeeded brilliantly in solving the problems that had built up over the years. In the process, by his own admission, he came close to committing murder; telephone directories and occasionally the telephone itself were uprooted. John was perceived, not unnaturally given his style and the rescue job he was attempting, as a fire-eating monster. No one saw the human behind the gruff exterior. At that time it didn't matter. However, as the factory moved into a period of growth and expansion, John recognised that he and the management team needed to make a conscious effort to change towards a more consensual style of management. People didn't feel empowered and they weren't about to stick their necks out when the blood still ran from the walls. John stood up in front of the total workforce of over 300 and said, 'We are going to have a different management style, we are going to change'. He introduced an attitude survey to take the temperature of the water and committed himself, in advance of the survey, to live by its results. This he and the management team have done, introducing exceptionally effective team briefings, management walk about and other consultative mechanisms. It took time for the workforce to be convinced, but they came to greatly respect John's integrity and open style.

Experiment with new ways of leading; you will be amazed how powerful your attempt to change can be.

Culture

When you put together all the day-to-day ways in which you, your managers and employees behave, you get *culture*. How the receptionist greets a visitor, whether managers are visible to staff, where managers eat and with whom, who goes or doesn't go to the pub, what people wear, all these things and many more provide the signals which people read as 'the way we do things round here'.

How would you and your managers describe your business culture?

The sum of your culture can provide a nutritious jelly or the culture can be treacle, the inertia which will stop your business from changing and growing – because, 'We've always done things that way'. Years after the death of Walt Disney, for example, his top management apparently met every new proposal with the comment, 'Walt wouldn't like it'.

If you want to make your culture work for rather than against you, take the example of Topnotch Health Clubs plc. The business was founded by CEO Matthew Harris, in April 1991, as an operator of health and fitness clubs targeted at the value for money, convenience sector of the market. Topnotch listed on the AIM in March 2000, and shortly afterwards, owned and ran 16 health clubs in the south of England. Matthew has a passion for the fitness industry which is demonstrated in his slogan 'Dare to be different', and which is reflected in every aspect of the business, from the lively attitude of staff, to the branding of premises (Power Zones/Planet Spin/The Iron Works), from the determination to make the fitness experience 'fun' for the customers to the bright red and blue book style annual accounts. Matthew's values are fundamentally around people, innovation, breaking convention and rapid growth. You can sense the culture the moment you enter his clubs; the management team is young, vibrant and passionately committed to the business. In a recent discussion of management team values, managers threw out boring motherhood statements as not adequately reflecting the 'buzz' of Topnotch. Instead they went for describing their Topnotch values in vivid images, 'If Topnotch were a planet, taste, element or animal what would it be?' For example:

'We will go boldly in creating ideas' (planet – Mars).

'We will have edge/freshness/zest/sharpness' (taste – lemon).

'We will be passionate, energetic, and encourage our teams to make the challenge and we will take the risk (element – fire).

'We will be rare, aggressive, powerful and challenging' (animal – tiger).

If, like Matthew, you can pull off the trick of 'daring to be different' so that every aspect of your external 'branding' matches your internal 'values' and behaviours, then you have true market differentiation.

One of the frequently used and productive ways of assessing culture is to get a group of your managers to brainstorm a list of words of impressions which sum up the characteristics of your business under the two headings of 'Where have we been?' and 'Where are we now?'. The results can be illuminating.

No prizes for guessing the name of this company:

Table 1.6.1 Brainstorming business characteristics example 1

What we used to be like	What we are now
● Penny a week ● 'Man from the…' ● Mum and Dad's insurance company ● Old fashioned ● Staid ● Down-market	● Changing ● Diversifying ● Big (biggest) ● Becoming up to date ● Still too deferential

Or this:

Table 1.6.2 Brainstorming business characteristics example 2

Historic	Now
● Best pilots ● Military attitudes ● Rigid hierarchy ● Introverted – no grasp of the market ● Decision by committee	● 'Putting people first' training programme ● Customer first ● No more military titles ● New rewards system ● Are top leaders in business or politics?

(Answers at the end of this chapter.)

Or you could assess your culture and try to place it in one of the following boxes (see Figure 1.6.5). Whichever box you end up in doesn't mean you can't change your culture. For example, the famous Abbey National deliberately tried to move from a 'process' culture towards a 'work hard, play hard' culture, more suited to a highly competitive and decentralised marketplace.

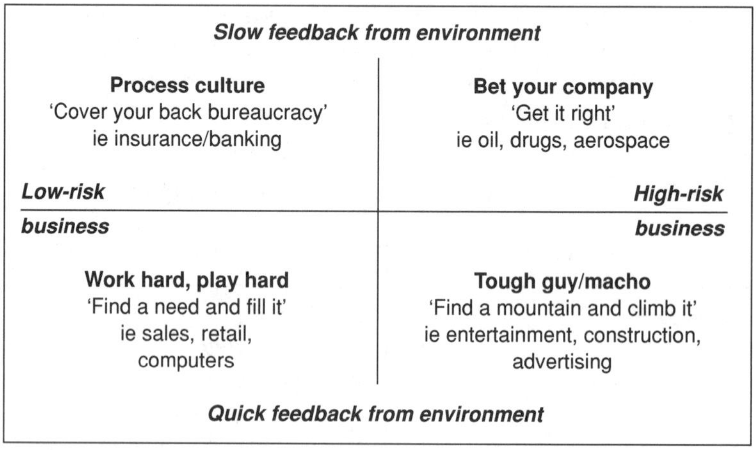

Figure 1.6.5 Four pure cultural types

Another aspect of culture which will emerge strongly should you decide to merge with or acquire another business is the potential for the expected business synergy to be eroded by culture clash. Apparently 70 per cent of mergers and acquisitions fail through people reasons, that is when cultures collide to such an extent that organisations cannot live together and the 'marriage' is doomed to end in divorce, or at best a strained incompatibility. For example:

HP

When HP (a very collaborative people-orientated culture) acquired Apollo, (an engineering-based organisation), it assumed that the Apollo people would be only too happy to join. In fact Apollo engineers saw it as 'dumbing down' their special values. Instead of an alliance that enabled HP to take on Sun direct, HP ended up refocusing its UNIX business on commercial servers.

The moral of this example is, take time at the 'due diligence' stage to assess culture 'fit', and put effort into managing post-merger integration.

Quintiles

To make sure that you achieve real and lasting synergy, do what the mighty Quintiles did when it acquired Innovex in 1997 (a merger of some 5,000 people with an equal sized organisation, now a combined business more than 10,000 people strong). Quintiles wanted to find out what the culture of the two partners really was. It carried out a 'culture diagnostic' across all 10,000 people worldwide, to establish cultural differences, from country to country and business to business, and to define the gap between what people saw 'now' compared with their 'desired' culture. This 'snapshot' gave a firm base of data on which to explore the differences and similarities of culture, and to create a new set of shared values.

Topnotch Health Clubs

At a different stage of growth, when Matthew Harris of Topnotch Health Clubs plc recently acquired six new clubs from Cannons, he took great pains to manage the integration process. His plan included the following:

- A carefully orchestrated raft of communications sessions on day 1, which introduced Topnotch vision and values, and outlined an 18-day Integration Plan.
- A determination that this would be a win–win situation, both for existing and new clubs. In a service business, you are buying people, and people can walk if they don't like what they see. It was felt that 'new' and 'old' clubs could learn from each others' experience. With this in mind, each 'new' club was allocated as the 'buddy' of an existing club, with a brief to identify each other's best practice.
- Interviews with both new and existing managers to explore their concerns. The new managers were in a state of shock, loss and disbelief, the existing managers were protective of their 'special' culture and just as scared of inevitable changes to established teams, who would have to 'norm', 'storm' and 'form' all over again.

An Integration Workshop was held at the end of the 18 days, to mourn the past, share values and forge a new team vision and values for the future.

Mergers are like marriages: you have to work at them. What are your three-week, three-month and first-year plans for achieving synergy?

Assessing structure capability

Structure is the skeleton of organisation. It tells you how work is divided up, who does what, and how the different roles relate one to another. Structure is more than 'the organisation chart of today'!

While your business can increase in size without changing its structure, Greiner suggests that the structure of your business will necessarily change at different stages of development (Greiner, 1972). Is your structure a straitjacket for the people who work within it? Does your structure reflect the problems you're trying to solve now or is it an inappropriate inheritance from the past?

It is always more difficult for old-style, well-established businesses to restructure to make themselves lean and fleet of foot. They carry too much investment in the way things used to be, and may end up with complex and impenetrable 'layers' of organisation, functional overlaid with a bit of 'matrix', decentralised business centres fighting centralised staff bureaucracies.

For newer start-ups, many of the old assumptions no longer hold, and the way is clear to set up radically different forms of organising. In the world of e-business, the requirement is above all for structural flexibility enabling a fast response to market opportunities that won't stay around for long. Massively high customer expectations drive the organisation in ways that are totally new. Customers have more and more upfront collaboration in working with their suppliers to design the products they want. Business structure must facilitate very tight links between front and back office, enabling all parts of the business from sales through production/marketing/technical/distribution to respond as one. If delivery is through a Web site, then inquiries will come from multiple points to multiple points within the organisation. Everyone in the organisation needs to have access to full information about each customer. People and what they know have become the source of competitive advantage. The old hierarchical structures, the equivalent of bricks and mortar buildings, can't flex to withstand the seismic changes of the 21st century. We need structures that move, often consisting of businesses split into fairly small, 'brand' based units, outsourcing all but their most 'core' competencies. Even the analogies have changed; clover leaf or doughnut patterns give way to star bursts from a central core, ever changing, moving out and reforming. The 'virtual' organisation does not need the built-in obsolescence of old-style tower block buildings. In the age of the Internet, some of the organisational trends we see are:

From	To
Managing assets	Managing information
Services internally sourced	Services outsourced
Command and control	Shared values
Internally driven	Customer driven
Product-based	Service-based
Hard issues	Soft issues
Functionally-based	Project-based

The age of the Internet is driving these changes but is also providing the solutions with:

- knowledge bases to share information internally and externally;
- electronic integration with service suppliers;
- automation of internal processes to give an integrated response to customers.

However, those managers in search of the ideal organisation structure – the Holy Grail – will be disappointed. In answer to the question, 'What is the right structure?' comes the reply, 'It all depends'. It all depends on the business environment you're operating in and how uncertain it is. It all depends on what kind of business you are historically and what kind of people you employ. The only statement we can make with any certainty of being right is that, whatever structure you have in place now, it won't be the one you need in the future. So before we start examining matrix structures, or business centres or centralised structures, it is worth asking yourself the following questions:

At what stage of development is my current business? (Greiner's Phases, 1,2,3,4,5).

How would I describe my present structure? (informal, functional, centralised, divisional, matrix).

What is the core capability of this business?

We will start to address these questions by looking at: how to divide things up; types of structure – advantages/disadvantages, and how to put things together again.

How to divide things up

When most people talk about business structure they mean: how are activities divided up into groups and functions, individual roles and responsibilities; how big is the span of control, and who is the boss of whom.

In terms of defining individual roles and responsibilities, the discipline of writing a job description is very useful for clarifying the job and helping recruitment.

Does everyone, including those on the board, have a job description and do they know exactly what is expected of them?'

Historically there has been a tendency to break jobs down into their component parts and specialise. At its worst extreme this has resulted in the archetypal production line job of putting the handles on a car door. The costs of over-specialisation include insularity, inflexibility, lack of team orientation and possibly poor motivation. Job enrichment has been a response to over-specialisation, in its attempt to build back into jobs a craftsman-type pride in having authority, doing a whole job, and working as a team. What is your own assessment: do you need more generalists or specialists, or both?

The evidence is that if you're an innovative organisation coping with rapid change and growth then you will do better to have broader and fewer job classifications which allow greater mobility and flexibility across functions. For example, it's been said that part of the inertia factor of General Motors in comparison to Toyota was that GM had 11 times as many job classifications as Toyota.

How do you group activities within your business? Ask yourself:

Are the various tasks in my business divided up in the best way?

The most commonly used dimensions are probably those exemplified by Figure 1.6.6.

The traditional principle is to group together like activities. Unfortunately, these groupings tend not to stay static as new market requirements force new kinds of responses. What therefore results is a rapid, complicated overlay of different types of structure. This can be very messy and can also involve making some difficult decisions, for example:

● Should quality control be centralised or put into specific business units?
● Should the sales function remain centralised?
● How should business units relate one with another?
● What should the role of the head office be?
● What exactly are the decision-making line functions and what are the purely advisory staff functions?

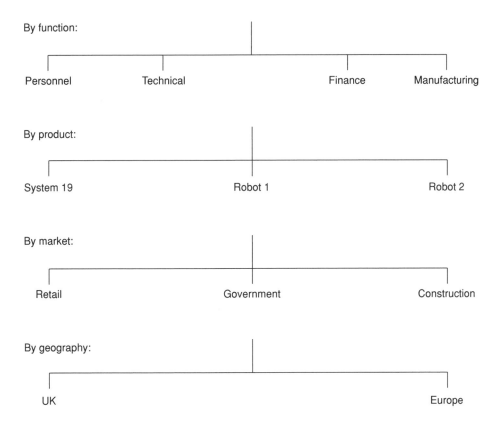

Figure 1.6.6 Typically used organisational dimensions

Finally, there are the old chestnuts – the rules to do with span of control. Urwick Orr has a lot to answer for! In the 1920s he established a rule of thumb which said that no manager should have more than a maximum of five or six direct reports. This reinforces the one person, one boss principle and allows for clarity and strong control by the manager. However, there is a very big price tag. Obviously, the narrower the span of control, the more levels of hierarchy must exist. The more levels of hierarchy there are, the more difficult it is to get sensible communication up and down the organisation: 'send reinforcements we're going to advance' very soon becomes 'send three-and-fourpence we're going to a dance'.

It is said that if an organisation has five levels of management and the president communicates a message from the top, then the percentage of information recalled by each level will be as follows:

Level 1	63 per cent
Level 3	40 per cent
Level 5	20 per cent

Small wonder that an engineering firm of 250 employees, with seven levels of hierarchy, reported communication problems.

The advice circulating around most businesses is 'cut out as many levels as you can and go for a flatter organisation'. Some businesses are being asked to 'cut out levels of management without increasing the span of control'. This can be something of a conjuring trick.

Certainly there needs to be some limit to the number of direct reports. Obviously, one cannot conscientiously carry out an infinite number of appraisals. However, as the role of manager changes from policeman/controller to conductor/orchestrator, the issue is much less important than managers think.

Types of structure: advantages/disadvantages

Greiner's model is a useful way of reminding ourselves that there is no one right answer. Neither matrix, nor business centre (son of strategic business units – SBUs) is the universal answer – it's a case of 'horses for courses'. Let's rapidly recap Greiner's development cycle. In Phase 1, the business is small, entrepreneurial, outward looking and its structure minimal and informal. There aren't the resources for dedicated resources, so everyone ends up doing a bit of everything. During Phase 2, the need for strong direction around formal systems and standards argues for a functional structure where manufacturing is separated from marketing, and marketing from sales, where a hierarchy of titles and specialised positions is built up. However, as the organisation becomes larger and more diverse this centralised structure becomes cumbersome and actually restricts the business from moving quickly into new markets.

Thus the demand for greater autonomy leads to more delegation and a decentralised organisation structure. In this decentralised structure, greater responsibility is given to business unit managers, profit centres are established and top executives at the head office try to restrain themselves to 'let go' and manage by exception.

The new decentralised structure works until there is a crisis of control – when the top managers start to panic and feel that they are losing control over field operations. Decentralised units are merged into product groups, the head office restaffs itself with specialist advisers, but the daily operating decisions remain decentralised. However, a lack of confidence gradually builds up between line and staff, and between headquarters and the field – a crisis of red tape is looming, to which the response is probably a move towards a matrix structure of teams and functions across the organisation.

Clearly it all depends where you're at. The summary chart below (Table 1.6.3) is intended only to be used to check that the structure you are about to introduce is not going to create more problems than it will solve. There is plenty of room for creative thinking in devising new and flexible structures that work for you (project teams, quality circles, temporary groupings etc).

Table 1.6.3 No right structures, only appropriate ones

Type of structure	Identifying features	Advantages	Disadvantages
Informal	● Business start-up ● Few people ● Highly committed ● Little need for structure	● Fun ● Market orientated ● Responsive	● Can be disorganised ● Attention to detail lacking ● Few systems in place
Functional/ centralised	● Functions are separated one from the other ● Vertical hierarchy ● Clear accountabilities ● Strong HQ	● Clarity of role ● Specialisation by function ● Systematic	● Unresponsive to business/market change ● Communications up/down and across suffer ● Compartmentalisation and empire-building
Decentralised business units	● Focus on business accountability ● Unique business mission ● Business manager calls the shots ● HQ manages by exception	● Motivates managers ● Responsive to customers ● Flexible	● 'Robber Barons' may go out of control ● Problems of integration of different strategies ● Problems of HQ control
Product groups	● Daily operating decisions remain decentralised ● HQ takes a more active and specialist role in coordinating plans and investment strategy	● HQ people are comfortable ● A global response to markets and competition may be more possible ● Strategies are integrated	● Cumbersome red tape ● 'Us' and 'Them' builds up between field and HQ ● Conflicts arise

Type of structure	Identifying features	Advantages	Disadvantages
Matrix	• Dual chain of command: two bosses (everyone had a mother and a father) • A 'Business Results' manager on one axis and a 'Resource Manager' on the other hold equal	• New and exciting; can build in flexibility • Allows organisation to respond to two sectors simultaneously (ie market and technology) • Suited to uncertainty and complexity	• Difficult for managers to get used to • Tendency towards anarchy • Power struggles inevitable • Severe 'groupitis' can occur • Role ambiguity inevitable

Table 1.6.3 *continued*

How to put things together again

The problem with organisations is that they are like Humpty Dumpty; having divided them up into little bits in the interests of efficiency, it is often very difficult to put them together again in such a way that they will actually work. So for differentiation gone mad read this delightful 'spoof' McKinsey report on the Royal Festival Hall.

McKinsey report on the Royal Festival Hall concert

The four horn players are seriously under-employed and their number should be reduced. In fact, if their workload was shared out among the other players they could be dispensed with altogether.

The 12 first and second violins were observed to be all playing the same notes. This duplication of effort should not be tolerated and the group could be cut drastically. If the sound becomes too thin it could easily be amplified electronically to whatever level is desired.

The playing of semiquavers was seen to be a considerable, and in our view unwarranted, effort. It could even lead to a demand for payment at piece-work rates. If short notes such as quavers and semiquavers were grouped together, by rationalising the score, into more economic units, a less qualified workforce, and even students, could be engaged without the loss of efficiency.

In some passages there is far too much repetition and we recommend a thorough reprocessing of the material. For example, it serves no useful purpose for the oboe to repeat passages that have already been fully dealt with by the violins. If all such superfluous passages were eliminated, the concert, which at present lasts up to two hours, could be adequately completed in approximately 20 minutes. The unproductive interval could then be dispensed with.

The conductor does not fully grasp today's concepts of management science as applied to orchestral activities, and he is apprehensive that artistic standards might decline. In this unlikely event, there would be compensating financial savings, since audiences, who are only, after all, a major distraction to the smooth functioning of the operation, would decline. Although improbable, this would merely call for parts of the concert hall to be shut off, thereby bringing added cost savings in electricity, personnel, ticket printing etc, on the one hand, and an essential improvement of acoustics by reduction of the background noises.

At the worst, the whole enterprise could be shut down, with consequent major economies in artist fees... and we could then all retire to the bar.

The experts now say that it is integration rather than dividing things up (differentiation) which is the key organisational challenge. Indeed, it is inevitable that as the business gets older and bigger and moves up the Greiner growth curve, every reorganisation demolishes old barriers only at the cost of creating new ones. The list of potential barriers is chastening; if we are not careful we create alienation: between the first and the second floor/between male and female/between secretaries and managers/between line and staff/between field and head office/between sales and marketing/between UK and European.

No wonder we all need as much help as we can get in coordinating activities. Ask yourself:

How fast can I get a coordinated response to a customer problem?

How is integration achieved at present at different locations, and across different functions such as sales/marketing/production/distribution?

Traditionally, integration was achieved through the manager at the top of the hierarchy personally taking control. As the business grows more complex and diverse, this becomes more and more difficult. The solutions lie somewhere in the area of teamwork.

When you look at your organisation ask:

Do people work individually or in teams?

Does local team solidarity work against identification with the whole business?

Do teams cooperate or compete with other teams in your business?

There are some clues. Corporate vision, which is shared by everyone, integrates (as in the consultancy group McKinsey). A strong set of shared values or culture integrates (like McDonalds). Informal networks help to integrate (Tandem beerbusts, get-togethers everywhere in the world at 4pm every Friday afternoon).

Project teams across disciplines build integration; job rotation and mobility also help to integrate.

The essence of the challenge is to create team identity at both a local level and also at a corporate level. Teamworking is the shape of the future.

When Mike Arama, chairman of a chain of 15 petrol stations was looking for a new accountant, he felt it was not only vital that the candidate should have good technical skills, but that he should fit in with the existing close-knit team. The behaviour-based test Arama chose to use was the Belbin Self-Perception Inventory (Belbin, 1981). It was developed by Dr Meredith Belbin in conjunction with the Henley Management Centre to give individuals a simple means of assessing their best team roles. Dr Belbin's research led him to identify eight dominant types of team behaviour*.

Assessing systems capability

Systems are the nerves of the organisation, the processes and connections that can switch the organisation on – or stop anything happening at all! Organisation systems are generally considered boring, but the truth is they can be very powerful levers for change. Systems can be sexy!

You will already have looked at many of your day-to-day operating systems to do with sales forecasting, budgeting and invoicing etc. We now ask you to do the same with regard to your people systems. We'll consider people systems under three headings: reward systems; people maintenance systems; communications.

Reward systems

Earlier on we rather crudely stated that, 'What gets measured, get produced. What gets rewarded gets produced again'. Getting your reward systems right will be crucial to moving your business in the direction you want. Unfortunately, it is not a case of plugging in to one sort of reward system (for example, bonuses or share options) and expecting that to work forever. As you go through different phases of growth, the behaviour you will be looking for will change and so must the way you reward it. This is an area requiring constant monitoring and as much imagination as you can apply in devising many types of rewards.

---

* The full Belbin Interplace System is available from Belbin Associates, 52 Burleigh Street, Cambridge (tel: 01223 264975; Web site: www.belbin.com). Belbin has since produced modified versions of this work, which are also available from Belbin Associates.

How do you currently reward people for achieving goals?

Are you rewarding appropriate behaviours?

Let's look at two small businesses that are moving from Greiner's Phase 2, growth through direction, in Phase 3, growth through delegation. What are the issues concerning how they reward behaviour?

Flexiform is moving fast towards creating a general manager culture where the people rewarded will be those who can manage their people and grow their business team. The chairman has put a lot of effort into reward systems and they are now generally regarded as OK. There is a good bonus system in which all share and it works well. However, money is only a short-term motivator; many people would like to see 'little and often' rewards. Rewards could be more immediate, perhaps quarterly rather than annually. Managers see value in having the freedom to give small, unexpected rewards to their people. The company is good at the little signs of recognition which mean a lot – the bunch of flowers, blowing a hooter when a new client is signed up and the occasional dinner out. They recently paid out very happily a large cash sum for the best slogan to encapsulate their mission statement. As one manager says, 'It certainly made everyone at least read it'.

Farmtext, on the other hand, is just hitting the rapids. Everyone is used to working every hour that God sends – but now the promises of jam tomorrow are starting to wear thin. Managers at all levels are voicing a strong concern that the rewards do not match the demands made of them. It's felt that there comes a time when you can't take liberties with people, cancel holidays and work weekends. One younger manager sums it up: 'Recognition of our efforts is the message, we fuel growth, and we're all dead keen to grow the business! What's the reward?' There isn't a lot of money about, but the problem is a real one if the business is to retain its best people. The management team is looking hard at putting together the right package: it's not just basic pay, nor promotion prospects, but also status and recognition, and above all some form of profit sharing and ownership.

Reward structures are always a challenge for growth businesses; make sure you are rewarding the behaviours the business needs now, and be constantly innovative in inventing new financial and non-financial incentives.

As you test out your reward systems, ask yourself what it is that you're expecting from people, and is this what is being produced and being rewarded? It's very easy to find that you are expecting one thing (such as profitable growth) and rewarding another (sales revenue). Don't be frightened of discriminating between good and bad performance; accountability for results must go with growth. How imaginative are you being in rewarding your people? Are you, for example:

- Paying enough?
- Linking rewards to performance?
- Giving cash bonuses, including instant ones?
- Rewarding team performance as well as individual effort?
- Putting people's pictures on bulletin boards and in newspapers?
- Making excellence awards?
- Rewarding those who know and use your vision?
- Giving free tickets to the theatre/match/concert?
- Giving gift certificates?
- Promoting technical and managerial stars?
- Giving badges (like IBM's 'Golden Banana' award)?
- Giving good people autonomy?
- Giving different work assignments, or job rotation?
- Saying 'Thank you'?
- Sending people to business schools?
- Having celebrations?
- Giving a share of the business?

People maintenance systems

We know that people are the key; that means it pays to keep them healthy. Personnel policies can seem set in concrete, but changing them as you grow is absolutely possible and essential if you are going to stay fit. This means taking a good look at your recruitment policies, your induction programme, your training, who you're promoting and how you appraise people:

How do I go about recruiting for key positions. Am I satisfied with the results?

How much training do I give all staff, myself included?

On what criteria do I promote people?

Do I regularly appraise all staff performance in a way that staff find helpful?

You can bet that at least one of these plates is wobbling dangerously and about to fall off its stick. Just as the perfect lifestyle is a myth, so you'll never get the perfect package of personnel systems. When you take a look at what you've got you'll probably find it's only good in parts. There follow some examples of how to get moving on recruitment, induction, training and appraisal.

Recruitment

Farmtext is growing into new markets. It needs new skills in the area of finance, marketing and perhaps personnel. These skills don't exist internally; Farmtext staff will have to recruit from outside, but they are experiencing a lot of difficulty recruiting, not only because the company is in a country area and not only because they are looking for specialist skills. They just don't know how to recruit. They need job descriptions and person specifications; clearer job criteria; they need to match the job with the person instead of taking whatever they can get; they need to increase their ability to make good people decisions. They need a framework for a selection profile and an interview process

Induction is a golden opportunity for making a good and lasting impression. Innovex runs an orientation programme for all its new recruits; it demonstrates that they and the company are something special. It tells the Innovex vision. The chairman pours the tea and teaches on every programme – that's how important it is and how special is their culture.

Training everyone on an ongoing basis is something Innovex believes in. This year their managers will all go through a core programme of management training and will add on any elective they need. A minimum of 8–12 days' training a year will be the rule. The chairman takes himself off to business schools. All the secretaries and administrative staff will have video and in-house training on being appraised, on word processing skills, on basic finance. The trained will become the trainers.

Appraisal is the keystone to management performance. If you haven't got an appraisal system, get one; if you've got one, review it. As in the case of many young companies, John Green of Green Systems has found that his appraisal system has become archaic and is no longer consistent with where he is taking the business. Interviews are rushed, linked to salary reviews; the process is of tick boxes and no comments; and appraisal is against qualities not results. It's a one-way tell, not a dialogue. Nothing much happens afterwards. The new appraisal scheme will reflect the new needs of the business. It will hold people accountable against business objectives. It will reward those who reflect the Green Systems vision and values. It will be a full two-way conversation where both parties have their own agenda. It will result in action and training and career development – it will build the managers of the future.

Communications

Finally, a seemingly innocuous question:

How good are your internal communications?

Once you're past the euphoria of Phase 1 growth we suspect that your answer is likely to be 'Not very'. Communication problems are a classic consequence of growth. In the early days you don't need anything very formal, you are probably a small team, openly involved in sharing information and playing bar billiards together.

The troubles come as you get bigger and people no longer come together on a regular basis, new people have joined who don't have the same shared history, and none of you have time for meetings. Cracks begin to appear in the communication downwards, in communications across from one department to another and in the extent to which anyone listens to the ideas coming up through the organisation.

The state of your communications is a good barometer of your corporate health. Once this goes, look out for fragmentation, 'them and us' behaviour, lack of team identity, frustration about goals, patchy information flow, politicking and cliques. It's a paradox that once your organisation is past a certain size even informal communications need formalising. Communications never happen unless there are the disciplines and mechanisms to make them happen.

Are you satisfied that you have in place at least some of the following very simple mechanisms:

- ways of cascading briefing groups downwards on a regular basis;
- management by walk about (MBWA);
- informal get-togethers (eg Tandem 'beer busts');
- regular management meetings;
- twice yearly 'State of the Nation' get-togethers for the whole team;
- quality circles or cross boundary think-tanks, problem-solving meetings;
- presentations by one department to another;
- social occasions: Christmas parties, away days, theatre outings, visits to the pub;
- a weekly happy-hour meeting of all staff;
- somewhere to eat where people can relax and mix.

People	Skills and attitudes	• Will existing skills be adequate or do these need to be built up before the business can grow? • What is the labour turnover rate compared with competitors/last year? • Are levels of sickness/absenteeism high or low? • Do I know why my people are leaving?
	Management capability and style	• Do I have sufficient managers to run my business well? • How much growth could they handle without becoming overstretched? • Is there anyone who can run the business in my absence? • If a key manager left is there someone to fill his place? • How much can I delegate? • What is my personal management style and that of my managers?
	Culture	• How would my managers and myself describe the organisation culture?
Structure	What kind of structure exists?	• At what stage of growth (Greiner) is my business? • How is my business currently controlled? • How would I describe my present structure?
	How to divide things up	• Does everyone have a job description and know what is expected of them? • Are the various tasks divided up and grouped in the best way?
	How to integrate	• How is integration achieved at present? • Do people work individually or in teams?
Systems	Reward systems	• How do I recruit for key positions?
	People maintenance systems	• How much training do I give all my staff (myself included)? • On what criteria do I promote people? • Do I regularly appraise staff performance?
	Communications	• How good are internal communications?

Figure 1.6.7   Checklist of questions for organisation audit

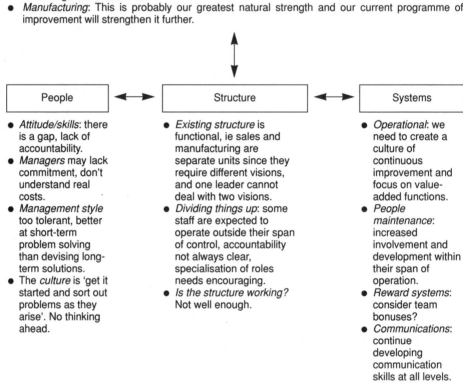

Figure 1.6.8 Organisation capability of Ebac Ltd

Organisation analysis (worked example)

John Elliot set up Ebac Ltd more than 20 years ago in Bishop Auckland, to sell domestic and industrial dehumidifiers and bespoke air conditioning. The business grew vertically into manufacture and product design. The business grew rapidly in the 1980s in both turnover and profit, with annual sales and profits then exceeding £10m and £1m respectively. Despite or possibly because of these good figures, the company was heading out of control, culminating in two years of losses totalling over £1.5m. But the worst thing is that when profits disappear so do the bankers. The cash shortage was much worse than the loss of profits. John says that there can be no doubts that the problems were all self-inflicted, even though they could have been lessened by a longer-term perspective from the banking fraternity. John goes on to say that there is, however, a benefit in the apparent inability of bankers to relate to business! Businessmen must fully explain their plans, which means they must think them out, in advance. To do this a structure is required. Figure 1.6.8 shows John Elliot's initial analysis of the organisation capability of Ebac Ltd.

Assignment 11

Assessing your current capabilities

Environment
(Write down the key external challenges from Assignment 2.)

Strategy
(Write down the major directions in which you are trying to move the business.)

People (current characteristics of skills and attitudes, management capability, style and culture)	Structure (how do you divide things up, what about teamwork?)	Systems (the essence of your existing reward, people maintenance and communication procedures)
1	1	1
2	2	2
3	3	3
4	4	4
5	5	5
6	6	6

Figure 1.6.9 Template for showing organisational ability

Assignment 12

Preparing an agenda for organisational change

Fits or misfits: your agenda for change

Going back through the present characteristics of your organisation (as outlined in Assignment 11) add a ✓ or a × to represent whether each of these features are 'fits' or 'misfits' with the challenges you face. The misfits should give you your agenda for change and should indicate where your primary challenges lie. Outline each misfit as you would in preparing a brief for a consultant. Four items are probably as much as you can realistically handle. What lever for change will you need to pull – primarily people, or systems, or structure – to tackle the challenges?

Answers to culture questions (pages 123 and 124) are:

1. Prudential Assurance Company Ltd.
2. British Airways.

Part 2

Where are we going?

If you have worked through the assignments at the end of each of the previous six chapters, you should by now have a good feel for your current strengths and weaknesses. The financial and people resources available to support future strategies should be apparent.

In Part 1, the position audit to determine the key factors in 'where we have been', you have been looking again at your product/service's external market and competitive environment. For each business you have been encouraged to define the target customer segments you need to serve, as this is at the heart of successful modern marketing.

Wong, Saunders and Doyle's Anglo/Japanese study (1989) found that, sadly, 47 per cent of British firms (as against 13 per cent of Japanese) acknowledged they were unclear about the principal customer categories and their special requirements (giving comments like, 'We do not see the market as being made up of specific segments. Our market is made up of the whole industry. Anyone in the market can be our customer'). Not surprisingly, the British competitors were increasingly pushed to the sidelines of their market, comprising largely lower-potential segments as opposed to the high-potential or up-market sectors targeted by the Japanese.

Equally, in the competitive environment, Japanese companies have shown themselves to be as much competitors in export markets as at home, in stark contrast to their more 'stay at home' British counterparts (see Table 2.0.1).

While a strong home base is indispensable, the opening of world markets and the new opportunities and competitive threats this will pose for British companies mean serious consideration must be given to the actions required by the new environment. British companies have led in company acquisitions in Europe and

Table 2.0.1   SME business orientation in 2000

	UK	France	Germany	Euro Av
National	48	29	28	36
European	41	53	62	52
International	11	19	10	12

Source: Cranfield Working Papers, 1993

in the United States in recent years, but is this the most cost-effective way to deal with the situation for your business?

Amberley

International trade leads to business growth

Amberley plc, for example, a British-owned company specialising in rising damp treatment, overcame language and legal, employment and promotional problems in France to successfully extend its depot network and direct selling methods across Europe. By sustained internal growth it has achieved profitable operations in three major continental countries and only now is considering acquisitions, most probably in the UK, by backward integration with companies supplying chemicals for its damp-proofing treatment.

There is much anecdotal evidence to suggest that those SMEs who do export can outgrow those who do not.

Within your own business unit's internal strengths and weakness audit, the main objective has been to clarify again the key product or service differentiation which led to the establishment of the business, and which needs to be constantly refreshed if its product life cycle is not to come to a premature end.

Many British companies, according to Wong, Saunders and Doyle, were weak at differentiating their products from competition, or possessed little competitive advantage. Only 20 per cent of British companies claimed they were 'good at product differentiation' compared to 53 per cent of the Japanese. On measures of research and development, design, process development and volume production capabilities, the British competitors consistently emerged the weaker.

Yet if Perrier can turn a commodity, water, into a well-differentiated brand by clever use of each element of the marketing mix, this ought to make us sceptical of those who claim differentiation cannot be achieved. To make it worse, the Perrier product was largely developed by an Englishman, Lord Northcliffe, before it was acquired by Gustave Leven in 1946!

Perrier

Anything can be made better and different

Perrier is presented as a top-quality product (hence total withdrawal and subsequent relaunch after the benzene scare). Perrier has product differentiation (with distinct green bottle, bubbles, twists of lemon/lime) and is priced high pricing to match quality and provide margins to justify distinctive promotions which vary from country to country (for example, using humour in the UK). The product is distributed worldwide from its single, magical, source: 'La Source', near Nimes, in south-west France. The whole 'marketing mix' is clearly being focused on health conscious, wealthy and younger target consumers.

Similarly, many Japanese companies have succeeded by adherence to the basics of the marketing mix: making good-quality products (which they were not famous for even 25 years ago, proving that it is a process that can be learnt), continually extending their range to meet the changing preferences of their customers, and investing in their distribution channels (stocks, technical training, dealer support for promotional spending).

All these lessons from Part 1 now need to be summarised in Part 2, Chapters 7 and 8, to help us clearly decide 'where we are going', ie for each of our business units, what our marketing options are and what our marketing strategy should be. At the same time we will review our financial options, and the management and people issues that will influence our strategic choices.

7 *Marketing options*

Your marketing options come, in the first place, from your audit of your business strengths, weaknesses, opportunities and threats (SWOT analysis). A SWOT should be prepared for each of your business/product activities and should be:

- a summary of the key elements in your business (Assignments 2–8);
- brief, concise and interesting, without being too abbreviated;
- focused on the real issues facing your company;
- action-orientated, so that positive proposals can be envisaged.

Each strength should be something you can build upon; each weakness, something that seriously needs to be corrected, as the following example from Autoglass suggests (Figure 2.7.1).

	Strengths	Weaknesses
1. Customers	We have a unique position with UK insurance companies	We are weak in the garage repair sector
2. Product	We provide a unique 24-hour, 7 days a week service to motorists	We lost some customers because answerphone system not alive
3. Place	We have strong depot representation in South	We are weak in depot representation in North
4. Promotion	Insurance companies give us good coverage to all insured motorists	We need to further develop a customer friendly Web site (www.autoglass.co.uk)
5. Price	Our prices, with our fast service, are competitive with garages	We are a price follower not leader
6. Finance	Our Southern depots are earning a minimum 25% return on assets	Our new start-up depots in Midlands are losing money
7. Operations	We have well-motivated managers through profit sharing scheme	Employee turnover is high because of irregular hours

Figure 2.7.1 SWOT analysis 1: strengths and weaknesses (Autoglass Windscreen Repairs Ltd)

In the same way, your summary of opportunities and threats should give you the confidence, and in some cases the justification, to plan future marketing actions, as the following environment analysis for Autoglass suggests (see Figure 2.7.2).

	Opportunities	Threats
8. Market	Growing steadily at real 3% pa	Slow market growth does not favour rapid expansion
9. Political	Government favours changing MOT regulations to include windscreen inspection	Entry into EU is encouraging cheaper windscreen imports from France, disrupting our traditional UK suppliers
10. Technology	Energy crisis encourages motor manufacturers to fit lighter bonded laminated windscreens (favours specialist fitters)	Switch by motorists to laminated windscreens threatens to make our stocks of toughened windscreens obsolete
11. Competition	Shows no signs of becoming organised enough to approach insurance companies	Our market share would be threatened if car accessory company (eg Kwik-Fit) diversified into windscreens

Figure 2.7.2 SWOT analysis 2: opportunities and threats (Autoglass Windscreen Repairs Ltd)

If the SWOT analysis has been carefully drawn, marketing actions and options can be developed (see Figure 2.7.3).

Critical success factors (CSFs)

The financial costs and benefits of these options clearly need to be determined, in terms of both revenue and capital needs (see Chapter 9). Before this, however, to focus attention on the marketing priorities facing your company, you should endeavour to finalise your marketing options analysis by determining and ranking the CSFs that are vital for your company's success by looking at your performance from a major customer's point of view (see Figure 2.7.4 on page 150).

By weighting each factor out of 100, and scoring your own company's current achievement and that of your competitors out of 10, even though this may be subjective, you should develop a clearer understanding of the priorities each marketing option entails. (Weighted averages derive from multiplying scores times weighting percentages.)

One problem with a quite open subjective assessment of your own and competitors' performance on CSFs is that companies frequently rate themselves ahead of, or at least equal to, main competitors (as Figure 2.7.4 shows for

SWOT ref	Action	Target date	Who actions
SWOT 3 Improve depot coverage in North of England	Investigating opening two new depots in main population centres, Manchester and Leeds: ● Contact estate agents ● Visit suitable sites ● Cost and prepare plans ● Select and train staff ● Open two depots	 Nov 15th Dec 1st Jan 2nd Jan 15th Mar 31st	PJB/RJB PB/RB
SWOT 7 Reduce employee turnover by recruiting staff and provide suitable training to NVQ2 standard for automotive glazing	Approach Training Centre, Birmingham to: ● Draw up approved training programme ● Obtain Training Centre approval ● Fit out one depot (Neasden) as training centre; cost and approve ● Recruit suitable applicants ● Post trainees to two new depots	 Oct 15th Nov 15th Jan 2nd Mar 31st	PS/CB

Figure 2.7.3   SWOT action plan (Autoglass Windscreen Repairs Ltd)

Autoglass). Care should be taken through market research with customers, for example, to see if they agree with both your assessment of the key success factors and how your company and competitors compare in these areas. (In the Autoglass example, the number one customer is key insurance companies, hence CSF 1 was to extend depot coverage to meet their main need, whilst 'consumers' (motorists) expressed buying preferences based upon 'screen availability' above 'friendly service' and 'image', hence CSF priorities 2, 3 and 4).

Assignment 13

SWOT analysis

Using the information gained in going through the marketing position audit, summarise the key market/business strengths and weaknesses of your business and the principal opportunities and threats you see ahead of you (see Figure 2.7.5 and Figure 2.7.6).

If you operate in a number of very different markets you will need to do a separate SWOT analysis for each business.

Competition position			Main Competitors (0–10)		
Critical Success Factor (CSF)	Importance of CSF (% weighting)	Autoglass	Windscreen Enterprises	Bridgewater Glass	Associated Windscreens
CSF 1 Achieve improved depot coverage to meet insurance co's national requirements	50%	7	5	4	7
CSF 2 Control windscreen and glass stocks to limit capital investment	25%	6	7 (aided by Laddaw)	5	7 (aided by C Pugh)
CSF 3 Develop competent staff for new depots, by setting up Training Dept	15%	4	3	3	3
CSF 4 Achieve national recognition while controlling promotional expenditure	10%	7	5	3	5
Total + weighted averages	100%	6.3	5.2	4.0	6.2

Figure 2.7.4 Critical success factors (Autoglass Windscreen Repairs Ltd and competitors)

	Strengths	Weaknesses
1. Customers/Market segment		
2. Product/Service		
3. Place (Distribution)		
4. Promotion (Advertising)		
5. Price		
6. Finance		
7. Operations (Sales)		

Figure 2.7.5 SWOT analysis 1: own company compared to competition

	Opportunities	Threats
8. Total market		
9. Political government/environment		
10. Technology		
11. Competition		

Figure 2.7.6   SWOT analysis 2: key opportunities and threats existing in current environment

CSFs for your business

From your SWOT analysis, and looked at from major customers' point of view, establish priorities for action by highlighting what are the CSFs for your business, and rank your current achievement on these factors versus your major competitors' (see the Autoglass example in Figure 2.7.4).

Competition position			Main Competitors (0–10)		
Critical Success Factor (CSF)	Importance of CSF (% weighting)	Your own business	(1)	(2)	(3)
CSF 1					
CSF 2					
CSF 3					
CSF 4					
Total	100				

Figure 2.7.7   Sample CSF table

Weight each factor out of 100; score your business and each competitor out of 10. Typical CSF 1 should be around 50 per cent, being the main way in which your business will stand or fall in your market sector. Check that customers agree with your assessment.

8 Marketing strategy: focus and priorities

SWOT and key success factor analysis is the essential first step in determining your marketing options. The next step is to apply some strategic analysis to your products/services and markets. It would not be sensible, for example, to invest heavily in products nearing the end of their life cycle; there are several useful tools which can be used to help develop a good strategic perspective. One is the Boston matrix, developed by the Boston Consulting Group in the early 1970s (McDonald, 1994). This suggests that a company's products should be classified according to their ability to generate or consume cash, against two dimensions of market growth rate and market share. This process is summarised in Figure 2.8.1.

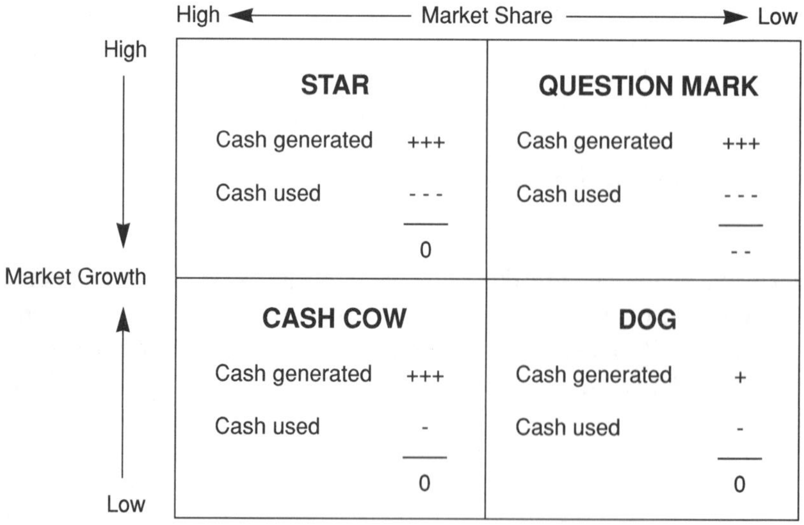

High ◄─────── Market Share ───────► Low

	High		Low
High	**STAR**		**QUESTION MARK**
	Cash generated +++		Cash generated +++
	Cash used - - -		Cash used - - -
	0		- -
Market Growth	**CASH COW**		**DOG**
	Cash generated +++		Cash generated +
	Cash used -		Cash used -
Low	0		0

Figure 2.8.1 The Boston matrix

The concept behind this 'product portfolio' approach, is, of course, to seek to use cash generated by 'Cash cows' to invest in 'Stars' and a selected number of 'Question marks', while considering disinvestment for 'Dogs'. Cash flow is used, rather than profits, as it is the real determinant of a company's ability to develop its products/services. Investment is directed in favour of achieving market share or growth while maximising cash flow, as shown in Figure 2.8.2.

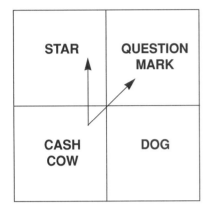 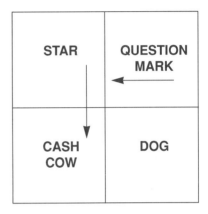

Figure 2.8.2 Matrix suggests investment direction

Some companies have used business strengths instead of market share, and market attractiveness instead of market growth; the strategic investment concept is the same, divesting from the 'Dogs' area and investing in 'Stars', and selectively in the other two boxes. You should endeavour to rank your products in this way, plotting them on the matrix, using circles to denote the approximate size of sales of each business unit. The direction in which these circles should be moving should influence your strategic investment decisions. Remember, however, that the analysis is only directional and that market and company circumstances can change quite rapidly.

Doulton Glass saw its product portfolio change quite dramatically in three short years, 1979–82. Its double-glazing (DG) activity, from being a fast growing 'Star', with increasing investment and depot network, became in 18 months a 'Dog' as market growth halted and market share was lost in a bitter, competitive discounting war. Disinvestment of DG became imperative to staunch cash out-flow and to permit selective new investment out of 'Cash Cow' glass merchanting (M) into the 'Question mark' products, safety glass (SG) and automotive (A), where market growth was being stimulated by safer glazing regulations and market share could be achieved by acquisition of small competitors (see Figure 2.8.3).

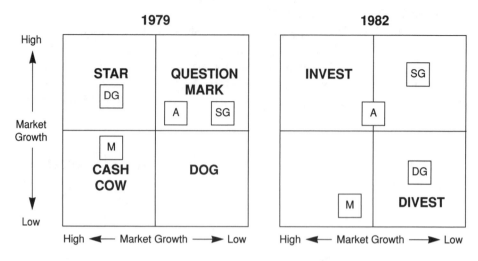

Figure 2.8.3 Product position in matrix changes over time

Another helpful tool is the checklist shown in the marketing strategy chart (Figure 2.8.4).

The chart illustrates the two major strategic options to pursue for each business unit: improved productivity, and increased volume.

These directions are not mutually exclusive, but each has a different strategic focus.

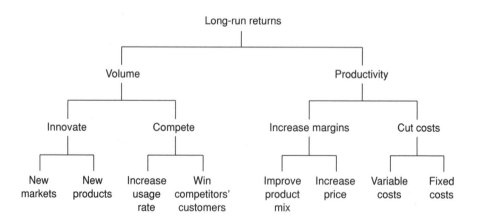

Figure 2.8.4 Marketing strategy: the strategic options summary

Improved productivity

Improving productivity is a constant requirement for a growth-minded business, not simply an activity during periods of economic recession (when it is still, nonetheless, important – much better than adopting the 'turtle position' ie 'getting off the road and pulling in your head and your hands!'). Productivity needs to be improved by acting on both your costs and your margins.

Cutting costs

Costs need to be constantly controlled and balanced against the needs for good quality and good service. In particular, you need to separate and act on your variable and your fixed costs:

- Variable cost cutting is always in evidence in recession; witness the automotive and banking staff cuts in the early 1990s. Some employers aim to keep flexibility: for example, Fiat in Italy chose to lay off 65,000 car workers (half of its workforce) for one week per month, to cut production levels by 40,000 vehicles. Fiat saw no point in permanent job cuts when the future (then influenced by the Gulf War) was so hazy.

   Other companies sought actual pay cuts rather than redundancies, together with tight control on expensive overtime. Focusing attention on the 20 per cent of items that make up 80 per cent of your costs will probably yield biggest results.
- Fixed cost reductions, similarly, should not include scrapping investments in technology that could bring economies and extra nimbleness in the figure (like flexible-manufacturing facilities, where, for example, Peugeot has invested in product lines that can turn out two models at once). Many firms, following Japanese practice, increase their use of sub-contractors to help offset increased risk.

Cobra Beer

At the end of his five-year contract with the Mysore Brewery, Cobra MD Karan Bilimoria decided to sub-contract beer production with his specific recipe to Charles Wells at Bedford. Slightly higher production costs were more than offset by more consistent quality and lower distribution costs. Consumer tests on his new and forceful advertising slogan, 'The beer from Bangalore brewed in Bedford', showed no adverse customer reaction to the change.

Equally, alliances between firms aimed to reduce fixed cost investments can be advantageous. In the soft drinks industry, Perrier provide distribution for Pepsi in France, while Bulmers reciprocate for Perrier in England, avoiding the need for extra investment in warehousing and transport.

Increasing margins

Increasing margins may be the result of the variable cost control actions noted above, through better buying (quantity discounts, payment term discounts), or by increased investment. It can also result from external market appraisal leading to changes in your product mix sales or even from increased prices.

Product mix analysis requires that your accounts give you accurate costs and gross margins for each of your product/service lines.

Autoglass Ltd, at a time of depressed sales, recognised the extra margin from fitting laminated compared with toughened windscreens. An incentive scheme for fitters, combined with display aids for customers emphasising the extra benefits of laminated versus toughened, saw an increased proportion of laminated sales in a static market, and a marked improvement in gross margins.

Increasing price is always difficult; you know what to do when cutting prices to stimulate demand: you make a lot of noise and publicity! Some people think that you should take the opposite approach, with increased prices being silently passed through to suppliers and customers alike. But this is rarely the way to generate long-term loyalty. Better companies seek to combine increases with improvements in service or product offerings. Even the Post Office, when increasing prices by 1p, frequently seeks to announce improved services, for example the reintroduction of Sunday collections. Equally, warning suppliers of planned increases may enable you to reduce slow moving stock and build longer-term customer/supplier loyalty.

Margins can also be improved by checking that unnecessary discounts are not given away, eg when slow payers are allowed prompt payment discounts.

Increasing volume

A systematic approach to building sales volume was devised in the form of a matrix by Igor Ansoff as shown in Figure 2.8.5 (Ansoff, 1986).

Developing new products for new markets is clearly a difficult and high-risk strategy; if instead you keep one of the variables constant, with either an existing product or an existing market, you are ensuring, in military terms, that 'you are keeping one foot on the ground' and reducing risk. The lowest risk is in competing more strongly with existing products and existing markets. The two strands of strategy in terms of priority are therefore: to compete more strongly; and to innovate, with new products and new markets.

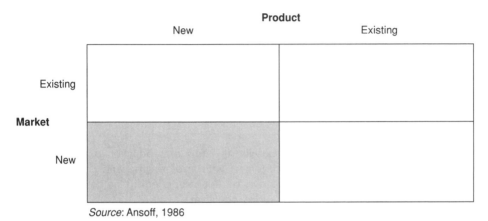

Source: Ansoff, 1986

Figure 2.8.5   Growth matrix

Compete

Competing more strongly with existing products within existing markets may be less glamorous than launching new products into exotic markets, but it usually ensures better returns. What is required is to sell more to existing customers – to increase their usage rate – then to capture customers from competitors.

Increased usage rate is possible because customers have a life cycle curve just like products, winning their early business (courtship) does not mean that you are their only supplier. Winning more of their business (wedding) is clearly a priority.

Equinox Furniture Design, a UK producer, supplied UK retailers with small 'top-up' orders, as overseas suppliers insisted on minimum orders of at least a dozen items. Equinox decided to offer customers an incentive to place minimum orders of five of each product. This virtually doubled the company's 'sell-in' to many existing customers, while still leaving it competitive with overseas suppliers, in terms of size of minimum order.

Equally, deadlock and divorce can loom with existing customers if you do not actively seek to maintain the marriage relationship; setting up computer links to facilitate direct customer ordering, carrying out joint promotions, or simply sharing information may be the way to build customer loyalty and sales. None of these actions require the expensive promotional costs for attracting new customers, which is why increasing usage rate has to be the most attractive method of building sales volume.

Winning competitors' customers again means following a low risk strategy of working with existing products in existing markets. Gaining entry to a competitor's customer is never easy, unless they are in the wedlock–divorce stage. To know this requires constant market intelligence, to reveal when a competitor's quality is down, deliveries are late or a trusted sales person has left. Your attention should always be to focus on added value rather than price: there is no point in growing unprofitably.

Equinox Furniture emphasised its flexibility in terms of production and small order delivery in order to gain entry to customers with foreign suppliers. Prices were not discounted. Only when it was accepted as a trusted supplier did the company seek to improve orders by offering minimum order incentives.

As you seek to win competitors' customers you may also be seeking to convert the sizable army of non-users of whatever you and your competitors sell. This usually involves seeking referrals from existing customers, sometimes by offering incentives, and can also involve buying mailing lists of customers with similar socio-economic groupings as your present customers (as Choc Express did from other mail order companies).

Innovate

Innovation, involving new products and new markets, is clearly high risk. But there are exceptions:

- Establishing new markets may mean simply taking existing proven products/services into a new geographical area, as Amberly plc successfully achieved by taking British rising damp cures and selling methods on to the Continent. The challenges involved coping with languages (when dealing, for example, with recruitment), adapting promotional methods (using multinational advertising agencies) and expanding under control (using good accounting systems).

  Or establishing new markets may mean simply expanding the range of your existing products, as with Doric Signs, which was able to extend its basic range of stove enamelled railway platform signs into multiple station information display panels, usable also in public parks and for signposting the Greenwich Millennium Exhibition. In this situation companies are basically expanding their 'core' businesses, the ones they know best. (Sir Graham Day, chairman of Rover and of Cadbury's once described a core business as 'one you can bet on'. Peters and Waterman describe it as 'sticking to your knitting'.)

● Finding new products may equally mean simple line extensions of your existing core businesses.

Autoglass realised early that success in establishing a windscreen replacement business would still leave seasonal troughs in their fitting business. By expanding into side windows (vandal area) and glass sun-roofs (peaking in the season of lowest windscreen replacement activity) the company was able to build a balanced product line, with good labour utilisation, concentrated nonetheless on 'automotive glass'. Even glass polishes and cleaning items provided a useful added contribution.

You should clearly be seeking to extend your existing product lines and seeking new market segments for your existing business. Yet major successful companies, like the Disney Corporation with its development of theme parks and hotels, or Sainsbury's with Homebase, are clearly able to launch new products and enter new markets, the most risky combination of all. How is this done? By hastening slowly and sometimes by acquisition, ie careful market testing in one's own premises, listening to one's own customers and employees (such as Stu Leonard's Dairy in Peters and Waterman's classic example (1985b)) and careful acquisition of proven earnings.

Beware synergy, which should really be spelt sinergy, unless you can actually quantify the extra value added – for example in better buying by quantity discounts, reduced price competition through acquiring significant market share – both of which Autoglass finally achieved in buying its major competitor, Windshield Enterprises. Careful test marketing has to be the key, as in new products/new markets Murphy's Law prevails: if a thing can go wrong, it will.

Lucius Cary, the successful owner of *Venture Capital Report*, invested £5,000 seedcapital to help David Vint develop a prototype of his new wax-filled hot water bottle. The 'Huggie', as it was labelled, was designed to provide a safer alternative to the traditional hot water bottle. A good working prototype resulted in a further £100,000 investment in manufacturing facilities and although the Christmas launch went well, a large number of Huggies were returned as faulty. Many of the thermostats did not work properly, also the wax oil filling started to penetrate the skin of the bottle when stored for a time. With hindsight, Lucius admitted, 'We were trying to break too much new ground'. The inventor, David Vint, remains unabashed: 'If we had £200,000–£300,000 more, I think the product would be a worldwide best seller'. The assets of the business were bought from the liquidator by an industry competitor.

The careful process of screening new ideas, developing the product and thoroughly test marketing prior to launch is both time-consuming and expensive. But much less expensive than jumping all those hurdles and rushing into the market. Hastening slowly but surely must be the key.

None of the above marketing strategic options may sound very exotic, particularly when compared with startling change of direction by Boddingtons, for example, where the brewing interests of the 200-year-old company were sold, with reinvestment in private nursing homes!

Perhaps the most daring strategic change in Europe since the second world war by a single man was the way in which Antoine Ribaud transformed BSN from being one of Europe's leading flat glass manufacturers into a leading European branded food company! This extraordinary achievement, by an extraordinary man, came after his failure to take over the leading European flat-glass manufacturer, St Gobain. Thwarted in this attempt, Antoine sold his low-yielding glass business to his major competitors and invested the enormous proceeds into the higher-yielding branded food business.

Extraordinary strategies and strategists do exist; for the growing business incremental options, such as we have outlined above, come first. When totally frustrated, however, as Antoine Ribaud was, or when all incremental options have been exhausted, you may need to completely rethink! If you divested all your businesses, what new diversification would you seek? Are the green pastures next door really greener? Antoine Ribaud proved it can be done.

Assignment 14

Strategic options

1. Try to position your products/services in the Boston matrix (see the example in Figure 2.8.1).
2. What are the directional implications from your products/services of the Boston matrix analysis?

3. Consider the opportunities you have to improve productivity in your business. List them under the headings of 'cutting costs' and 'increasing margins'.
4. List the ways you can increase volume in your business under the headings of 'competing more strongly' and 'innovating'.
5. Write down your diversification or divestment possibilities.

9

Choosing between alternatives

Growing the business will require a mixture of strategic options. These include: doing more of what you do now, for broadly similar types of customer – only better; launching new products, line extensions and new services; entering new markets and market segments; and possibly diversification, which can loosely be described as doing something you know nothing about for a customer you know even less about. Diversification is, by its very nature, the most risky strategic option of all, and should not be entered into lightly. Usually, only the terminal decline of your core business is a signal that diversification is essential.

Michael Peters and Partners

Problems caused by diversification

Michael Peters headed the first design company to be floated on the Stock Exchange. He graduated from the London College of Printing before obtaining a masters degree in fine arts at Yale University. He returned to London to join Collet Dickenson Pearce as creative director of the design department. Peters formed Michael Peters and Partners, a design consultancy specialising in corporate identity, and floated 13 years later to give the company's 60 employees a stake in the business at a reasonable price. For two or three years the company was very much the darling of the stock market. It was only when Peters started to diversify that things went disastrously wrong, and the company had to call in the receivers.

Two years after floating, Peters and his small management team went on what can best be described as a diversification binge. They moved into retail design, exhibitions, conference and event management, and even human resource management. For a business that was undermanaged itself, that was pretty rich.

Some of the companies that Peters bought to anchor his diversification around were successful, but many were not. But things went disastrously wrong when they expanded into the United States, a market that has been the graveyard for many UK companies. Trying to make the company's management team which had been used to working in the brand and corporate identity business manage activities it was not familiar with – some of them 3,500 miles away – was a recipe for disaster.

Following the receivership, Peters and his team are back to running their core business as plain Michael Peters Ltd; in Peters' words:

> We are once again back to basics, working with those clients who have always worked with us in our core brand and corporate identity business. That's what made us famous in the first place, and that's where we made our money. It has been a very painful experience, but I've learnt a big lesson. From now on, we'll be sticking firmly to what we know best.'

Terrapin

Understanding a diversified group

Often the only person who understands the logic of a diversified group is the boss. Neither the customers nor the staff have a clue.

Profits collapsed at Terrapin, the modular-buildings maker, during the final years of Harry Bolt's long chairmanship. As founder, Bolt refused to hand over management control until a few months before his death at 86.

Bolt's early thinking served the company well after the war, when he used aluminium made for building aircraft to create frames for portable prefabricated homes. Suited to mass production and capable of being folded so that four units could be carried on one lorry, these were quickly joined by buildings used by civil engineers rebuilding the national road network. The company later moved into education, supplying classrooms to house growing pupil numbers.

But eventually Bolt's domination of strategy became a barrier to new ideas.

Bolt had built up a diversified paradox. Whilst having sales of less than £20 million per annum, the company operated eight subsidiaries. They offered products and services ranging from long-term building rental and prefabricated construction, to contract furnishing and industrial space heating. The paradox is that sales effort was concentrated in an area within two hours' drive from Milton Keynes.

Perhaps we should leave the last word on diversification to a former boss of Tesco, who worked his way from being their first management trainee to become MD then, 12 years later, chairman. He pursued a single-minded policy to expand Tesco's food business in the UK. He is quoted as having said: 'My business experience tells me that you have got to get hold of a market and not move until you have squeezed every last drop from it'. Over that period Tesco overtook Sainsbury's as the UK's leading supermarket group, a lead that it is constantly extending.

Acquisitions, as a means of implementing any of these 'generic' core strategic options, is examined in a later chapter.

Analysis of strategic options

So much for developing strategy, now for the hard choice of which to pursue. If you have done a thorough job you should now have more options than either your management or financial resources could sensibly pursue – at the same time, at any rate. It is the comparison that will help you to choose the most desirable avenues.

Is the strategy compatible with your strengths?

As well as the greater risk associated with moving away from market penetration strategies, the further away you move from your own strengths, the less likely you are to succeed. The work done in preparing the position audit, and the marketing SWOT analysis, can be summarised to help you reduce areas of subjective judgment to something resembling the quality that numeric comparisons can provide.

Let us suppose you make and market rugby shirts and you are considering whether to move away from supplying just the club/supporters market, where you are strong at present, and to get into the fashion market for rugby-type shirts as well. Here you will be up against quite different competitors and the criteria for success in the market place will be different too.

The first step in making your decision is to review what you think are the critical factors for success (see CSFs, Chapter 7) – in other words what any company has to do right to succeed. For example, price might be important in the traditional rugby shirt market, but when it comes to the fashion market, image may be the deciding factor. Do not just rely on your opinion, ask customers in the market what they think, both about the critical factors and about your rating against each factor.

You can research these factors either by questionnaire or by face-to-face discussion with a reasonable number of customers and potential customers. Do not just rely on your salespeople's opinion; they always see price as the deciding factor. From Table 2.9.1 you can see that you and, more importantly your customers, rank image as being the most important factor and price the least important in this market.

You can reflect this relative importance by giving each factor a weighting, with the total for all factors being 100 per cent. In this example your customers feel that half the consideration in their purchase decision is given over to the image of the rugby shirt, and price accounts for only 10 per cent. You now need to rate your company and your main competitors against each CSF. So, for example, if your main strength lies in having an extensive product range, much more so than your competitors, you might rate this 9 out of 10, as you might also

Table 2.9.1 Critical success factors (CSFs)

CSF	Weighting %	Strengths and weaknesses	
		Your rating (out of 10)	Your main competitor's rating (out of 10)
Product range (choice)	20	× 9 = 1.8	× 7 = 1.4
Price	10	× 9 = 0.9	× 6 = 0.6
Quality and durability	20	× 2 = 0.4	× 9 = 1.8
Image	50	× 2 = 1.0	× 9 = 4.5
	100	4.10	8.30

rate your keen competitive prices. Unfortunately, if your product quality and garment durability characteristics are low and you have no fashion reputation, ratings on these factors might drop to only 2 out of 10.

Weighing all these factors up by rating yourself out of 10, you end up with a score of 4.10 compared with your competitor who has 8.30. (This is done by multiplying your rating out of 10 by the weighting factor expressed as a decimal: in Table 2.9.1, for example, for product it is $0.2 \times 9 = 1.8$.) Your competitor has an inferior product, whose stitching would not last a minute on the pitch, and it is overpriced. Sadly, the competitor is a wizard at quality and its shirts are the envy of every fashion-conscious female! As these two factors combined make up 70 per cent of reasons why people in this market buy, it gives your competitor an overwhelming advantage. You can repeat this exercise for all your major competitors.

So much for strengths and weaknesses; it still needs to be seen if there is an opportunity worth pursuing. The first step here is to define what constitutes a desirable opportunity. Let us suppose your main aim is to break out of the low-growth, low-profitability commodity rugby shirt market and into a faster moving sector. Then growth and profit would feature high on your shopping list of the factors which make for an attractive market to move into. (See Table 2.9.2).

Once again you could weigh the importance of each factor and get some scores and these might then be weighted to account for 60 per cent (25 per cent growth rate + 35 per cent profitability) of your reasons for seeing a market as attractive.

Now you need to develop a set of scoring criteria for each factor. If the market was under £5 million in size, or delivered a profit below 10 per cent, it would be fairly undesirable. This would be scored zero. A large market with over £50 million per annum sales and profit of over 15 per cent would be very attractive,

Table 2.9.2 Market attractiveness

Factor	Weighting %	Scoring criteria			Score	Result
	A	10	5	0	B	A × B
Market size	15	£50m	£5–49m	under 5m	10	1.50
Growth rate	25	15%	10–14%	under 10%	10	2.50
Competitiveness	20	Low	Medium	High	5	1.00
Profit margins	35	Over 15%	10–15%	under 10%	5	1.75
Seasonality	5	Low	Medium	High	7	0.35
	100%					7.10

and so would be scored 10. By multiplying the weighting in column A by the score in column B and dividing by 100 (to return the percentages in column A to decimals so you can use them in multiplication) we arrive at a market attractiveness factor of 7.1. This makes the fashion rugby shirt market an attractive market to go for, being well above the average of 5.0.

The final stage in the analysis of options is to put these results on a chart, plotting business strengths against market opportunity. Here you can see that while the fashion market is attractive, your strengths as seen by the market do not really lie there. If you do want to enter that market then you need to tackle your image and improve your product quality. That may be easier said than done.

Yardley

Radical changes of strategy are very difficult

Yardley, one of the oldest perfume and cosmetic firms in the world, was placed into receivership after being in business for 228 years with £120 million debts blamed on its 'rather stodgy' image.

The Essex-based company, which had been a household name for generations, and held three Royal Warrants, collapsed after a year of trying to shed its old-fashioned image. Founded in 1770 and one of England's ten oldest companies, Yardley attempted to reinvent itself with a £2.5 million series of racy and suggestive advertisements featuring the supermodel Linda Evangelista. Unfortunately, the pictures of the semi-naked model chained in a cell did little to improve sales in the Middle East, where there were enthusiastic followers of Yardley's decorous 'Olde English Rose' look.

The real power of strategic analysis is to help you choose between competing ideas. Suppose that rather than go into the UK fashion market for rugby shirts, you also had the chance to go into the French traditional rugby shirt market (Figure 2.9.1). By going through a similar exercise for the French market segment you might come up with a strength factor of 8 and a market opportunity of 7. Not quite such an attractive option, but you have nearly twice as many strengths to exploit that opportunity.

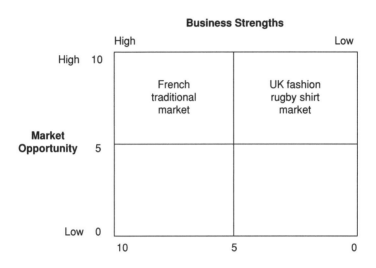

Figure 2.9.1   The opportunity/strength matrix

You can follow this through to evaluate as many optional strategies as you like. But you must remember to keep the market opportunity criteria the same throughout. You may, and indeed probably must, vary the CSFs for each market you are examining. For example, exporting to France may have 'Britishness' as a CSF which may not feature at all in the home market.

The final spin-off is that an analysis forces you to identify the CSFs in your market, by getting your customers to tell you what they think. And it makes you spell out what constitutes an attractive opportunity in a way that should make your choices more rational, and easier to communicate to your management team. That must be very much more thorough than relying on a wet finger to test which way the wind is blowing.

Will the strategy help you to achieve your prime objectives?

If your prime objective is to increase your return on investment from 10 per cent to 20 per cent then pursuing any strategy that does not return at least 20 per cent is going to make life very difficult for you.

Tandem

Having piles of cash is not always ideal

Tandem Computers, who briefly made it to the Fortune 500, pursued mutually exclusive strategies. They wanted to increase their return on investment (ROI) to 25 per cent and so use money efficiently, but would only pursue market strategies which resulted in quick cash paybacks. They succeeded in their marketing strategies, and piled in the cash until it filled up half their balance sheet. But as they could only get 12 per cent on the money market for their cash, the other half of their capital employed had to realise 38 per cent ROI to bring the average up. This in turn led them into more and more risky areas.

Dairyborn

Having the right strategy can make all the difference

Robert Segesser, MD of Dairyborn Foods, the cheese component business, came on the Cranfield Business Growth Programme and turned his company objectives on their head afterwards.

For five years he built sales – £3 million a year's worth – without making much profit. Then he defined the company's principal objectives as being to move its profit margin from 16 per cent to 25 per cent. This moved the business into what he likes to refer to as 'margin-protected' business: in other words, things that only Dairyborn can do, that customers want badly and will pay for. Segesser believes that, if his customers get to the future before he does, they will leave him behind. He has to create solutions for customers' problems before they even realise they have them.

Refocusing on solving problems rather than selling cheese, and aiming for profit margin growth rather than turnover growth alone, has transformed the firm into a business with £15 million a year sales and £2 million a year profit. From being worth little, a few years later the company turned away a potential suitor with £20 million on the table.

Remember that your new strategies must help you meet your objectives in terms of growth rate, market share, profitability etc.

Is the strategy within your mission?

Having spent a lot of time developing a mission statement that everyone believes in, there is not much point in pursuing strategies that lie outside it. Remember, your mission is supposed to be narrow enough to give you focus and wide enough to give you scope for growth.

Blooming Marvellous

Blooming Marvellous, the UK designer maternity wear company, could be forgiven for revising their mission only if women gave up having babies, or once 500,000 out of the 700,000 women who have babies each year in the UK were in one (or two!) of their outfits.

It is wise to 'stick to the knitting' – at least until you are deep into Phase 4: growth with strong management.

Are acceptable levels of risk involved?

All new strategies involve taking risks. Risks can be loosely classified into those you have to take, those you do not have to take, those you cannot afford not to take and those you cannot afford to take.

The first type of risk basically describes the nature of the business you are in. If you're a bookmaker, it is no good worrying that your money is all on a horse! Some risks are not integral to the business and so you do not *have* to take them: for example, the risk of currency changes, up or down, can be laid off by someone in international trade. It means your costs may be a little higher, and you will not win if currencies move in your favour, but you will not make expensive mistakes either. Whichever route you take, it will have virtually no effect on the customers' desire for your product or service.

There are other risks you cannot afford not to take. For example, if all your main competitors are spending heavily on new product development, or on improving their point of sale tills and sales analysis equipment, then by doing nothing you may be left too far behind to be competitive.

Finally, some strategies call for such a high resource commitment that if they do not succeed the whole company is prejudiced. These are the risks you cannot afford to take.

Sock Shop

Don't make a bet if you can't afford to lose

Sophie Mirman was just 27 when she founded Sock Shop and 33 when she lost it. At one stage she had an empire with a paper value of £72 million, which at the time made her the 188th richest person in Britain. When the company floated, its shares were over subscribed by 530 per cent.

City pressure for expansion encouraged Mirman to look for new opportunities abroad. She opened 17 shops in the United States, which she now admits was her worst mistake. The company's formula of outlets in inner city stations, which worked well in the UK, failed in the United States. There it was an invitation to local drug addicts to steal the takings several times over.

The company's expansion into the US market led to high gearing, at a time when interest rates doubled in one year.

In Mirman's words, 'We turned left instead of right, when we went into the American market'. The company's failure in the United States caused its 103 UK outlet business to go into administrative receivership. All Mirman and her husband partner, Richard Ross, walked away with was the £2.5 million they took out on flotation.

Mirman and Ross now run Trotters, offering couture for kids aged from nought to ten, shoes, accessories, toys and hairdressing in a bright fun setting designed to entertain children. Since they started they have only opened two shops, both in London's Kensington area. Their move into mail order is based on their 25,000 customer database, and was an opportunity that took them three years to plan and exploit. Trotters Online, their latest venture, sticks to their customer base, up to 11-year-olds, and was meticulously planned before its launch date.

Barriers to entry

Any new strategy can be significantly more attractive if, by pursuing it, you make it more difficult for new competitors to enter the market, or for existing companies to stay the course.

Waterstone's

Intangibles can be barriers too

Tim Waterstone's strategy of seven-day, late-night trading and of having well-educated, knowledgeable staff, all on substantial bonus schemes, transformed the UK bookselling market. W H Smith could not match this strategy. They tried, but their unionised staff were less than enthusiastic about the proposed opening hours – so they bought 51 per cent of Waterstone's, making Tim Waterstone a multimillionaire in the process. Sweet revenge for a man who was fired by W H Smith eight years earlier.

The time value of money

While reviewing your company's plans for the future, you and your management team may come up with a number of exciting new business opportunities. The only trouble is that, before they can be exploited you may have to invest in new equipment, and perhaps even some extra space. This seems reasonable enough – after all, you have to speculate to accumulate. The key question is, what is the right proportion of money to spend now, to receive a given amount of profit in future years?

The example in Table 2.9.3 illustrates a typical problem. The proposition is that you should invest £50,000 capital to make £80,000 over the next five years: a clear profit of £30,000, apparently a satisfactory situation as the return is 60 per cent (($30 \div 50$) × 100). The cash will come in and out as shown.

Table 2.9.3   Cash flow of investment

Year	Cash out (a) £	Cash in (b) £	Net cash (b–a) £
0	50,000	–	(50,000)
1	5,000	15,000	10,000
2	5,000	15,000	10,000
3	12,500	37,500	25,000
4	12,500	37,500	25,000
5	5,000	15,000	10,000
			10,000
			30,000

This is based on a £50,000 investment now, followed by some cash expenses and cash income in the future. In other words, this is a typical business buying in materials, adding value and selling mainly on monthly terms.

Present value

You may by this stage have a nagging feeling that receiving £10,000 in five years' time is not worth quite the same as the identical amount coming in next year. And you would be right.

If you were offered a pound in a year's time you would instinctively value it lower than a pound today. The exact amount lower would depend on how much return you want for your money. So, for example, if you want to make 20 per cent profit, you would only pay about 80p now for each pound payable in a year. If you were going to receive the £1 on offer in two years' time you would value it even lower – and so on as time progressed.

The concept that explains this diminution of value with time is called 'present value'. It is calculated by using a mathematical equation which fortunately you need never know, as tables are readily available (see Table 2.9.4), or you can find the information stored in most financial calculators (eg Hewlett-Packard's).

Table 2.9.4 Present value table

Year	Percentage			
	14	15	16	17
1	0.877193	0.869565	0.862069	0.854701
2	0.769468	0.756144	0.743163	0.730514
3	0.674972	0.657516	0.640658	0.624371
4	0.592080	0.571753	0.552291	0.533650
5	0.519369	0.497177	0.476113	0.456111

Table 2.9.4 is an extract which shows the present value of a pound received in one to five years' time, on the assumption you want to make between 14 and 17 per cent return on your investment.

Let us return to our example to see how present value works in practice. Let us assume that we want to make at least 17 per cent return on the investment we are to make. Accordingly we would select the present value factor at 17 per cent, from Table 2.9.4, and put the appropriate factor against each year of the life of the investment (see Table 2.9.5).

Table 2.9.5 Present value of cash flow of investment

Year	Net cash flow (a)	Present value factor @ 17% (b)	Net present value (NPV) (a × b)
0	(50,000)	1.000	(50,000)
1	10,000	0.855	8,550
2	10,000	0.731	7,310
3	25,000	0.624	15,600
4	25,000	0.534	13,350
5	10,000	0.456	4,560
	Net present value		(630)

Take the present value factor for each year and multiply it by the net cash flow. (The net cash flow is arrived at in Table 2.9.3.) This gives the net present value of the cash that this investment generates. In this case it comes to £49,370 (8,550 + 7,310 + 15,600 + 13,350 + 4,560), which is £630 less than the £50,000 we put in (year 0 is now and £1 now has a present value of £1, hence the factor 1.000). So if you had expected to make 17 per cent return on your investment, you would have been disappointed. You would have been even more upset if you were anticipating 60 per cent, as first indications suggested.

The real rate of return

The present value concept tells us whether or not an investment is going to achieve a given rate of return. (You can arrive at that rate by looking at your past achievements, your competitors' performance, or by setting a challenging objective.) However, it will not tell you an important thing to know – what return you are actually going to get for your money.

Going back to the example, all we know is that the net present value (NPV) is negative, as the target rate of return has not been achieved. To establish the exact rate of return we would need to recalculate the present values using a low enough percentage to make the net present value a positive sum. So if we were to plump for 14 per cent, the figures would look like Table 2.9.6.

Table 2.9.6 Present value of cash flow of investment, PVF at 14%

Year	Net cash flow (a)	Present value factor @ 14% (b)	Net present value (NPV) (a × b)
0	(50,000)	1.000	(50,000)
1	10,000	0.877	8,770
2	10,000	0.769	7,690
3	25,000	0.675	16,875
4	25,000	0.592	14,800
5	10,000	0.519	5,190
	Net present value		3,325

Once again, by adding up the sum of the present value of cash flows from years one to five, and deducting it from the cash going out at the start of the project, we arrive at the NPV. In this case it is a positive figure, so we know the project makes a return greater than 14 per cent and less than 17 per cent, the two rates we have tried.

We can deduce the actual rate by doing the following sum:

Interpolating Equation

$$\begin{array}{l}\text{The Internal} \\ \text{Rate of} \\ \text{Return (IRR)}\end{array} = \begin{array}{l}\text{Lowest} \\ \text{Trial} \\ \text{Rate}\end{array} + \left[\frac{\text{Positive Cash Flow}}{\text{Range of Cash Flow}} \times \frac{\text{Difference between}}{\text{High and Low Rates}} \right] \%$$

$$= 14 + \left[\frac{3,300}{3,996} \times 3 \right] = 14 + 2.47 = 16.47$$

Now that we have a slightly more meaningful piece of information on the proposed project profitability, we know it will make a real return on the money invested of 16.47 per cent. We can then compare that with the other projects we may have in mind in exactly the same way as you could, for example, compare the, say, 6 per cent return offered on a current bank account, with the 12 per cent on offer from a one-year building society bond.

Nothing is certain

The danger with the NPV technique is that in producing very precise figures – 16.47 per cent, for example – it can give you a false sense of security. You could be forgiven for believing that what you have forecast will actually happen in much the way that you expect.

No one can see five years into the future with any great degree of accuracy, although you can often get an idea of the type of events that might occur, and some order of their magnitude. For example, if you set out to buy and run a car, at the outset you will know its approximate cost to within 10 per cent, its working life within a year or so and the running costs such as insurance, road tax, repairs and petrol, also to within 10 per cent. If, after doing all your sums, the car you would like is within your budget only if petrol costs do not rise more than 10 per cent per annum, or if you can be certain that it will last five years rather than the more likely four, then you are probably making a bad decision.

It is exactly the same with capital budgeting: you need to subject your figures to what is known in the trade as 'sensitivity analysis'; in other words, to find out how sensitive a particular project is to a particular likely event. Returning to our earlier example, suppose that 16 per cent was an acceptable return, but we wanted to see what the project could stand up to, we could rerun our calculations as follows.

Let us assume that the revenue flow is going to build up more slowly than we think, although over the life of the project the expenses and revenues will be the same, ie £50,000 out and £80,000 in (see Table 2.9.3).

We can now see that this project is so sensitive to a 20 per cent (£8,000 versus £10,000) drop in profits in the first two years, that it would not make economic sense to invest. The big question now is how likely your forecast is to be 20 per cent out.

Table 2.9.7 Sensitivity analysis

Year	Net cash flow (a)	Present value factor @ 16% (b)	Net present value (NPV) (a × b)
0	(50,000)	1.000	(50,000)
1	8,000	0.862	6,896
2	8,000	0.743	5,944
3	25,000	0.640	16,000
4	25,000	0.552	13,800
5	14,000	0.476	6,664
	Net present value		696

While some of the arithmetic in the above examples may have been cumbersome, the concept once grasped is simplicity itself. A pound received tomorrow is worth less than a pound today, simply because of what you could do with the money if you had it at your disposal now. So the only meaningful way to compare pounds out now with pounds received in the future is to discount the value of those future sums in line with your profit expectations.

If you still budget for your capital expenditure ignoring present value, it is unlikely that many of your business investment decisions will make the profit you expect.

Softer investments

Not all new strategies call for increases in fixed assets, as the two examples below illustrate.

Dairycrest

Advertising costs can drop to the bottom line

Heavy advertising of Cathedral City and Davidstow cheeses allowed Dairycrest to hold the prices of its branded products despite a sharp fall in the price of milk.

The company managed to pocket most of the benefits from the 12 per cent drop in milk prices by spending £1 million a month advertising its main brands on television.

This year, it intends to spend £12 million on television advertising (a 50 per cent increase on the previous year's budget) to help it to move away from the commodity cheese market.

The company has increased margins from 5 per cent to 5.8 per cent by selling a higher mix of its more expensive cheeses, and by not passing on all cost savings to supermarkets.

Branded produce, which includes Frijj, now represents 40 per cent of group sales, but about 75 per cent of profits.

Dairycrest spent £6 million on advertising in the first half-year, up from £3.75 million spent in the same period last year. Profits have risen from £18.7 million to £20.7 million.

Atrium

New solutions to old problems

Patrick Dormoy's up-market furniture business has solved the problem of what to do with yesterday's products to make room for today's.

The company has a £5 million a year turnover, using its central London premises as a showcase for designers and architects to take their clients. Once a year traditionally Atrium held a sale to clear out old furniture. What was not sold was either warehoused or left in the showroom. The problem with 'annual sales' was that they disrupted the normal and valuable business of showing clients today's products. The solution was to invest in a virtual showroom, which allows customers, via the Internet, to browse 365 days a year on what is in effect a permanent sale.

Both these 'softer investments' can and should be subjected to the critical appraisal that any other option for growth would be.

In Dairycrest's case, the sums are quite simple. Is an extra £4.5 million spent on advertising worth the extra £2 million it makes in profits? That in turn depends upon how long it will be able to retain the higher margins once the advertising reverts to the original levels. In other words, is their expenditure an investment, or just an increase in overheads?

Assignment 15

Checking your options

1. Check your strategies out against the criteria described in this chapter and any others you have, and then list them in your order of preference.
2. Make sure your preferred strategies make up a reasonably balanced port-folio.
3. Make sure the likely sales and profit levels, if achieved, will meet your growth targets. (We will look at this in more detail when we make the fore-casts and projections in the business plan in Part 3.)

10 *Financing growth*

Whatever strategic direction you propose to pursue, it is almost certain to require money. By now you will have discovered that a healthy business has an equally healthy appetite for cash. For the first years of a business's life its strategic choices are invariably limited by the availability of funds. Once it gathers momentum and begins to plan its strategic direction, the 'corset elastic' is usually the limited availability of good opportunities and the management to exploit them successfully. The constant search for funds is not in itself a cause for concern. Businesses, after all, exist in part at least to turn money into goods and services, which can be sold on for a profit. It usually takes a while for the business cycle to move from strategic ideas to profit and so, as long as you are growing, more money will be needed.

What should concern you, however, is where that money comes from. There are two main sources of money, internal and external, with a number of sub-divisions of each sector. Getting the right balance of funds from these different sources is the key to profitable growth – and perhaps even to survival itself.

Internal sources of funds

Surprisingly, many businesses have much of the money they need to finance growth already tied up in the firm. It may require a little imagination and some analysis to uncover it, but the financial position audit should have given some pointers to how this might be done. Look at the accounts for High Note in Table 1.4.3 (see page 64). Here you will see that the company is employing 46 per cent more capital in year two to generate additional sales of only 30 per cent. The problem in this example is that High Note has more than doubled its money tied up in fixed assets and is getting very little in return. You should start by looking very carefully at all your capital assets to see if they really are essential to the business. In addition, when you develop your growth strategies, consider carefully both the amount and timing of any major capital expenditure, otherwise you could end up scrambling for business at any price just to cover costs.

Richard Edward Ltd

Expanding the capital base too fast

Richard Edward Ltd was started when John and David Moger paid £220 for an elderly little litho press and installed it in a garage. David could not actually lay his hands on his share of the cash at the time and John claims still to be waiting for the £110. The company grew steadily with turnover moving from £254,000 in year 2 to £641,000 in year 4. Within 10 years the company had turnover of £2 million in the original printing business and just under three quarters of a million pounds in a new mailing and print finishing business.

The Moger brothers were in an expansive mood. The business they had built up was thriving: to invest in better property and better equipment seemed a sensible thing to do. They spent £855,000 on new premises and almost £1 million on two new presses.

Within 12 months the company's interest bill wiped out its profits. John Moger confessed at the time: 'We are not making anything at the moment, we are just hoping to survive'. Desperate to keep the presses going, they searched for any work, from contracts from government departments down to a few letterheads or a bundle of business cards.

John Moger now admits that his business had grown so fast that there was little time for contingency planning. 'We were a bit too busy,' he said.

Squeeze working capital

Working capital is a further area rich in possibilities for squeezing to release cash for expansion. Debtors and stocks are perhaps the most fertile areas to start. According to figures prepared by a reputable forecasting consultancy, Spain, Italy and Portugal topped the list of Europe's slow payers. Around a quarter of SMEs in these countries wait between 90 and 119 days for the settlement of bills.

The best payers were in Finland, where the average was 27 days, followed by Poland (31) and Denmark and Norway (32). The UK has the highest proportion of companies with an average payment period of between 45 and 59 days.

Do not take too much comfort from new UK legislation to allow firms to charge interest on late payment. In Spain, where the contractual period for payments is 68 days, the average time for payments is 74 days.

Holliday Chemical Holdings

Good IT systems can cut production costs

Holliday Chemical Holdings, a Huddersfield-based chemicals manufacturer with UK turnover of £33 million, spent £160,000 on a computerised materials requirements planning system which allowed it to plan production schedules in its two UK plants (employing 367 people).

Michael Peagram, head of the new management team which bought into Holliday, used tighter controls on purchasing and the computerised systems to cut £1 million from the company's stocks of £8 million. Stocks had been allowed to grow as turnover quadrupled but that was an unsustainable cash drain.

Sophisticated computer systems may be appropriate for a company the size of Holliday but smaller businesses can achieve considerable improvements by making relatively simple changes in the way they purchase and monitor their stocks of raw materials. Holliday itself is buying in chemicals on a monthly rather than a quarterly basis where possible to reduce its own stocks.

Mercado Carpets

Computers can't make decisions for you

Mercado Carpets, a Leeds-based carpet wholesaler, has computerised its stock control procedures but combines this with what John Wharton, joint MD, calls 'gut feel' to decide on the types and volumes of carpets to be purchased. Wharton estimates he devotes five hours a week to stocks and purchasing.

Mercado normally carries between £4 million and £5 million worth of inventory in its warehouse compared with an annual sales level of £26 million. Acquired by its present management by means of a buy-out, the company employs 168 people.

Wharton keeps stocks low by buying, where possible, from suppliers with short delivery times, though shipment delays mean he is forced to hold 12 weeks' stocks of carpets from his US suppliers. In the wake of the buy-out, Wharton persuaded his major suppliers to extend their payment terms by one month.

For businesses that have failed to monitor stock levels closely, the introduction of tight controls can prove daunting. A 'quick and dirty' way of making improvements can be achieved by grading stock as A, B or C according to the value of individual items or of the total number held. Attention is then focused on items in the A category which can provide the greatest savings. These items can then be subjected to regular stock-takes; patterns of demand can be studied to see how frequently orders are placed, if there are peaks and troughs, or whether demand is seasonal. Managers can then decide the quantities they require and when to place their next order or start their next production run if they are making the item in-house. B and C items can be brought into this programme once it is well established.

Much of the cost of many products is incurred in the final stages of manufacture so big stock savings can be made by holding stocks of semi-finished items: only put the finishing touches to an item when the customer wants it.

Companies frequently maintain larger stocks than are necessary because a new order is triggered automatically when stocks fall to a certain level. These trigger points should be re-examined for each product to see if lower levels can be set.

Make more profit and plough it back

Another internal source of finance is to make your present business more profitable and plough that profit back to grow your business. That may sound a little trite, but many businesses find that whilst they have been very good at growing turnover, they have been less clever with growing profits. Out of 15,000 UK companies in the £1 million to £50 million a year turnover band, only 960 had grown profits and turnover by an average of 25 per cent in each of the preceding years. The vast majority had either stood still or, worse, grown sales at the expense of profits and margins. With sales growth and margin erosion come the certainty that the business will need more and more cash injections for lower and lower returns: not exactly a winning formula.

Jato Dynamics

There is no point growing the top line if you can't grow the bottom line

'Four years ago, I made the mistake of growing the company for its own sake rather than to make additional profit. We ended the year with a pre-tax loss of £233,000. I don't want to do that again', states Jake Shafran, who founded Jato Dynamics more than 14 years ago. The company markets data on the specification and price of virtually every new car sold. This service, now Internet-based, can provide customers with an immediate analysis of the likely impact of price and specification changes. The company made £533,000 profits on sales of £9.8 million. It employs 215 people worldwide, with 99 at its head office in Harrow, north-west London.

Five steps you can take to unlock the extra profit potential in your business are described below:

- *Recognise the iceberg.* Just as the small tip of the iceberg showing above water conceals an enormous mass below, the small(ish) percentage of profits the average business makes (typically under 10 per cent of sales), conceals a great volume of money being used to arrive at that profit.

It only requires a few percentage points reduction in costs to improve profits dramatically, as Table 2.10.1 illustrates.

Table 2.10.1   The effects of cost savings on profits

Before		After 2% cost saving		Extra profit		But if sales drop...	
£000	%	£000	%	£000	%	£000	%
1,000	100	1,000	100	–	–	714	100
950	95	930	93	–	–	664	93
50	5	70	7	20	40	50	7

In the example given in Table 2.10.1, the last profit-to-sales figure was 5 per cent. Costs, the 'below the water line' mass, are 95 per cent. By reducing those costs by a mere 2 per cent, bottom line profits have been increased by a massive 40 per cent (this is a simplified example from a real life case).

This extra profitability can be used to finance extra investments, saved as a reserve for bad times, or it can be used to compensate for lower sales. In the example above, when costs are reduced by 2 per cent, turnover from sales can drop by over 25 per cent, to £714,000, before profits will dip below £50,000. That should take care of even the most unpleasant sales dip.

Now much of this will come as no surprise to you; after all, most of this is your money so naturally you are well informed as to where it goes. But the people who work for you have probably never considered (or been given the chance to consider) the phenomenal impact that relatively small savings in costs can have on the bottom line. So why not tell them? You could start by giving your key employees a copy of the above table and inviting their comments.

● *Use the 80/20 rule*. Obviously you cannot leave the whole responsibility of reducing costs exclusively to the people who, after all, created the costs in the first place. Just as with any other business, task objectives have to be agreed and strategies adopted.

Fortunately, here you have the 80/20 rule working in your favour. This rule states that 80 per cent of effort goes into producing 20 per cent of the results. Look at Table 2.10.2 below, which was prepared for one company on a recent business training programme. This more or less confirms the rule, as 18 per cent of customers account for 78 per cent of sales.

Table 2.10.2 The 80/20 rule in action

Number of customers		Value of sales		Value of potential sales	
	%	£000	%	£000	%
4	3	710	69	1,200	71
21	18	800	78	1,500	88
47	41	918	90	1,600	94
116	100	1,025	100	1,700	100

A quick glance at figures in your own business will in all probability confirm that 20 per cent of your customers account for 80 per cent of your sales, and yet your costs are probably spread evenly across all your customers. Salespeople tend to make their calls in a cycle that suits their administrative convenience, rather than concentrating on customers with the most potential.

Interestingly enough, when the salesman in the company used in the above example was asked where he thought his sales in two years' time would be coming from (see last column in Table 2.10.2) he felt that his top 18 per cent of customers would account for 88 per cent of sales (up from 78 per cent of actual sales this year). And yet an analysis of his call reports showed that he spent over 60 per cent of his time calling on his bottom 68 accounts, and planned to continue doing so. This activity-based rather than results-based outlook was being used to make out a case for an additional salesperson. What was actually needed was a call grading system to lower the call rate on accounts with the least sales potential. So, for example, accounts with the least potential were called on twice a year and phoned twice, whilst top grade accounts were visited up to eight times a year.

This grading process saves costs as phone calls are cheaper than visits; it eliminates the need for an additional salesperson, which at first glance the projected growth would have justified; and it even frees time so the salesman can prospect for new, high potential accounts.

The 80/20 rule can be used across the business to uncover other areas where costs are being incurred that are unwarranted by the benefits. In some areas you just need to open your eyes to see waste. Did you know that the average executive spends 36 minutes a day looking for things on or around the desk? This can waste up to £10,000 a year for a fairly senior person – you, for example. The same survey, conducted for the British Institute of Management, revealed that a quarter of the 500 executives they questioned spent 11 hours a week in meetings, equivalent to 13 weeks a year. Few were satisfied with their investment.

The chances are that if you are anything like many other UK chief executives you feel that you and your management team waste too much time on the wrong priorities. It is not that managers are not working hard enough – on average they work 20 per cent more hours than a decade ago. It is just that organising time and daily priorities in a world in which there has been a 800 per cent increase in business information, and the average manager is interrupted every eight minutes, is difficult to say the least. But the 'cost' of wasting time is very real, in two senses. First, you end up buying more management than you need, and that cost has to be spread across your products. Secondly, people are too busy doing the wrong things to have time to do the right things.

- *Use zero-based budgeting.* The 80/20 rule is helpful in getting costs back into line, but what if the line was completely wrong in the first place?

When you sit down with your team and discuss budgets, the arguments always revolve around how much more each section will need next year. The starting point is usually this year's costs, which are taken as the only 'facts' upon which to build. So, for example, if you spent £25,000 on advertising last year and achieved sales of £1 million, the expense would have been 2.5 per cent of sales. If the sales budget for next year is £1.5 million, then it seems logical to spend £37,500 next year. That, however, presupposes last year's sum was wisely and effectively spent in the first place, which it almost certainly was not.

Zero-based budgeting turns the cost argument on its head. It assumes that each year every cost centre starts from zero spending and, based on the goals of the business and the resources available, arguments are presented for every pound spent, *not just for the increase proposed.*

- *Use training to reduce mistakes.* According to one senior banker, basic mistakes by employees account for between 25 and 40 per cent of the total costs of any service business, and not just in banking. It is certainly true that people learn from experience, and the more often they do a job, the faster and better they get at it (up to the stage that indifference sets in, of course)! What a pity, however, that so many of Britain's smaller firms let their employees practise on their customers, losing money and goodwill in the process.

Training people, on a regular basis, in all aspects of their jobs, is a sure-fire way to reduce mistakes, and get costs down and customer satisfaction up. This is doubly important with the high staff turnover that is all too common today. Some short-sighted employers say: why train them when they stay for such a short time? Answer: it costs 2 per cent of salary to train them which is less than 10 per cent of the cost of their mistakes, if Frost is right. And once trained, who knows, they may even get enough job satisfaction to want to stay; just think how much you will save if that happens.

Training can be one of the fastest payback routes to cost reduction. One study carried out recently by a major American corporation concluded that its productivity was improved by 5 to 20 per cent simply by explaining to people why their jobs matter. This single action saved it a net US$9 million, after training costs, over the previous three years.

Allen

Even small mistakes can prove very expensive

Allen, the construction company, revealed that management blunders had cost the group about £1 million in operating profits. Errors in tenders submitted at the end of one year had meant that margins on some contracts were considerably reduced, a fact that only came to light as the work progressed the following year. Donald Greenlagh, the chairman, said that 'heads have rolled' and that the mistakes were due to failures of management rather than company policy.

Pre-tax profits for the six months to September 27 of that year still showed an increase from £7.1 million to £8.9 million and turnover up more than 30 per cent to £166.6 million from £126.8 million. Earnings rose to 15.01p a share from 12.29p. The interim dividend rose to 5.1p from 4.38p. Profits could have been over 11 per cent higher, had these mistakes not occurred.

● *Ensure that making higher profit is an incentive.* Lots of companies have incentive schemes, but most end up rewarding the wrong achievement. Some firms actually reward people by how much they spend! So, for example, buyers with the biggest budget get the highest pay and perks. Production staff are paid for greater output and salespeople for more sales, whether or not either activity is particularly desirable at the time it is achieved. In one company (whose name has been withheld to protect the embarrassed) one of the largest creditor items on liquidation was the salespeople's commission.

There are many reasons for giving people intermediate incentives, such as sales commission, but unless you build profit targets into your goals and incentives, nine times out of ten you will end up with the wrong result. You get nothing if the company does not make a satisfactory profit, so rewarding others if they do not make money is only encouraging an illusion of reality.

Building incentives for everyone around the profit you make focuses the whole business on customers and costs, and that has to be good. It will make everyone look for cheaper ways to do things, ways to eliminate waste, more effective ways to spend their time (and your money), and ways to get more money out of more satisfied customers – in short, all the ways to unlock the profit potential in your business.

Medic Aid

Everyone can help to do things better

This case study shows how one participant on a Cranfield business growth programme – Mark Kirby of Medic Aid – managed to increase his profit per unit of output. Medic Aid grew from £2 million turnover per annum to over £4.5 million within 18 months of Kirby attending the Cranfield programme. Staff at Medic Aid took a detailed look at everything they did with a view to increasing the profitability of every hour they worked. Each process was examined and made the subject of a brainstorming session. For example, one part of the manufacturing process of the company's nebulizer products required several hundred plastic parts to be tipped onto a table. Invariably 50 or so fell off the table and were either damaged or took valuable seconds to recover. By putting a 3-inch-high plastic rim around the table, at a cost of £5, the company saved two hours' production time per week. Several hundred simple ideas like this reduced the total production time for one key product by nearly 40 per cent.

The overall effect was quite staggering. At long last Medic Aid managed to grow both profit and sales. Unit profitability got progressively bigger when the Profit Improvement Programme (PIP) was introduced, and within 12 months the company was making six times as much profit as before.

One final thought on internal sources of finance: do you really need to do everything yourself? If you do not you could release all the working capital and fixed capital tied up in that process and use it for better things.

Mark Kirby of Medic Aid subcontracted his low value added production processes to a subcontractor who could actually make them cheaper than he could. The subcontractor took on the commitment to buy raw material and hold stocks, and Kirby used the factory space saved for better things.

The Nighthawk case study gives another example of how this concept can work successfully.

Nighthawk Electronics

You don't need people to make money

No manufacturing. No salesmen. No research and development. Tina Knight has grown her company from a standing start to a turnover of £2 million a year as much by deciding what not to do as by what she has to sell.

She is MD of Nighthawk Electronics, based at Debden, Essex. The company supplies switches for computer equipment, the kind of gadget that, for example, allows half a dozen personal computers to use one printer between them.

She says, 'I didn't want to get into manufacturing myself, but I save myself the headaches. Why should I start manufacturing as long as I've got my bottom line right? Turnover is vanity, profit is sanity. I have run companies for other people and I do not have to grow big just for the kudos'.

Instead, Knight contracts out to factories in Derby and Bedford. She feels she still has control over quality, since any item that is not up to standard can be sent back She also has the ultimate threat of taking away trade, which would leave the manufacturers she uses with a large void to fill. 'We would do so if quality was not good enough. Many manufacturers have under-utilised capacity.'

Knight uses freelance salesmen on a commission basis. She explains: 'I didn't want a huge salesforce. Most sales managers sit in their cars at the side of the road filling in swindle sheets. R & D is another area where expenses would be terrific. We have free-lance design teams working on specific products. We give them a brief and they quote a price. The cost still works out at twice what you expected, but at least you have a measure of control. I could not afford to employ R & D staff full-time and I would not need them full-time. Our system minimises the risks and gives us a quality we could not afford as a small company'.

Indirectly, the tight-knit staff of eight at Debden control and provide work for about 380 elsewhere.

Debt and equity

There are two fundamentally different types of external money which a growing company can tap into: debt and equity. Debt is money borrowed, usually from a bank, and which one day you will have to repay. While you are making use of borrowed money you will also have to pay interest on the loan. Equity is the money put in by shareholders, including the proprietor, and money left in the business by way of retained profit. You do not have to give the shareholders their money back, but they do expect the directors to increase the value of their shares, and if you go public they will probably expect a stream of dividends too. If you do not meet the shareholders' expectations, they will not be there when you need more money – or, if they are powerful enough, they will take steps to change the board.

Why is borrowing attractive?

High gearing is the name given when a business has a high proportion of outside money to inside money. High gearing has considerable attractions to a business which wants to make high returns on shareholders' capital, as the example in Table 2.10.3 shows.

Here the business is assumed to need £60,000 capital to generate £10,000 operating profits. Four different capital structures are considered. They range from all share capital (no gearing) at one end, to nearly all loan capital at the other. The loan capital has to be 'serviced', that is, interest of 12 per cent has to be paid. (The actual amount of the interest rate will change both the ROSC and the interest cover, but the principle behind the sum is the same.) The loan itself can be relatively indefinite, simply being replaced by another one at market interest rates when the first loan expires.

Table 2.10.3 shows that ROSC grows from 16.6 to 30.7 per cent by virtue of the changed gearing. If the interest on the loan were lower, the ROSC would be even more improved by high gearing, and the higher the interest the lower the relative improvement in ROSC. So in times of low interest, businesses tend to go for increased borrowings rather than raising more equity, ie money from shareholders.

At first sight this looks like a perpetual profit growth machine. Naturally owners would rather have someone else 'lend' them the money for their business than put it in themselves, if they could increase the return on their investment. The problem comes if the business does not produce £10,000 in operating profits. Very often, in a small business, a drop in sales of 20 per cent means profits are halved or even eliminated. If profits were halved in this example, it could not meet the interest payments on its loan. That would make the business insolvent, and so not in a 'sound financial position'; in other words, failing to meet one of the two primary business objectives.

Bankers tend to favour 1:1 gearing as the maximum for a small business, although they have been known to go much higher (a glance at the Laker accounts will show just how far the equation can be taken, with £200 million plus of loans to £1 million or so equity). Gearing (9) can be more usefully expressed as the percentage of shareholders' funds (share capital plus reserves), to all the long-term capital in the business. So 1:1 is the same as saying 50 per cent gearing.

What is the right balance of debt to equity?

A company's gearing will be continuously changing with the growth opportunities it sees ahead, the current cost of money and the availability of equity and

Table 2.10.3   The effect of gearing on ROSC

Capital structure		No Gearing – £	Average Gearing 1:1 £	High Gearing 2:1 £	Very High Gearing 3:1 £
Share capital		60,000	30,000	20,000	15,000
Loan capital		–	30,000	40,000	45,000
(at 12%)					
Total capital		60,000	60,000	60,000	60,000
Profits					
Operating profit		10,000	10,000	10,000	10,000
Less interest on					
Loan		NONE	3,600	4,800	5,400
Net profit		10,000	6,400	5,200	4,600
Return on share capital	=	10,000	6,400	5,200	4,600
		60,000	30,000	20,000	15,000
	=	16.7%	21.3%	26%	30.7%
Times interest earnt	=	N/A	10,000	10,000	10,000
			3,600	4,800	5,400
	=	N/A	2.8X	2.1X	1.9X

debt capital. At certain times it is hard to raise more money from shareholders: for example, when the general stock market is depressed, or if your profit performance is not up to the mark. Banks or other lenders may be your only hope. Conversely, when the conditions are right, companies frequently raise more share capital to fund growth, well in advance of needing the cash.

Verson International

Take the money when you can

When Verson International, the West Midland-based machining manufacturer, raised £10 million of extra share capital via a rights issue, Tim Kelleher, chairman and chief executive, said the issue, which will halve gearing to close to 53 per cent, would give the group the flexibility to make further acquisitions in the following 12 months.

Bankers would generally favour a 1:1 relationship between borrowed funds and share capital. But the nature of the risks involved in your business strategy is a more important factor to consider, rather than pursuing this symmetrical pair of numbers. A more useful way to look at the debt–equity relationship is to compare money risk to business risk (as shown in Figure 2.10.1).

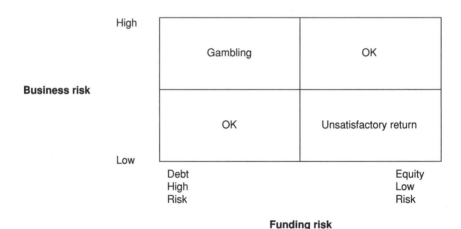

Figure 2.10.1 Funding matrix

If your business sector is generally viewed as very risky, and perhaps the most reliable measure of that risk is the proportion of firms that go bust, then financing the business almost exclusively with borrowings is tantamount to gambling. Debt has to be serviced whatever your business performance, so it follows that in any risky, volatile market place one day you stand a good chance of being caught out. Building firms are a good example of companies in a high-risk business sector who almost always use high-risk money. The fallacy is to believe that, because houses were thought to be a risk-free investment, building them was a safe enterprise too. It is no surprise that building firms top the bankruptcy rolls in both boom years and recessions.

If your business risks are low, the chances are that profits are relatively low too. High profits and low risks always attract a flood of competitors, reducing your profits to levels that ultimately reflect the riskiness of your business sector. As venture capitalists and shareholders generally are looking for much better returns than they could get by lending the money, it follows they will be disappointed in their investment on low-risk, low-return business. So if they are wise they will not invest in the first place, or if they do they will not put any more money in later.

With the funding matrix in mind you can begin to work towards a balance of debt and equity that is appropriate for your business. Very often you will find it attractive to raise both sides of the equation at the same time, as Helene has done.

Helene

You can raise debt and equity together

Helene, the clothing maker and textile merchant, has announced a £2.62 million rights issue to fund its expansion. The company plans to offer 14.4 million new shares at 20p each on a one for four basis. The share price shed 1p recently, to close at 24p.

Monty Burkeman, chairman and joint MD, said the company's sales had grown by 50 per cent last year to £62 million; the pre-tax profit was £4.1 million. In the first five months of this year turnover was 22 per cent ahead of the comparable period. 'We need to finance it' he said.

Burkeman explained that Helene needed to have the capacity to get orders ready for its retail customers, who would have arranged to take delivery at any time over a three-month period. The issue has been fully underwritten by Allied Provincial Securities. Helene has also arranged a £5 million unsecured term loan with the National Westminster Bank.

What financiers look out for

Successful entrepreneurs with a proven track record can have as many problems raising finance for their ventures as can the relative novice. Bob Payton, who founded the highly successful Chicago Pizza Pie Factory, related an experience making exactly this point.

Chicago Pizza Pie Factory

Even a good track record won't guarantee financial backing

I now have a 10-year track record in the hospitality business. My company had a turnover of £10 million this year, and made a profit of £1 million. But the one constant problem I have had for the past 10 years has been raising finance to put my ideas into practice. Getting the £4.5 million for my latest venture, Stapleford Park, a country house hotel in Leicestershire will, by the time it opens in May, have taken three years. It has been as difficult and as gut-wrenching as trying to raise £35,000 for my first place, the Chicago Pizza Pie Factory.

Originally EMI agreed to back my first venture. We'd shaken hands on the deal and I had ordered the ovens and gone off to the States to learn how to make pizza. When I came back I got a 'Dear John' letter. They'd decided, on reflection, not to go ahead. I have that letter still, framed and hanging on the wall in my office. After a lot of trouble, I finally raised the money elsewhere and went ahead. EMI were subsequently proved to be wrong.

Financiers' needs

Anyone lending money to or investing in a venture will expect the entrepreneur to have given some thought to the financier's needs, and to have explained how they can be accommodated in the business plan.

Bankers, and indeed any other providers of debt capital, are looking for asset security to back their loan and the near certainty of getting their money back. They may well want guarantees from the founder and his or her family.

City Herbs

The banks look after themselves first

City Herbs grew into a £5 million-a-year business employing 80 staff in a state-of-the-art refrigerated warehouse in Spitalsfield Market, east London in just 14 years. When Maggie Lawless started the business, her bank manager of 15 years patted her on the head and refused her a start-up loan, advising her to 'stick to her knitting'.

The company found a slightly more sympathetic bank and developed a fleet of 10 trucks, delivering not only herbs, but also lettuces, potatoes, tomatoes, grapes and many other products. But Lawless was still wary when it came to bank managers.

Nobody running their own company must delude themselves that their cosy relationship with their bank manager is protective for anyone else but the bank. They can be enormously helpful in many ways. But they lend money to make money. And they are not risk-takers. Our bank had no qualms about asking our youngest son, on reaching his 18th birthday, to sign away his inheritance rights.

Bankers will also charge an interest rate which reflects current market conditions and their view of the risk level of the proposal. Depending on the nature of the business in question and the purpose for which the money is being used, they will take a 5–15 year view.

As with a mortgage repayment, bankers will usually expect a business to start repaying both the loan and the interest on a monthly or quarterly basis immediately the loan has been granted. In some cases a capital 'holiday' for up to two years can be negotiated, but in the early stages of any loan the interest charges make up the lion's share of payments.

Bankers hope the business will succeed so that they can lend more money in the future and provide more banking services, such as insurance, tax advice and so on, to a loyal customer. It follows from this appreciation of a lender's needs that they are less interested in rapid growth and the consequent capital gain than they are in a steady stream of earnings almost from the outset.

As most new or fast growing businesses generally do not make immediate profits, money for such enterprises must come from elsewhere. Risk or equity capital, as other types of funds are called, comes from venture capital houses, as well as being put in by founders, their families and friends. Because the inherent risks involved in investing in new and young ventures are greater than for investing in established companies, venture capital fund managers have to offer their investors the chance of larger overall returns. To do that, fund managers must not only keep failures to a minimum, they have to pick some big winners too – ventures with annual compound growth rates above 50 per cent – to offset the inevitable mediocre performers.

Bankrupt Clothing Company

VCs have their share of failures

Bankrupt Clothing Company, the jeans and casual-wear retailer owned by 3i, lived up to its name and went bust. The group and its seven stores collapsed into administration and Coopers and Lybrand were appointed to find a buyer.

The failure was an embarrassment to 3i, which had backed the £4.6 million buy-out of the business just the previous year. The company's name always raised eyebrows from landlords who wondered how sensible it was to lease their stores to a chain promoting bankruptcy.

Peter Campbell was installed as MD with a brief to boost sales, but they did not rise from about £11 million. In an effort to boost turnover, the group launched Gaff, a new concept, but it closed recently owing to a lack of demand. A fashion operator who supplied the chain said: 'Another one bites the dust. The bottom has fallen out of the jeans market'.

Typically, a fund manager would expect from any 10 investments one star, seven also-rans, and two flops. It is important to remember that, despite this outcome, venture capital fund managers are only looking for winners, so unless you are projecting high capital growth, the chances of getting venture capital are against you.

Not only are VCs looking for winners, they are also looking for a substantial shareholding in your business. There are no simple rules for what constitutes a fair split, but the generally accepted rules suggest the following starting point:

For the idea	33 per cent
For the management	33 per cent
For the money	34 per cent

It all comes down to how much you need the money, how risky the venture is, how much money could be made – and your skills as a negotiator. However, it is salutary to remember that 100 per cent of nothing is still nothing. So all parties to the deal have to be satisfied if it is to succeed.

VCs may also want to put a non-executive director on the board of your company to look after their interests. If this happens, you will have at your disposal a talented financial brain, so be prepared to make use of him or her, as this service will not be free: you will either pay 'up front' in the fee for raising the capital, or you will pay an annual management charge.

As fast-growing companies typically have no cash available to pay dividends, investors can only profit by selling their holdings. With this in mind, the VC needs to have an exit route such as the Stock Exchange or a potential corporate buyer in view.

Unlike many entrepreneurs (and some lending bankers) who see their ventures as lifelong commitments to success and growth, VCs have a relatively short time horizon. Typically, they are looking to liquidate small company investments within three to seven years, allowing them to pay out individual investors and to have funds available for tomorrow's winners.

So, to be successful your business must be aimed at the needs of these two sources of finance (see Figure 2.10.2).

There are many useful directories and guides to all the sources of funds for a growing business. It would be superfluous to list them again here, or to describe such terms as overdraft, loan, hire purchase and so on. We have concentrated rather on covering the areas that, in our experience, growing firms have often neglected and should certainly address if they are planning significant growth.

Lenders (any safe bet)	Investors (winners only)
• Security and low risk	• High risk but high returns
• 5–15 year horizon	• 35% compound growth minimum
• Ability to pay back loan and interest immediately	• Short time horizon, 3–7 years
• Conservative growth	• But no payments until the end of the deal
• Small sums, with frequent top-ups	• Exit route evident at outset
• No share of future profits but want a loyal long-term customer	• – Back to founders – Trade buyer – USM etc
• No management involvement, but may want to criticise from the wings	• Substantial shareholding – For the idea: 33% – For management: 33% – For money: 34%
	• Hands-on involvement
	• Large sums, with few top-ups

Figure 2.10.2   Financiers' needs

Debt capital

The banks are the principal sources of debt capital. However, the days when you could expect to cultivate a lifetime relationship with either a bank or a bank manager are long gone. Banks are into market segmentation and profit generation, so you need to be prepared to (a) shop around and (b) manage your relationship with the bank carefully.

As a rough guide, if you are with the same bank for over five years you have not pushed them hard enough. There are myriad things to negotiate with your bank, and there is even a new breed of consultants who advise on banking relationships.

Small Firms Loan Guarantee Scheme

The scheme guarantees loans from banks and other financial institutions for small businesses with viable business proposals which have tried and failed to obtain a conventional loan because of a lack of security.

Loans are available for periods between 2 and 10 years on sums from £5,000 to £100,000 (£250,000 for businesses which have been trading for more than two years). The Department of Trade and Industry (DTI) guarantees 70 per cent of the loan (85 per cent for businesses trading for more than two years). In return for the guarantee the borrower pays the DTI a premium of 1.5 per cent per year on the outstanding amount of the loan. The premium is reduced to 0.5 per cent if the loan is taken at a fixed rate of interest.

The commercial aspects of the loan are matters between the borrower and the lender.

Leasing and hire purchase

Leasing is a way of getting the use of vehicles, plant and equipment without paying the full cost at once. Operating leases are taken out where you will use the equipment for less than its full economic life: for example, a car, photocopier, vending machine or kitchen equipment. The lessor takes the risk of the equipment becoming obsolete, and assumes responsibility for repairs, maintenance and insurance. As you, the lessee, are paying for this service, it is more expensive than a finance lease, where you lease the equipment for most of its economic life and maintain and insure it yourself. Leases can normally be extended, often for fairly nominal sums, in the latter years.

The obvious attraction of leasing is that no deposit is needed, leaving your working capital free for more profitable use elsewhere. Also, the cost is now from the start, making forward planning more simple. There may even be some tax advantages over other forms of finance. However, there are some possible pitfalls, which only a close examination of the small print will reveal. So do take professional advice before taking out a lease.

Hire purchase differs from leasing in that you have the option to eventually become the owner of the asset, after a series of payments.

Hire purchase and leasing companies have their own association, which can provide details of suitable forms. Further information can be obtained from: Finance and Leasing Association, Imperial House, 15–19 Kingsway, London WC2B 6UN (tel: 020 7836 6511; fax: 020 7420 9600; Web site: www.fla.org.uk; e-mail: info@fla.org.uk).

Factoring and discounting

Factoring is generally only available to a business that invoices other business customers for its services. Factoring can be made available to new businesses, although its services are usually of most value during the early stages of growth.

Factoring is an arrangement which allows you to receive up to 80 per cent of the cash due from your customers more quickly than they would normally pay. The factoring company, in effect, buys your trade debts and can provide a debtor accounting and administration service. In other words, it takes over the day-to-day work of invoicing and sending out reminders and statements. This can be a particularly helpful service to a small expanding business. It allows the management to concentrate on expanding the business, with the factoring company providing expert guidance on credit control, 100 per cent protection against bad debts and improved cash flows.

You will, of course, have to pay for factoring services. Having the cash before your customers pay will cost you a little more than normal overdraft rates. The factoring service will cost between 0.5 and 3.5 per cent of the turnover, depending on volume of work, the number of debtors, average invoice amount and other related factors. You can get up to 80 per cent of the value of your invoice in advance, with the remainder paid when your customer settles up, less the various charges just mentioned.

If you sell direct to the public, if you sell complex and expensive capital equipment, or expect progress payments on long-term projects, factoring is not for you. If you are expanding more rapidly than other sources of finance will allow, this may be a useful service. All other things being equal, it should be possible to find a factor if your turnover exceeds £25,000 per annum, though the larger firms will look for around £100,000 as the economic cut-off point. Further information can be obtained from: Factors and Discounters Association, Administration Office, 2nd Floor, Boston House, The Little Green, Richmond, Surrey TW9 1QE (tel: 020 8332 9955; fax: 020 8332 2585; Web site: www.factors.org.uk).

Shareholders' funds: equity

There are three principal vehicles for attracting new investors to help finance your growth plans.

Venture capital

Venture capital (VC) is a means of financing the start-up, development, expansion or purchase of a company, whereby the VC acquires an agreed proportion of the share capital (equity) of the company in return for providing the requisite funding. VCs often work in conjunction with other providers of finance in putting together a total funding package for a business.

Venture capital is a relatively new industry in the UK, although its origins go back to the late 18th century, when entrepreneurs found wealthy individuals to back their projects. Now venture capital is a global business with over 600 active VCs in the United States and a further 200 or so across Europe and Asia.

The funds being invested by VCs has exploded in the past five years. (See Figure 10.2.3). In the first quarter of 2000 over $22.7 billion went into start-ups in the United States alone.

But just because there is a lot of money about it doesn't mean it's easy to get. One VC, Accel Partners in the United States, went on record to say it received 25,000 business plans asking for finance last year and invested in only 40.

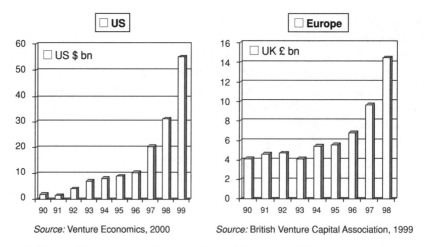

Source: Venture Economics, 2000   *Source:* British Venture Capital Association, 1999

Figure 2.10.3 Venture capital in the United States and Europe, annual investment

Until recently the returns that VCs made were not exactly startling. In the UK the average return on high technology investments by VCs over the life of the investment was 23 per cent. In the United States the average return across all sectors ranged from a low of 2 per cent in 1990 to a high of 44 per cent in 1995. But in 1999 something startling happened. According to *Venture Economics* (2000), VCs in the United States made a 147 per cent return. That was brought about mostly by their Internet investments turning into initial public offerings (IPOs) in less than 3 years after investments were made. This compared with the seven years plus that it took before, with the exit route more likely to be a trade sale on a much lower multiple. Turning this nominal return back into cash is another thing again.

Venture capital is a medium- to long-term investment, not just of money, but of time and effort. VCs aim to enable growth companies to develop into the major businesses of tomorrow. The British Venture Capital Association's *Guide to Venture Capital* (BVCA, 1998) describes how the process of venture capital can work for you.

The British Venture Capital Association (BVCA) represents every major source of venture capital in the UK. It has some 200 members, and produces an annual directory, which describes the investment interests of every VC. The Association also produces a directory of Business Angels. Contact: The British Venture Capital Association, Essex House, 12–13 Essex Street, London WC2R 3AA (tel: 020 7240 3846; fax: 020 7240 3849; Web site: www.bvca.co.uk/). The Web site provides extensive information on venture capital in the UK and on the services of the Association which represents every major source of venture capital in the country.

The new dentists

Venture capitalists like exciting opportunities with the right risk–reward ratio

The days when dental patients sat in dingy waiting rooms and thumbed through three-year-old copies of *Punch* are over. A revolution is sweeping through the £2 billion industry as it takes on the characteristics of big business. Dentistry is rapidly changing from being a fragmented cottage industry into one divided up among corporate chains. The pace of consolidation is similar to the transformation that has taken place in eye-care and nursing homes.

A handful of entrepreneurs and venture capitalists are leading the shake-up, buying up surgeries at the rate of one a week. 'The rules are being rewritten,' says Tarquin Desoutter, MD of Dencare Management, which owns 50 surgeries in the south of England and is backed by the VC Advent. 'The market is moving rapidly and we aim to double in size by the end of next year.'

Desoutter is not alone. Luke Johnson, the financier who turned Pizza Express into a national chain, is now the biggest owner of surgeries. His network of 100 employs 300 dentists under the umbrella of Integrated Dental Holdings (IDH), which is backed by 3i, DLJ Phoenix and Murray Johnson. In the past year alone, IDH has made 20 acquisitions.

Other players include James Hull, a 38-year-old dentist who is building up a chain of 26 outlets under the JD Hull brand, with backing from 3i. He is followed by Whitecross, a former public company taken private by Apax. Whitecross, run by Paul Mendlesohn, has 14 practices with 50 surgeries and has commitment from Apax to invest another £30 million in the sector. The company aims to have 200 outlets within five years.

The logic behind this wave of mergers and takeovers among Britain's 18,000 dentists is compelling. Cuts in NHS subsidies have made it harder for single outlet dentists to earn a good living and invest in new equipment. At the same time, increasing bureaucracy has put greater demands on dentists' time and patients want a better quality service.

Faced with these challenges and rising overheads, many opt to sell to a larger group that can exploit economies of scale and install state-of-the-art equipment. Some companies, such as IDH, also own laboratories making bridges, crowns and false teeth to sell through their networks.

The new entrants point to the explosion in dental spending in America, where the market is worth £30 billion a year. A high proportion of this is for cosmetic dentistry and, by 2005, this is expected to reach £50 billion. At £2 billion (of which £1.5 billion is paid for by the NHS), dental spending in Britain is a fraction of this and the growth opportunities could be enormous.

Business angels

For small sums of money, from £10,000 to £100,000, you could contact a business angel. An angel is a private individual who is willing to put their money and perhaps their efforts into your business. Various industry estimates suggest that upwards of £6.5 billion of angels' money is looking for investment homes, although the sum actually invested each year is much smaller than that. Not only will angels put in smaller sums of money than conventional venture capital providers, they will be more prepared to back start-ups and riskier projects – if the chemistry is right. They may even want some hands-on involvement in your business.

So how do you get in contact with an angel? You will need to use an introductory agency or 'marriage bureau' such as LINC, who circulate to subscribing investors a regular bulletin of abbreviated information on business projects. If you are seeking finance through LINC you should submit a business plan indicating the amount of finance required (sample plans and counselling services are available). Once this has been accepted as a bona fide proposal, you will be charged a small fee for as many bulletin entries (around 50 words) as are felt necessary. Also a longer, two-page summary business plan will be prepared to help any inquirers requesting further details. Contact points for the business angels' network are to be found in the BVA's *Guide to Venture Capital* (BVCA, 1998).

The Chief Executive Partnership (CEX)

Business angels often hunt in packs

CEX is a slightly different type of business angel. It pools money from senior industrialists – the partners – for investment in small companies. Chairman Nicholas Garrow describes the operation as industrial investing and is not kind about venture capitalists as a breed.

CEX's 40 partners are more than just sources of cash. Drawing on their range of industrial skills, Garrow or Fraser Marcus, CEX's MD, both formerly corporate financiers at Salomon Brothers, the US investment bank, will also take a board seat.

The rest of the partners are senior figures such as Sir Bryan Nicholson, chairman of BUPA, who do not have the time for a non-executive position, but who will act as sounding boards at various stages of an investment.

'We have far greater involvement than the venture capitalist who finds a chairman after the deal has been done to keep an eye on the thing and make sure the preference shares are being serviced', says Garrow.

This year CEX bought a 73 per cent stake in PDP Couriers, a specialist international air courier, in a transaction valuing the company at £3.2 million. Garrow had no doubt that founder David Golder remained 'totally enthused by the business'. Garrow, now chairman, has in turn impressed Golder: 'He is very analytical and has come up with some very good suggestions as to how to expand the customer base'.

CEX has raised £15 million from partners so far. It has achieved an exit from three of its eight investments, including from Leada Acrow, sold to plant hire company Ashtead, making an eight-fold return on equity over three years.

Enterprise Investment Scheme (EIS)

The Enterprise Investment Scheme (EIS) is intended to make it attractive for private individuals and pools of funds to invest equity capital in small firms. The EIS replaced the Business Expansion Scheme on 1 January 1994. The EIS is available for new equity investment in qualifying UK unquoted trading companies, whether or not they are incorporated and resident here, and to investors liable to UK income tax, whether or not they are resident here. The main features of the scheme are as follows:

- It offers income tax relief at 20 per cent on investments up to £150,000 per annum.
- It allows capital gains tax exemption on disposal of shares.
- It allows relief for a loss on disposal against either income or capital gains tax.
- Investor(s) can be paid directors and still qualify if not connected with the company or its trade before eligible shares were issued.
- There is no investment limit per company per annum.
- The minimum holding period is five years.
- Investment must be in an unquoted company carrying on a qualifying activity for a minimum of three years.
- Companies invested in must have no more than £10 million maximum assets value before investment and £11 million after.
- There is unlimited deferral relief where chargeable gains are invested in eligible shares.
- Up to £25,000 of investment made by an individual can be carried back to the previous year, if made in the first half of the tax year.

The scheme does not extend to investment in property development; farming, market gardening and forestry; hotels, guest houses and residential homes. These notes are a guide to the scheme as it operates at present. The government makes changes to the scheme fairly frequently, so to see if your company could be eligible as an EIS investment vehicle you would need to speak to your accountant and to the Inland Revenue.

Pure Entertainment

Some investment schemes have attractive tax incentives for investors

Twenty-five-year-old Harry Holmwood started Pure Entertainment, the central-London-based video games company, with five friends: 'I had to buy every how-to-start-a-business book I could find', he laughs. The team used the Enterprise Investment Scheme to raise £160,000 start-up capital from parents' friends. 'We didn't need all that much, just enough for computers and salaries,' says Holmwood, 'and everyone took a pay cut anyway.' The investors also came in useful for financial and legal advice.

The group may be young, but they sure know their games. Lunatik, for which they received a £600,000 advance from the major games publisher Eidos, features unique 3D graphics. Eidos has been impressed enough to take a 26 per cent stake in the company. Holmwood has already turned down one offer to buy the business.

Prior to forming Pure Entertainment, Holmwood had a good career developing at Sony. So why did he start his own business? 'It's just not as much fun working for a big company. Here we can try out our own ideas. And we have no problem recruiting new staff. Everyone wants to come and work for us'.

There is a gentle but determined air about Holmwood. Projected turnover for Pure Entertainment this year is £1.5 million and the company has a steady revenue stream from royalties. In the future, Holmwood wants Pure Entertainment to publish its own games, rather than just developing them for others.

Going for an initial public offering (IPO)

There are two possible types of stock markets on which to gain a public listing. A full listing on the London Stock Exchange, The New York Stock Exchange or any other major country's exchange calls for a track record of making substantial profits with decent seven figure sums being made in the year you plan to float, as this process is known. A full listing also calls for a large proportion of the company's shares being put up for sale at the outset. (In the UK this would be at least 25 per cent of the company's shares.)

In addition, you would be expected to have 100 shareholders now and be able to demonstrate that 100 more will come on board as a result of the listing. This is rarely an appealing idea to entrepreneurs, who expect to see their share price rise in later years, and are loath to sell off so much of the business at what they believe to be a bargain basement price. There is also the threat of a takeover with so many of the shares in so many other people's hands. However, if an IPO appeals, the US market may be the best place to float. The value placed on new companies on those stock markets is between three and five times that of UK and European markets (see Table 2.10.4 below).

Junior markets such as London's Alternative Investment Market (AIM), or the Nouveau Marché in Paris are a much more attractive proposition for entrepreneurs seeking equity capital. It has been possible for some time for new, small and often unproven businesses to be 'floated' on a junior stock exchange.

AIM was formed in November 1995 specifically to provide risk capital for new rather than established ventures, and it has an altogether more relaxed atmosphere than other markets. AIM is the largest junior market in Europe. Over 400 firms are listed and some £4.5 billion of new equity capital has been raised. AIM is particularly attractive to any dynamic company of any size, age or business sector, which has rapid growth in mind. The smallest firm on AIM entered at under £1 million capitalisation and the largest at over £500 million. The formalities are minimal, but the costs of entry are high and you must have a nominated adviser, such as a major accountancy firm, stockbroker or banker. For further information about AIM contact: The London Stock Exchange, Old Broad Street, London EC2N 1HP (tel. 020 7797 1000; Web site: www.londonstock exchange.com).

Going public also puts a stamp of respectability on you and your company, enhancing its status and credibility and enabling you to borrow more against the security provided by your new shareholders, should you so wish. Your shares will also provide an attractive way to retain and motivate key staff. If staff are given, or rather are allowed to earn, share options at discounted prices, they too

Table 2.10.4   Where to float... and why it matters

Market	Number of stocks	Floatation cost	Entry requirements	Minimum market capitalisation	Comparable price earnings ratios PEs
Alternative Investment Market (AIM)	350	£0.5m	Low	None	1
London Stock Exchange	2,500	£1m+	High	£1m+	1
TechMARK	200	£0.75m+	High	£50m+	×3
New York Stock Exchange	2,600	£7m	Very high	£12m+	×2
NASDAQ	5,500	£6m	Very high	£10m+	×5

can participate in the capital gains you are making. With a public share listing you can now join in the takeover and asset-stripping game. When your share price is high and things are going well you can look out for weaker firms to gobble up – and all you have to do is to offer them more of your shares in return for theirs: you do not even have to find real money.

Royal Blue

Managing expectations carefully

For John Hamer of software producers Royal Blue, flotation was the last thing on his mind when, as newly appointed chief executive, his most pressing task was to renegotiate the terms of a loan they had defaulted on.

> I took over in the middle of the recession with the aim of turning us from a software services company into a software products company which would stand a better chance of differentiating itself in the market. But yes, the first task was to persuade 3i, the lenders, that it was in their interest to keep us in the game – which they did. Of course, although we felt that the strategy was the right one, we didn't actually have the products – even in concept form.

What Royal Blue did have, however, was the right strategy. Within a year product ideas for equity market trading systems, call centres and help desk systems were all at the prototype stage. Three years later they were all selling successfully, the corner had been turned and profits were seen to be steadily growing.

Indeed, profits had grown so much that the company could make a £1 million acquisition in the United States using cash funds. Within 5 years the company that had lost £250,000 on revenues of £3.5 million was turning over £21 million and making pre-tax profits of £3 million. It now employs 300 people.

So what did flotation represent for Hamer and his management team?

> The idea seemed attractive but the actual decision to go for it was quite interesting. The basic problem was that no one – the investors, directors and staff with shares in the company – was particularly keen to sell their shares to allow a float. In the end we all had to agree to sell 20 per cent of our existing shareholdings.

Of course, having made the decision, expectations and fears within the organisation need to be managed carefully:

> You must let people know as much as you can as soon as you can, because there's a long haul between making the decision and popping the champagne corks; for a start you need to decide where to list. At the end of 1996 we started talking to brokers in London – and I must say that at that time, before the software sector took off, quite a few were simply not interested or could not see the future potential. However, enough were and we narrowed the field down to three. The advisers we chose had two obvious advantages: firstly, I'd read in sector newsletters that they had recently floated other software businesses and, secondly, when it came to the beauty parade, they were the ones who really understood the business.

In retrospect he also stresses two further points in the choice of adviser:

> I think it becomes quite clear that you get what you pay for, and although our total advisers' bill came to around £1 million, I think that when you relate this to our market capitalisation of £50 million you can see that you actually get very good value. This leads to my next point: our advisers, Hoare Govett, worked long hours with us – you need to choose people you know you will get on with because you will be placed together in close proximity, under considerable stress, for quite a time.

Hamer had heard that the due diligence and verification process was hard work but he did not realise quite how much. 'Everything in that prospectus has to be verified. I even found myself writing to Leeds University for a copy of my degree certificate'.

And that was just the start. When it comes to seeking investors, Hamer recommends a strong constitution and commends a quality he had not previously known about: 'We found ourselves making 50 one-hour presentations in a space of two weeks, and trying to be at your best for each is a real test. It is at this point that you also come across the concept of broker distribution – the real test for them'.

Donatantonio and Sons

You don't have to be a new business or even in high technology to get listed on AIM. Food importer A Donatantonio and Sons floated on the London Stock Exchange, offering 30 per cent of its shares for sale at 70p each. The exercise is raising £3.2 million and values the company at £10.6 million.

The money mainly funded a move from the Wood Green, north London, premises to a new headquarters in Hertfordshire.

The company, established in 1902, moved to the Wood Green site – a former Bassetts factory – in 1975. A company director told *The Grocer*: 'With our expanding business in food ingredients, we have simply outgrown our building'.

The importer has a staff of 26 and is this year forecasting £850,000 profit on sales of £9.2 million.

As you draw up your flotation plan and timetable you should have the following matters in mind:

- *Advisers.* You will need to be supported by a team which will include a sponsor, stockbroker, reporting accountant and solicitor. These should be respected firms, active in flotation work and familiar with your company's type of business. You and your company may be judged by the company you keep, so choose advisers of good repute and make sure that the personalities work effectively together. It is very unlikely that a small local firm of accountants, however satisfactory, will be up to handling your flotation.

- *Sponsor.* You will need to appoint a financial institution, usually a merchant banker, to fill this important role. If you do not already have a merchant bank in mind, your accountant will offer guidance. The job of the sponsor is to coordinate and drive the project forward.
- *Timetable.* It is essential to have a timetable for the final months during the run up to a float – and to adhere to it. The company's directors and senior staff will be fully occupied in providing information and attending meetings. They will have to delegate and there must be sufficient back-up to ensure that the business does not suffer.
- *Management team.* A potential investor will want to be satisfied that your company is well managed; at board level and below. It is important to ensure succession, perhaps by offering key directors and managers service agreements and share options. It is wise to draw on the experience of well-qualified non-executive directors.
- *Accounts.* The objective is to have a profit record which is rising but, in achieving this, you will need to take into account directors' remuneration, pension contributions and the elimination of any expenditure which might be acceptable in a privately-owned company but would not be acceptable in a public company, namely excessive perks such as yachts, luxury cars, lavish expense accounts and holiday homes.

  Accounts must be consolidated and audited to appropriate accounting standards and the audit reports must not contain any major qualifications. The auditors will need to be satisfied that there are proper stock records and a consistent basis of valuing stock during the years prior to flotation. Accounts for the last three years will need to be disclosed and the date of the last accounts must be within six months of the issue.

Can anyone float?

Certainly AIM is a very broad church. The following are just a few of the more unusual ventures that have been floated here.

Dmatek

The company name stems from the forename initials of the three founders: Doron Dourat, Michael Goldstein and Avishai Erell. Based in Israel, Dmatek developed an electronic monitoring system mainly used to keep track of convicted criminals allowed to live outside prison, although it had applications in community care and remote medical monitoring. It is big business: the UK's prison service costs taxpayers around £1.8 billion a year.

Why so unusual? Dmatek's product was a transmitter built into a bracelet strapped to an ankle of the subject. It sent a signal to a receiver unit, with which the authorities can keep track of the subject's whereabouts.

Most of the company's income was derived from the United States but the system was also sold in Sweden, Latin America and Australia; Dmatek was the leading developer of the technology for Europe.

Ambient Media Corp

This company sold advertising through two media: the reverse side of automated teller machine (ATM) receipts and the reverse side of supermarket delicatessen queue tickets. Ambient helped clients sell their own products or services. By working with NCR, up to 80 per cent of ATMs could be targeted in the UK.

Why so unusual? Using such common media as bank and till receipts for advertising is a novel way of providing information to a captive audience. Separately, in conjunction with Nottingham City Council, Ambient launched a new scheme, TOUCH, a loyalty card used in shops and leisure facilities.

Ambient also owned a printing subsidiary called Indigo that produced such titles as *Pregnancy Plus* and *Good Times*.

Dentmaster

Specialising in removing vehicle dents, Dentmaster performed better than most since floating on AIM in 1996. It raised £1.18 million through a placing of 3p a share. The stock hit 5p after it predicted that it would exceed a forecast 41 per cent EPS rise for the year to 30 June 1998.

Why so unusual? Its dent-removal technique was novel. Bumps are smoothed flat without scratching paint thus avoiding the need to respray.

Clipper Ventures

Ofex-quoted Clipper was a round-the-world sailing event company offering landlubbers the chance to circle the globe for a mere £22,750. Destinations included Nassau and Brazil. Clipper's executive chairman, Sir Robin Knox-Johnston, was the first person to sail single-handed around the world non-stop.

Why so unusual? Sailings take place only every two years, so profit seesawed up one year and down the next. Clipper built up its corporate hospitality business to smooth the figures.

Jumbo International

Bouncy castles and balloons were Jumbo's staple business. But it was not all fairs and birthday parties. Its products were used for advertising and promotions – such as an inflatable burger for Burger King.

Why so unusual? Jumbo produced balloons sealed without knots. Chairman Walter Goldsmith was formerly chairman of Flying Flowers.

Downtex

Downtex makes duvet covers and bed linen. It floated on AIM in July and is run by brothers Jonathan and David Mond. They originally formed the company through a management buy-out from Casket in 1990.

Why so unusual? Downtex aimed at football fanatics. Soccer-crazy kids could buy duvets, pillowcases and wallpaper to decorate their bedrooms entirely in their team colours.

West 175 Enterprises

The company floated on AIM two years ago, raising £1.5 million. It specialised in producing cookery programmes for the UK, US and other overseas markets.

Why so unusual? Cookery programmes' popularity created a burgeoning media sub-sector presenting opportunities for production companies to cash in. West 175 later signed a 17-year 50:50 joint venture with the BBC.

The rewards of floating

Since junior stock markets such as AIM were introduced, several thousand entrepreneurs have become millionaires.

Computacenter

Computacenter's flotation will make about 30 of its employees millionaires, in addition to founders Philip Hulme and Peter Ogden, who will each emerge with shares and options worth up to £295 million. Those who will reap financial benefits include chief executive Mike Norris who has a stake worth up to £21 million, and finance director Tony Conophy, with a holding worth up to £12 million.

Philip Hulme, chairman, and Peter Ogden, a non-executive director, are also selling £59 million of shares in the placing and donating £50 million to charity from the proceeds. Hulme is donating the entire £30.5 million proceeds from his share sales while Ogden is donating £18.5 million, or two-thirds of his £28.5 million proceeds.

The beneficiaries of the two men's donations have yet to be decided. Hulme and Ogden started the business in 1981 with capital of about £60,000. A spokesman said Hulme did not need the money and considered donating to charity an appropriate way to allocate his sale proceeds, while Ogden already donates to educational charities.

Norris and Conophy are among some 700 Computacenter employees who hold shares and options with an average value of £250,000 at 610p a share, the mid-price of the price range of 550p to 670p announced recently.

VC Apax sold 21 million shares worth about £128 million and was left with 8.6 per cent, while investment group Foreign and Colonial is selling 4 million shares worth

£24.3 million and will retain 4.6 per cent. Hulme and Ogden will remain the biggest shareholders with 23 per cent.

The penalties of floating

So much for the rewards of flotation. The penalties are equally awesome, and they can happen before you even get a listing, as described below.

Nord Anglia Education

Kevin McNeany, founder and MD of Nord Anglia Education, spent four months and £300,000 preparing his company for a flotation. On the day before the price of the issue was due to be announced, McNeany decided that his company, which runs 16 private schools and five language schools, was being valued too cheaply and cancelled the flotation.

'I wasn't willing to accept the price because it was 20 per cent less than what had been suggested before' says McNeany, a former teacher who, over the past 18 years, has built up a company with turnover of £8.2 million and pre-tax profits of £610,000.

'My financial advisers said: "You can't do this", I said: "I am"', recalls McNeany. Disappointed, despondent and £300,000 poorer, McNeany took the train back to Manchester from London to renegotiate credit lines with his bankers which he had thought the flotation would render unnecessary.

The next penalty is that public companies come under the greater scrutiny of a larger and more perceptive investment community.

Soundtracs

Soundtracs, an AIM listed electronics company, was forced in September 1998 to announce it had not disclosed a new director's string of previous failed directorships, or a reprimand from the Institute of Chartered Accountants (ICA).

When Richard Owen was appointed non-executive chairman of Soundtracs on 30 March 1998, the company disclosed only his previous directorship of United Trust and Credit, a merchant banking group which was active in bringing companies to the Unlisted Securities Market in the 1980s. Soundtracs was one of the companies it brought to market.

However, after consultations with the Stock Exchange, the company has now announced a further 11 present directorships held by Owen. It also said he was a director of Triumph Investment Trust, which went into receivership in November 1974. The debenture holder was believed to have been repaid in full, the company said.

Owen was also a director of WS186 1733, formerly known as Wembly Sportsmaster, when it went into receivership in October 1992. The debenture holders, including Owen, were repaid none of the £375,000 they were owed.

Owen was reprimanded by the ICA in November 1983 over his role as a director of Scotia Investments between 1974 and 1976. Soundtracs' shares were unchanged.

You may also find that being in the public eye not only cramps your style but fills up your engagement diary too. Most entrepreneurs find that they have to spend up to a quarter of their time 'in the City' explaining their strategies, in the months preceding and the first years following their going public. It is not unusual for so much management time to have been devoted to answering accountants' and stockbrokers' questions that there is not enough time to run the day-to-day business, and profits drop as a direct consequence.

The City also creates its own 'pressure' both by seducing companies onto the market and then by expecting them to perform beyond any reasonable expectation.

Aukett

The pressures of being listed on the stock market

Michael Aukett, chief executive of Aukett, the architectural practice, is not certain that he would not reconsider his options if he had his time again. After Aukett went public it maintained its steady promise for the year by turning in highly respectable interims. Profits shot up 24 per cent to £947,000.

Yet Mr Aukett says: 'The City is responsible for creating the hype that any size of business should go on the market, but architectural firms are basically too small. We don't begin to command any position under a market capitalisation of £50 million'.

With the benefit of hindsight, Mr Aukett believes now that he would have waited another three years to grow to a bigger size before tangling with the institutions: 'They seduce you to go in and when the market goes on its knees, they don't support you. How do our shareholding staff feel when they see the market dip?'

One final penalty worth mentioning is the apparent lack of a direct relationship between the business's profit performance and its share price. Confidence, rumour and the sentiment for certain business sectors which fall in and out of favour all play a part in moving share prices up and down, and in the end that is all public shareholders and city institutions care about. Polly Peck is a fairly vivid example of this problem. The auditor's report showed the company had made £161 million profit and the share price stood at 417p, making the company worth £2 billion on paper. By 20 September, the company's shares were suspended at 108p on the back of rumours about alleged share dealing irregularities. A month later the company went into administrative receivership and the shares were declared 'worthless'.

Whatever the downside risk on going public, it is as well to remember that several thousand private companies go bust for every public company that goes under. In the long run the only realistic way to get big, very rich and survive is to go public.

Nothing is forever

Hundreds of companies outside the FTSE 100 Index feel they are victims of a scornful market which is only interested in their larger brethren. Now they are fighting back. Armed with the support of venture capitalists, 12 companies took themselves private in 1998 and the market expects this trickle to become a flood.

The Capitol Group, a security business, and Brunner Mond, a chemicals company, announced plans to leave the stock market. Brunner Mond was floated in 1996 and has been sold for £145 million. Its shares had languished below its 175p float price for most of its public life. It took a bid from CVC, its former venture capital backers, for them to go to a premium of 190p.

Eric Kinder, chairman of Brunner Mond, is disappointed but philosophical about what has happened. He says:

> If you put the work into getting it right for a flotation and then it is reversed in only 18 months then that is disappointing. At least if it is your own performance you can do something about it. But we fulfilled all our prospectus promises and you cannot do any more than that. Brunner Mond is a great industrial company and it shows what regard the market has for great British industrial companies. At the end of the day, the share is only worth what people will pay for it. It may well be to the advantage of the company that we are private rather than languishing in the public market.

CVC, a leading venture capital house which maintained a stake of more than 20 per cent in the public Brunner Mond, certainly thinks so. It was drawn to the deal for a variety of reasons. It is close to raising its latest £1 billion plus fund and needs to invest it.

Ian Currie, a director at Apax, which took the Whitecross Group private in a £7 million deal, says: 'There is no investor interest in the smaller companies. They are undervalued and unrecognised by brokers and institutions. Whatever they announce does not move the price, which has led to this trend that will continue for at least another year'.

Brian Phillips, a director at NatWest Private Equity, which has raised a £350 million plus fund and taken Betterware and Healthcall private, says: 'Venture capitalists have a lot of cash and catholic tastes. We ask whether we can see value in businesses be they in the public or private sector'.

So long as the smaller companies shares lag the FTSE 100 Index, the trend will continue. Dibb Lupton Allsop, the City lawyers, which has been involved in 9 out of the 12 deals listed privately, estimates that 60 companies could be taken private in the next 12 months.

Even if you do not want to leave the market it may want to leave you.

Internet IPOs

An IPO used to take about six months to execute, but the Internet has changed all that. Now a dot.com can expect to get listed in 13 weeks. Unless of course the index has crashed. In April 2000, dozens of would-be IPOs were stalled on the runway as the Nasdaq went into free fall. The chances of those companies who had to pull their IPOs ever coming back are low. Less than 1 in 10 firms who scratch their IPO ever get a second chance.

Although it may vary from exchange to exchange, the timetable for executing an IPO looks broadly like this:

Week 1. Pick underwriters to take your company to market. This involves listening to a dozen or more bankers tell you why they are number one in handling your type of IPO. It can be a wearying experience listening to perhaps three depressingly similar presentations per day. The bankers will all have done successful IPOs before, probably by the dozen, so it's likely you will be looking more for empathy than technical competence. At the end of the week you need to have chosen a lead and probably a couple of co-managers, to help spread the good word about your great business to the share-buying community.

Week 2. The lead manager begins drafting the company's prospectus. This involves sucking you, your management team and your accountants dry of background information. Your CFO will be involved full-time in this process, so better get some financial back-up in place to deal with routine matters.

Week 3. You and bankers collaborate on the prospectus. (By now fairly junior staff will be handling the process. The stars you met on the presentations in Week 1 have moved on to sell the next deal.)

This process can involve several eight-hour days with people from your law, banking and accounting firms going through the documentation line by line. It involves a delicate balance between outlining the risks whilst simultaneously describing the business and the investment prospects in a way that will appeal. You can see how other companies have gone about this process by looking at their filings on the Securities and Exchange Commission (SEC) Web site (www.sec.gov).

In the end this due diligence process should have flushed out any worries and concerns about you or your business.

Week 4. The lead manager files the registration document, known in the United States as an S1, with the SEC, or its equivalent in whatever country you plan to list.

Weeks 5–8. The lead bankers and you and your team prepare the presentation for the 'road show' (see Week 11) and wait for the SEC to digest your documents.

Week 9. SEC responds with 20 pages of nitpicking questions: 'What do you mean by "online response times"?' and 'Can you provide evidence that your client X is one of the largest drinks manufacturers in Spain?'. There may well be a second round of questions a few weeks later, but by then you will have got the measure of how to reply.

Probity is important in this whole process. What is required is transparency, the Nevada of the share-dealing community. World Online's float on the Amsterdam Exchanges (AEX) in the spring of 2000 is a salutary warning on disclosure. The company was at the time Europe's largest Internet service provider. It generated an enormous amount of interest among Dutch private investors, the company's home base, with 150,000 subscribing in the March IPO at a price of €43. Within six weeks the price was down to €14.80. The reason given for the slump in price was that World Online's chair, Nina Brink, had disposed of some of her shares to a US private equity fund Baystar Capital in December 1999, three months before the float. The price she sold at was €6.04 and Baystar sold in the first few days of trading at over €30. Brink was accused of making allegedly misleading statements during the offer period, and was forced to resign on 13th April. Unhappy shareholders are taking legal advice, but the company's bankers claim there was no wrong doing.

Week 10. The lead manager plans the 'road show' (see Week 11). You go to the bank and sell the company to their institutional salesforce. They then get to work with their clients to persuade them to subscribe for your stock. Everyone is bound by what are known as 'the Rules'. Rule 174 of the securities act governs the 'Quiet Period', which extends from due diligence to 25 days after the IPO. Over this period the company must be careful about not hyping the stock or doing anything that would lead to speculation about its performance in the press.

Rule 135 explains exactly what you can and cannot say to the press. It's generally best to say nothing. If one of your competitors is doing an IPO their Quiet Period is a good time to hit at them in the press, or to go out and buy a business you know they might want. They are in effect in limbo and can't retaliate.

This is where the institutional sales team come into their own. Via an ancient ritual of winks, nudges, passive verbs, rhetorical questions and comparisons, they get their story across. The lead banks sales team can be a mighty force indeed. Goldman Sachs, for example has some 400 front line salespeople in their

IPO team, and that can result in a very big message reaching a lot of potential investors.

Weeks 11–12. A glorified travel agent in the bank fixes up a punishing schedule, known as the 'road show'. This is the reverse of Week 1, when people were selling to you. Now you are selling the stock to institutional investors. This could involve as many as 80 meetings across three continents in 13 days. A lot can be said at road show meetings, but the only document that can be handed out is the S1 prospectus. Anything else could be a violation of Section 5 of the securities act.

Commitments start to come in from the institutions. 'I'll take 250,000, but only if the price is below US$20. At US$25 I'll only take 100,000.' The bank's syndicate manager has to make sense of this anticipated demand to come up with an IPO price.

Week 13. The day of the IPO. Assuming the Nasdaq has not gone into one of its habitual nosedives, the bank's market maker figures out the highest price someone will sell at and someone will buy at and sets a price, usually above the opening price and the price at which the institutions have bought. If the Nasdaq has plunged and you have to pull the IPO, it's like slipping down a long snake back to the bottom of the snakes and ladders board. You may get another crack at it in six months, or perhaps never. One entrepreneur likened doing an IPO to childbirth. Painful, glorious, but not to be done again.

Your company is now public, the bank collects 7 per cent of the proceeds, your employees are rich and you now have the funds and credibility to get back on with growing the business.

If the market maker has got the price too high, and the shares plunge quickly it will leave a sour taste in everyone's mouth. The pre-float shareholders can't realise their gain for months after the float, and having a paper profit slashed in half, as for example with lastminute.com's float, will not endear you to the staff.

The institutions will be sitting on a loss, and whilst they are grown up enough to take it on the chin, they will be very wary when you come back for more money. It is usually best to set the price at a rate that will see the shares rising in the weeks and months following a float. That makes for better press coverage too, which inevitably impacts favourably on customers, suppliers and potential employees.

Other ways to fund growth

Industry backers

Safetynet

Safetynet is a company that specialises in providing back-up computer services for companies whose computer systems are put out of action in the short term by fire, flood or even human error.

Set up 12 years ago by two former IBM salesmen, the company now has 230 subscribers, of whom only 19 have ever experienced a 'disaster'. The company's turnover is £3 million and pre-tax profits are around £1 million. Their 17 competitors are not doing quite so well, as none make any money, according to Safetynet's founders.

Compatibility being all important in the computer business, Safetynet has had to specialise. It is only interested in disasters affecting the medium-range IBM machines. The decision to concentrate on this area appears to have been influenced by the knowledge that IBM's AS 400 was going to prove a highly popular machine. (There are at least 500 of them in the City now). Convinced that they had hit upon a sound proposition, the founders had to convince others. VCs were not enthusiastic but another approach proved more rewarding.

Reasoning that their prime requirement would be equipment, they approached companies in the industry for support. Eventually, United Computers provided hardware in exchange for a 14 per cent stake. Bluebird Software, now IBM's largest agency in the mid-range but then a relatively new company which had bought its first computer from Paul Hearson, agreed to cover all the business's variable costs, and took a 26 per cent stake.

As Safetynet has grown, the founders have been able to buy out their early backers for more than £600,000. The two founders are now the sole owners of the company and seem happy to keep it that way. Talk of a flotation has stopped. 'We feel very cool about going public', says Paul Hearson.

Franchising

Have you ever wondered why Steve Bishko's Tie Rack is surviving in this turbulent economy of ours, and Sophie Mirman's Sock Shop has gone to the wall? Both are (or in Mirman's case were) niche retailers; both need small high-street locations; both founders came from Marks & Spencer and knew all about their product; neither product is essential for survival, like food; indeed, if anything, socks seem more essential than ties!

One of the key reasons lies in the different ways in which their respective businesses were funded and managed. All the Sock Shop outlets were funded by the company itself and in the last year of their life they were largely provided for by the banks. In Tie Rack's case the situation is rather different. Of their 135 outlets, 107 are effectively owned by the people who manage them. These franchisees, as Tie Rack's managers are called, have stumped up at least £60,000 each for the privilege of following the Tie Rack formula for business success. That is a fairly staggering £7 million of new money which is completely risk and cost free to Tie Rack. A similar sum would have cost Mirmam £1.25 million a year in interest charges alone – and it probably did, as £2 in every £3 in the Sock Shop was put up by the banks.

Material World

Miles O'Donavan's franchise Material World (named after the Madonna hit record, Living in a Material World), is a good example of how to turn a successful conventional business into a franchise. He is an up-market version of a market trader, buying up fabric manufacturers' ends-of-lines and seconds and selling them to an apparently appreciative public. 'It is a very simple business', he says. And he never doubted that it would succeed because, the way he looks at it, it is providing a service at both ends of the equation. Not only is he helping out those people who would love to make their home 'very Sanderson' but currently find themselves strapped for cash; he is also helping out the manufacturers who have to rid themselves of their surplus stock somehow.

This mutually beneficial system is already well established in the clothing business, where disposing of chain store cast-offs is the basis of several retail chains. O'Donavan, however, operates with goods from rather further up-market. Much of what he stocks would normally sell at £15 to £20 a metre, but he has a blanket price of £7.95 a yard. The fact that he sticks to yards is not just a hankering for days gone by, it gives him a 10 per cent price advantage.

O'Donavan woke up one morning and decided that with nine of his own shops he was about as exposed as he would like to be. Watching Coloroll and Lowndes Queensway sink without trace, he decided the time had come to share the risk with others. After a brief flirtation with the idea of venture capital, he plumped for franchising and has never looked back. His new franchisees have helped lift turnover from £1.8 million to £3 million in the present year and his business is now expanding fast both in the UK and in Europe. Best of all, he can sleep easy at night with the comfort of knowing his franchisees are as exposed as he is to the consequences of failure, something no Queensway store manager ever was.

Grant awards and other sources of finance

Unlike debt, which has to be repaid, or equity which has to earn a return for investors, grants and awards are not refundable. So, although they are hard to get, they are particularly valuable.

Business Links

The DTI provides various types of grant aid to small firms via the nationwide network of 240 information and advice centres. The Business Link Nationwide Signpost number is 0345 567765. Calling that number will get you to your nearest Business Link.

As well as providing general business advice on topics such as exporting, innovation, technology, design, marketing and training, each Link can tell you about any grants and awards that are relevant either to the area you plan to set up in, or to the type of business you are already in.

So, for example, if you are, or plan to set up in an assisted area (one chosen for special support) you may be eligible for Regional Selective Assistance (RSA). This is a discretionary scheme aimed at attracting investment and creating or safeguarding jobs in the assisted areas.

Grants of up to 15 per cent of eligible project costs are made to help a company to carry out an investment project within the assisted area. Qualifying projects are generally purchase of fixed assets, including opening of a new plant, modernising or adding new facilities to existing plants. Eligible costs can include:

- plant and machinery;
- some associated one-off costs, such as patent rights and professional fees;
- associated land, site preparation and buildings.

The amount of grant awarded will depend on the area and the needs of the project, the number of jobs safeguarded or created, and the impact the project will have on the economy. Each application is individually assessed, and needs to be able to demonstrate that the project would not go ahead in the same form without the grant assistance.

If you are involved in the development of a new technology then you may be eligible for a Small Firms Merit Award for Research and Technology (SMART), which is open to individuals or businesses employing fewer than 50 people. The grant is in two stages and can be for amounts as high as £100,000 or so, in total.

You may also get help with the costs of training staff, gaining quality recognition or carrying out market research to identify export opportunities. Your starting point to find out about these and other grants is the Business Link Nationwide Signpost number.

South West Regional Development Agency (SWDA)

If you plan to set up business in the country then the SWDA may be able to help with the conversion of redundant rural buildings. Over 4,000 old buildings have been put to work using such grants. In 1997, nearly £0.5 million in grants was provided by the now-defunct Rural Development Commission (since replaced by the SWDA) to help village shops prosper and flourish. For more information contact: South West Regional Development Agency, Sterling House, Dix's Field, Exeter EX11 1QA; tel: 01392 214747; fax: 01392 214848; e-mail: enquiries@southwestrda.org.uk; Web site: www.southwestrda.org.uk.

Assignment 16

1. Look hard at your working capital and see what opportunities there are to reduce the amount of cash tied up.
2. Review your fixed assets and see if there is any scope for savings.
3. Can you eliminate costs or increase efficiency in any part of your business?
4. Is there anything you do now or that your growth plans include, that it would be better to buy in?
5. Is there any form of funding, eg factoring, venture capital, that you are not currently using? If so, review these options and locate possible suppliers of these funds that could be interested in backing your growth plans.

11 Acquisitions, mergers, joint ventures and divestments

Before we look at the pros and cons of each of these strategic options in a little more detail, it would be as well to be clear on what each term means.

Acquisitions

An acquisition occurs when one company buys another – more often than not in a 'friendly' deal, but sometimes events are not so harmonious. After the acquisition, only the parent company usually exists in any real legal sense and the top management of the 'victim' usually depart quickly.

Mergers

Mergers are friendly bids where companies join forces and the separate identities of the businesses of the companies concerned continue after the deal is consummated. The Time Warner/AOL deal could be seen as one such marriage of convenience.

Worldwide mergers and acquisitions between them account for the equivalent of the assets of a small European country changing hands each year.

However, in the UK the volume of company sales is rather less. It is also, as you might expect, a very cyclical activity, with a higher level of activity during 'booms'.

Timing is everything. The best time to sell your company is when profits are high and growing. Therefore, it is critical to take the economic cycle into

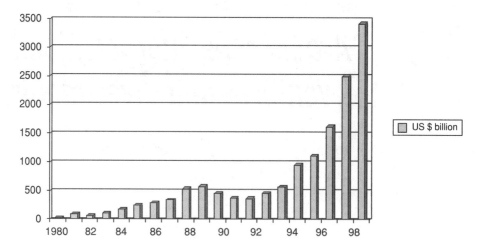

Source: Thomson Financial Securities, January 2000

Figure 2.11.1 Worldwide mergers

account when timing a sale. The evidence is clear – there are far fewer private company deals during a recession because profits are falling and there are fewer buyers willing to pay the entrepreneur's reserve price.

Joint ventures

These occur when two or more companies decide to set up a separate third business to exploit something together. There is no attempt to harmonise the whole of the two parent businesses, and the joint venture may be disbanded easily when the reasons they joined forces in the first place disappear. No shares in either parent company are changing hands, so there are not too many hidden problems.

Joint ventures are popular among small and growing firms. One Cranfield study (1992) revealed that over 15 per cent of small firms had plans to set up a joint venture with a European partner.

Epic International Media

The simple way to set up a European joint venture

Brighton-based Epic International Media, a company engaged in interactive computer-based training, has a UK turnover of £700,000 and a workforce of 14. It has formed a European Interest Grouping (EEIG) with Lang Learning Systems of Brussels and Mentor Consultants of Dublin. An EEIG is a legal formula which allows companies from more than one European community country to establish a joint business venture. The grouping is intended to be a simpler and more flexible way of setting up joint ventures and to avoid the need for the partners to choose a particular set of national laws – likely to be unfamiliar to at least one of them – to govern relations between them. The partners are not obliged to contribute capital to the company and there is no requirement either for formal meetings of members or the filing of annual reports or accounts. The EEIG itself pays no taxes; profits are shared among the partners and taxed in their hands. A drawback is the absence of limited liability.

VSW Scientific Instruments

An example of a different type of joint venture is VSW Scientific Instruments, a Manchester-based company with sales of £5 million and 100 employees. It is negotiating a cooperation agreement with Sofie Instruments, a company in Esomme, south of Paris, which makes a complementary range of equipment. VSW, which makes instruments for analysing surfaces, wants to start by distributing Sofie's products in Britain and Scandinavia, where it has a sales subsidiary; but is also interested in collaborating on the development of new products.

The European Commission's Business Cooperation Network is the largest player in the joint venture field. Each year more than 10,000 small- and medium-sized firms approach them for help. The network consists of 460 advisers – private consultants, chambers of commerce, development authorities – throughout the community who log their client's business profile with a central computer for matching with potential partners. Computer matching can be notoriously hit-and-miss but the commission estimates that several hundred businesses have found partners this way.

Examples of other types of joint ventures are as follows:

Toad

Toad, the car hi-fi and security company, hopes for a sales boost from its alliance with Autoglass, the windscreen replacement business that has more than 180 UK branches. Autoglass and Toad, which is chaired by the biotechnology entrepreneur Chris Evans, plan to offer a one-stop service letting customers replace broken car windows and stolen audio systems, and improve vehicle security.

John Lewin, Toad's chief executive, said that the alliance would put 'the two most professional businesses in both areas on one number'.

Autoglass has UK sales of £125 million and about 40 per cent of the glass replacement market. Under the deal, it will invest almost £1.5 million in Toad, half of it to buy

4.99 per cent of Toad at 25p a share, a premium to the 19p market price. Autoglass will also receive convertible preference shares and options that could later lift its stake to 20 per cent.

Toad will acquire Autoglass's £2 million-a-year car hi-fi business.

Psion

It is not often that a company's share price doubles on the day it gives a profits warning. But then not all companies announce in the same breath that they are embarking on a joint venture that will be responsible for the next generation of wireless communications equipment.

Psion, with Nokia, Motorola and Ericsson, three of the world's largest manufacturers of mobile phones, announced that they would use Psion's handheld computer operating system as the software base for a raft of new products.

A slice of such a potentially exciting future was enough to send investors into overdrive – ignoring Psion's warning of a continuing slowdown in the market for its Series 5 handheld computer. When rumours of a possible deal began to filter into the market, Psion shares trebled to more than 600p.

David Potter, Psion's chairman, saw the value of his family's 26 per cent share in the company jump from £40 million to £119 million.

His satisfaction at the reception to the deal will be all the greater considering the challenges Psion has faced – culminating in the shares hitting their lowest point since the end of 1995. Indeed, until this venture was announced many analysts had all but written the group off as a one-product UK company in a market targeted by some of the world's biggest computer companies.

'I think most followers of Psion had lost faith up until this deal', says one analyst. 'We could not see a way forward for the group given the weight of the competition in the handheld market.'

It was not always so. Psion has been one of the great success stories of British technology, developing from humble origins as a start-up in 1980 to become the world leader in the handheld computer market.

Potter, 55, founded the company after starting out in academia and dabbling as a professional investor. This combination of an intellectual mind and financial acumen has always stood him apart in the information technology industry, where good ideas and sound commercial sense often fail to come together.

'David's always been good on technology, but he also understands the markets he operates in', says one long-standing institutional investor. 'If he doesn't, he makes sure he finds out.'

The first Psion organiser was launched in 1984 and by the early 1990s the Series 3 was combining an electronic diary with a powerful word processor and spreadsheet capability. By the time the series 3a and 5 were introduced, Psion was clearly the leader in a market which was beginning to grow rapidly.

It was not just the consumer market in which the company was finding a successful niche. Organisers for the industrial market followed, and the company set up a separate software business to exploit the EPOC operating software used in Psion's computer products.

Potter says Psion is successful because it has remained at the forefront of innovation and development and consistently produced high-margin products for the top end of the market. Its Series 3c and 5 computers have won countless awards.

According to those close to the talks, Psion's strategy had been to develop EPOC as the industry standard operating system by signing up manufacturers one by one. Nokia secretly became the first, but only Philips had publicly signed up out of the rest of the industry.

However, attempts by the telecoms equipment groups to develop and implement their own systems for the new generation of wireless devices were also hitting problems. It was fast becoming clear that the industry needed one solution.

At the same time, the industry was becoming alarmed at the prospect of Microsoft CE becoming the dominant operating system. EPOC was the only viable alternative.

How big a business this will be for Psion remains the key question. It has a 40 per cent stake in Symbian, the new venture which will license EPOC. The four partners forecast annual sales of some 70 million units for which they would charge a license fee of between US$5 and US$10.

The new products would include 'smart' mobile phones which can send and receive data, handheld computers which utilise cellular technology to send and receive e-mail, and voice communicators small enough to wear like a watch.

The range of analysts' estimates of what this business will be worth is enormous, reflecting questions ranging from the likely consumer response to the new products to Microsoft's reaction to being largely frozen out. However, even on the most conservative estimates, Symbian could add about £15 million to Psion's annual pre-tax profits by 2001, doubling the group's current total. More optimistic forecasters say the additional profits could be well over £30 million a year. Mr Potter describes this joint venture as 'a defining moment for Psion'.

Divestments

Divestments occur when you sell bits of your business to other companies. Any rapidly growing firm ends up with bits of its business that either no longer make sense, or prevent the company from exploiting opportunities that better fit its new strategic direction. This pruning should be done regularly and promptly.

One £3 million company in the publishing industry launched an exhibitions business in a period of rather gung-ho expansion. They were offered £200,000 for the exhibitions business by a competitor, who as good as told them it was the wrong business for them to be in. They decided to stick with it only to discover a year later that it really was the wrong business for them – they struggled hard to get £40,000 for the same assets.

Going on the acquisition trail

Each year about 2,000 private companies changed hands and many times this number of unincorporated businesses also changed hands. The average size, in turnover terms, of the companies bought and sold was under £7 million per annum, with many having sales below £0.5 million. Forty-five per cent of the acquisitions were viewed as wholly amicable. There was a willing buyer and a willing seller, and no other parties were involved. Another 45 per cent were classified as partly contested, either because there were several interested buyers, or because the vendor resisted being taken over. Only 10 per cent of the acquisitions were hostile, with a bid being made over the heads of the vendors' board. These contested bids are the deals that make the headlines, but, as you can see, the reality is that an awful lot of quite small companies are changing hands in a fairly friendly way, for modest sums of money.

Table 2.11.1 Buyers' and sellers' assessment of the results of the acquisition

	%
Very successful	20
Successful	35
So-so	20
Unsuccessful	17
Very unsuccessful	8

When economic growth is virtually static, or if you want to achieve really dramatic growth, then buying someone else's business can be a very attractive option. But be warned. While acquisitions took place under friendly or fairly friendly conditions, only 55 per cent were eventually rated as successful or very successful by both buyers and sellers. So buying a company is certainly not always a sure-fire winning strategy.

Metalrax/Wagon

Acquisitive companies don't always grow the fastest

Wagon Industrial Holdings started out as a maker of railway buffers, but its core businesses in the 1980s and 1990s were industrial shelving systems and office furniture. Wagon was capitalised at £50 million and £125 million was spent on 50 global acquisitions over the 10 years to 1997. By then nearly £60 million had to be provided

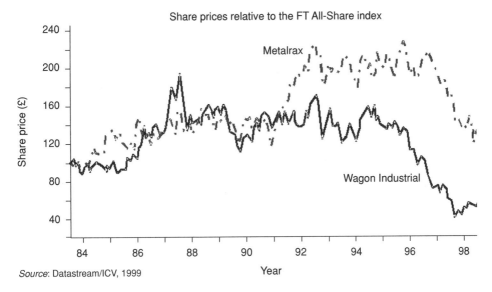

Figure 2.11.2 Metalrax/Wagon Industrial

to address the problems caused by the acquisitions, and the share price had collapsed. Metalrax, also a small maker of metal racking and storage systems, spent only £10 million on 10 acquisitions over the same 10-year period.

Profit margins in Metalrax have improved from 11.5 to 13 per cent. Earnings per share have quadrupled since 1984 and in 1998 the company took power to buy back its own shares with the £11 million of net cash held in reserve.

The share price, relative to the FT All-Share Index, is perhaps the most eloquent way of portraying the differences in performance. Whilst Wagon's management were busy firing employees from the companies they acquired – up to two-thirds of them in one case – and being fired themselves, Metalrax were building loyal teams. No one on the Metalrax board of seven has less than 19 years' experience with the company – and the top four have more than 30 years' experience each.

Kwik-Fit

Tom Farmer, who set up Kwik-Fit Exhausts and built it into a £500 million turnover business in 25 years, confessed that acquisition as an expansion strategy was his biggest commercial mistake.

'Expanding too rapidly through acquisition was probably the biggest business mistake I ever made.' Now, with over 1,600 outlets and a turnover of £0.5 billion, Farmer can afford to reflect on past errors of judgement.

From the outset we had a clear corporate identity with our blue and white logo and blue overalls, and excellent reputation with customers, and a good financial control system. By the late-1970s we were thinking of expansion.

Towards the end of 1979 we approached a competitor, Euro Exhausts, which had 51 depots south of Birmingham. We acquired the business in January 1980 for £10 million immediately doubling our size.

Now we felt we were really 'king of the castle', with a national business. We were also excited because our suppliers kept telling us about Euro's computer system and we thought we could just slide our way of controlling the business into their system. The biggest shock came when we discovered that their computer system just produced reams of paper and required even more administrative staff than we had.

We also wanted to change the company's name to Kwik-Fit Euro and create a single company identity. But they had a yellow-and-brown logo and brown overalls and this turned out to be a very contentious issue. Whose colours would win?

And we wanted the managers of Euro to do things our way. They didn't want to, so they left the company.

Three months later we were still struggling to put the thing together, desperately short of management, when another deal came along. I made inquiries and found that the Firestone Tyre company had 180 retail depots but was thinking of selling them to concentrate on manufacturing. A month later I met the MD in London and we did the deal that day. I had to – at £3.25 million it was a snip.

Flying back to Edinburgh I knew it would be a bit of a problem breaking the news. So I told the other managers we were a national company and had to keep on expanding. I'm a wee bit of an orator, and as I kept talking they were getting more and more excited. Then I dropped the bombshell and there was a stony silence. Then the boys starting flipping their lids.

In the end we did a deal with Dunlop Rubber, which paid £3.25 million for 82 of the depots. So in effect we got 98 depots free.

On reflection it was foolhardy to have attempted the Firestone deal. It was a good deal in the end but we were very lucky because I went in without proper planning. Our acquisition turned out to have no financial controls and terrible staff morale. Even worse, the Firestone mechanics wore red overalls and their signs were all red and white!

Prior to that deal we had produced profits of £4 million. Now our turnover had gone up fourfold but our profits fell to £1 million. I had to stand up and tell the shareholders that this was due to our investment in the future and all the other things you say at such times.

The whole thing caused us a lot of pain and grief at the time. It took two years of dedication and commitment to integrate the administration and financial controls, bring in a proper computer system and train staff.

What I learned is that you should never do anything just because it is a good idea. You must spend time on making sure it is a really good idea. Of course you can add instinct based on experience. But do not go on gut feeling – that is just a recipe for indigestion.

Of course not all acquisitions are disasters. Sometimes, as in the example below, they can be the making of the company.

Moxon Dolphin Kerby

Andrew Wilkinson was MD of the recruitment consultancy Moxon Dolphin Kerby, which had 50 employees. After a relentless stream of further acquisitions, today Andrew Wilkinson is chief executive of a group of companies with over 700 employees.

Two small acquisitions made in Manchester and in the Thames Valley in 1998 bring the total to 12 so far. The most notable have been MSL (one of the more respected names in executive search and selection) and Austin Knight (the UK's largest recruitment advertising agency).

Big is beautiful for Mr Wilkinson, certainly in terms of resources. Group turnover is over £150 million, with offices in Birmingham, Bracknell, Bristol, Cardiff, Edinburgh, Glasgow, Leeds, London, Manchester, Newcastle and Nottingham.

The group has more than 2,000 clients in the UK, of which 70 are FTSE 100 companies. Among the customers are Ford, Guinness Brewing, Pricewaterhouse-Coopers, Chelsea and Westminster Healthcare, IBM and Kent County Council. Wilkinson says growing is like wearing two hats:

> On one hand the UK market is still the same, but growing; clients will have the same team of people as before working with them, but possibly introducing new ideas, which is ideal. There will still be the same small team relationships, but we can put more resources into those relationships and invest money behind the scenes. Throwing new people at clients we do not think is right. It is important to remember that our business is a relationship business and we want to hold on to our customer base.

On the other hand, Wilkinson says, clients are doing more business across Europe and globally, which demands particular services:

> We are an owned global network of companies working together, rather than a series of piecemeal business partnerships. We doubled in size twice [in the space of a] year. The advantage of being bigger is that we have more resources, a bigger pool of people and a broader mix of services to offer, and they need to be shown to the clients.

Here is a seven-point plan to make sure that you can end up with a very successful acquisition, merger or joint venture.

1. **Examine why you want to buy.**

   Big companies end up on the takeover trail for matters of management ego as much as corporate strategy. Over 40 per cent of big companies listed 'sending signals to the City' as their principal reason for buying. A further 35 per cent put it down to the 'chairman's insistence'.

   Not surprising then that academic research concludes: 'Acquisitions are, on average, a poor investment for acquiring firms and indicate the ability of management of the acquiring firms to act on their own behalf and not in the shareholders best interest' and 'Given that the non-acquiring firms matched or out-performed the acquiring firms by a margin of two to one, it is necessary to consider other explanations for why firms engage in merger activity'.

For smaller companies the reasons to buy need to be rather more practical and down to earth. Sound reasons for acquisitions include:

- To increase market share and eliminate a troublesome competitor.
- To broaden your product range or give you access to new markets.
- To diversify into new markets acquiring the necessary management, marketing or technical skills to enable you to capture a reasonable slice of the market, relatively quickly.
- To get your business into another country or region.
- To protect an important source of supply which could be under threat from a competitor.
- To acquire additional staff, factory space, warehousing, distribution channels, or to get access to additional major customers more quickly than by starting up yourself.

You should produce a written statement explaining the rationale behind your reason to buy – before you start looking for companies to buy – otherwise you could end up pursuing a 'bargain' just because it seems cheap, that has absolutely nothing to do with your previously defined commercial goals. It is also worth remembering that companies available at knockdown prices are likely to need drastic surgery. So unless you fancy your chances as a company doctor, stay well away.

Winprime

Martin Blaney, MD of Winprime, a West London wholesaler of PCs and printers, says he has a list of gaps in his company's range which he would like to fill and a profile of the sort of business he would like to acquire.

'But a company of our size (170 employees and £40 million worth of sales) doesn't have a wonderful research document and reams of paper', he added. Blaney and his managers keep a close eye on what is happening in their industry and take up suggestions put to them by the City institutions who helped him get started.

'It is difficult to have some wonderful acquisition plan', commented Blaney. 'We are always talking to people and making contacts. We may hear of somebody in trouble.' Within 18 months Winprime made its second acquisition, buying Document Technology (DTL), a supplier of non-impact printers, when DTL's own plans to develop a portable printer failed.

Pointing

Hugh Charlton, MD of Pointing, a Northumberland-based manufacturer of food colours and flavours, says his company has a set of written criteria. These cover the product areas Pointing wants to add, the size and profitability of the target company and the markets and technology in which it is involved.

Pointing, a family company employing 95 people and with sales of £12 million, would be unlikely to spend more than £3 million on an acquisition, notes Charlton.

But even if you have a plan you must remain opportunistic, he adds. Pointing's most recent acquisition, a Manchester-based company making food ingredients, was found by David Garrick. 'We have a hit list but this was a company we were not aware of', says Charlton. 'It is in a peripheral area not specified in our brief.'

---

2. **Think about what you want to buy.**

On average, it can take one person more than one year's work to find and buy a private limited company. The more accurately you describe your ideal purchase the simpler, quicker and cheaper your search will be.

Just imagine trying to buy a house without any idea where you wanted to live, how much you wanted to spend, how many bedrooms were needed, whether you wanted a new house or a listed building, or if you wanted a garden. The search would be near impossible to organise, it could take forever, and the resultant purchase would almost certainly please no one. The same problem is present when buying a company. The definition of what you want to buy should explain:

– The business area/products/service the company is in.
– The location.
– The price range and the cash you have available.
– The management depth and the management style you are looking for.
– The minimum profitability and return on capital employed you could accept. It is worth remembering if the company you plan to buy only makes 1 per cent profit whilst you make 5 per cent, and you are of equal size, the resultant profit will be 3 per cent $[(5 + 1) \div 2]$.
– The image compatibility between your company and any target.
– The scope for integration and cost savings.
– The tax status.
– Other key factors for success. Outside of the factors listed above you may have vital reasons that if not achieved, would make the acquisition a poor bet. For example, if you want to iron out major cash flow or plant capacity cycles, there is little point in going for a business similar to your own. That will only make the peaks and troughs more pronounced.

Star Cargo

John James, chairman of Star Cargo, a privately-owned transport and freighting company, started takeover talks with 17 companies. For a mixture of reasons none of the talks came to anything.

There were owners who decided not to sell; businesses that appeared less attractive when more was learnt about them; and businesses that were clearly not worth the value put upon them by their owners.

But times proved more fruitful and Star Cargo, based in Harpenden, Hertfordshire, sewed up two deals. It bought Viking Shipping Services, a profitable company, from the receivers handling the affairs of its failed parent, and concluded six weeks of negotiations to acquire another small shipping firm a short time afterwards.

Despite the unpredictable outcome of takeover negotiations, Star Cargo, which had turnover of £16.6 million and 155 employees, was committed to making acquisitions as well as seeking organic growth.

'Negotiations can be enormously time-consuming and costly and can fail after you have gone a long way down the road', says James. 'But you have to put the effort in if you want to achieve results.' In the space of three years Star Cargo's efforts led to four acquisitions.

3. **Start looking**

Once you have a profile of the sort of company you would like to buy you can assemble your shopping list. Two sources are of particular use:

One Source UK, financial details of 360,000 UK companies, five years of accounts plus key ratios and basic company history and director information. It can search by company name, geographical location, SIC code, turnover and number of employees.

One Source Europa: similar in content to One Source UK but covers European companies. It provides accounts details in local currency, sterling and US dollars.

One Source provides summarised profit-and-loss accounts, and balance sheet data, a four year trend and some key rates of UK companies, the vast majority of whom are private. For each sector (for example window manufacturers, retail chemists, the toy industry, employment agencies or software houses), key performance ratios, growth rates and relative performance are analysed over a three-year period, or by getting the accounts direct from Companies House, you can sift through for companies conforming to your profile.

You could also read the financial press such as *The Times* on Saturdays, *The Sunday Times* business to business section, *The Daily Telegraph* on

Mondays or *The Financial Times* on Tuesdays. There are several hundred companies for sale each week in these papers. Alternatively you could advertise for companies yourself, or approach an organisation that handles the sale of other people's companies. Major accountancy practice or merger brokers are very active in this field. You could start by talking to your professional advisers

If this all seems like too much hard work you could brief a merger broker or merchant bank to search out prospective companies for you. This will not be cheap – anything around the 5 per cent mark is not unusual for smaller deals and professional advisers could add another couple of per cent to that figure.

If you are going to look overseas for a target company make sure you understand the possible additional obstacles in your way. For example, the rules and regulations in different countries are not the same (see Table 2.11.2). The motivation of the vendors is a major problem. Many continentals are much more interested in issues of tax, spreading wealth around the families and ensuring pension rights of annuities, factors which have to be considered when structuring the deal.

4. **Investigate and approach**

   Once you have your shopping list of prospective purchases you need to arm yourself with everything you can find out about them. Get their literature, samples, copies of their advertising, press comment and, of course, their accounts. Then go and see their premises and as much of their operation as it is possible to see. If you can't get in, get one of your salespeople in to look the business over for you. This investigation will help you to both shorten your shopping list, and put possible purchases into order of priority. Now you are ready for the approach.

   Although you are technically 'buying', psychologically you would be well advised to think of acquiring a company as a selling job. As such you cannot afford to have any approach rejected either too early or without a determined effort. You have three options as to how to make the initial approach and each has its merits. You can telephone, giving only the broadest reason for your approach – saying perhaps you wish to discuss areas of common interest. You could write and be a little more specific on your purpose, following that up with a phone call to arrange a meeting, perhaps over lunch. Finally you could use a third party such as an accountant, merchant bank or consultant. Reasons of secrecy could make this method desirable; or if executive time is at a premium there may be no other practicable way.

   The first meeting is crucial and you need to achieve two objectives. Firstly, you must establish mutual respect, trust and rapport. Nothing

Table 2.11.2   Mergers and acquisitions legislation in Europe

	Belgium	France	Germany	Netherlands	Spain	UK
Approval generally required for public takeovers	Yes	No	No(9)	No	Yes	No(6)
Approval generally required for takeovers by foreigners	Yes(1)	Yes(1)	No(9)	No	No(8)	No(6)
Limits on voting rights	Yes	Yes(2)	Yes(2)	No(5)	Yes(2)	No(7)
Board able to issue extra shares to its allies	Yes(2)	Yes(2)	Yes(2)	Yes(2)	No	No
National antitrust legislation (& 6)	No	Yes	Yes	Yes(4)	Yes	Yes(4)
Employee rights created by takeover legislation	No(3)	No(3)	Yes	Yes	No	No

worthwhile will follow without these. Then you need to establish in principle that both parties are seriously interested. Timescale, price, methods of integration etc, can all be side-stepped until later, except in the most general sense.

5. **Valuing the business**

Once you have found a business that you want to buy, and that is probably for sale, you will need your accountants to investigate the business in depth to see exactly what is on offer. This can take several weeks, and it is a little like having a house surveyed. You need to remember that accounts are normally prepared on the 'going concern basis', which implies the company is going to continue trading much as before. This means that the historical cost of fixed assets such as buildings, land, machinery etc, can appear in the balance sheet, rather than the market worth. After all, until you came along they hadn't planned to sell their fixed assets, but now the figures will have to be recast using different principles.

Ultimately, what you are buying is either extra profit or perhaps lower costs in your own business. You have to decide how much either is worth. Public companies usually have rules of thumb for each sector. For example, much of the retail sector is valued on a Price/Earnings of 12, which means retailers are seen as being worth 12 times last year's net profit. A private company in the same sector would only be worth two-thirds that figure, as their shares are less easily bought and sold. The worth of the assets in the business would also be important, and whatever the business, it is usually people – their knowledge and skills – you are buying, unless of course you are simply asset stripping.

Prices paid for private companies are monitored in a new three-monthly index prepared by accountancy firm, Stoy Hayward. The index is published in the magazine *Acquisitions Monthly* (tel: 020 7369 7498), and will enable owners of private companies to follow trends in unquoted company acquisitions and help them to assess a fair price for their own businesses.

Based on completed acquisitions, the index tracks the ratio between the purchase price of private companies sold during a 3-month period and their historical earnings. The price/earnings ratio of the index of private companies is usually about 20 per cent lower than the trading P/E multiple of companies in the FT 500 Index for the same period. This reflects the value placed on liquidity.

There is no great science in valuing business, it is just a rather messy art – and in the process you can always work out if it would be cheaper to start up from scratch yourself. That will give you an outer figure for your nego-tiations.

6. **Limit the risks**

   Buying a business will always be risky. If you have done your homework and got the price right with any luck the risks will be lessened. Here are some specific things you can do to lessen the risks.
   - Set conditional terms: for example, you could make part of the price conditional upon a certain level of profits being achieved;
   - Handcuff key employees: if most of the assets you are buying are on

two legs, then get service contracts or consultancy arrangements in place before the deal is signed;

- Establish non-competitive clauses: make sure that neither the seller nor his key employees can set up in competition, taking all the goodwill you have just bought;
- Check tax clearances – obviously you want to make sure any tax losses you are buying, or any tax implications in the purchase price are approved by the Inland Revenue, before committing yourself.
- Establish warranties and indemnities: if, after you have bought, you find there is a compulsory purchase order on the vendor's premises and the patent on his fantastic new product is invalid, you would quite rightly be disappointed. Warranties and Indemnities set out those circumstances in which the seller will make good the buyer's financial loss. So if there is anything crucial that looks worrying, you could try to include it under this heading. Not unnaturally, the seller will resist, but you need to be firm on key points.

7. **Manage the acquisition**

However well-negotiated the deal, most acquisitions that go wrong do so because of the human factor, particularly in the first few weeks after the deal is made public. Some important rules to follow are:

- Have an outline plan for how to handle the 'merger' – and be prepared to be flexible. (Interestingly enough, only one buyer in five has a detailed operational plan of how to manage their acquisition – but 67 per cent of those being bought believe the buyer has such a plan so it is psychologically important.)
- Let business go on as usual for a few weeks, as you learn more about the internal workings of the company. Then you can make informed judgments on who or what should go or remain in post. Ninety per cent of successful acquisitions follow this rule.
- Hold management and staff meetings on day 1, to clear as much misunderstanding as you can. Do as much of this yourself as you possibly can.
- Never announce takeovers on a Friday. Staff will have all weekend to spread rumours. Wednesdays are best – just enough time to clear up misunderstandings, followed by a useful weekend breathing space.
- Make cuts/redundancies a once-only affair. It is always best to cut deep, and then get on with running the business. Continuous sackings sap morale, and all the best people will leave before it is their turn.
- Set limits of authority, reporting relationships and put all banking relationships in the hands of your own accounts department, as quickly as possible.

Dynaction

Acquisition strategies – nothing can be ruled out

Two French entrepreneurs, Henri Blachet and Christian Moretti, a Hanson and White in miniature, have spent the past eight years building a mini-conglomerate in France by acquisition that has confounded the sceptics. Dynaction, their holding company, which controls 32 small firms, turned in a profit of FF173 million, (around £0.5 million per company), over 50 per cent up over two years.

Their philosophy is based on three maxims. The first is that boring businesses are best. Rather than buy small companies in sexy sectors like high technology or luxury goods, Dynaction bids for firms in dull ones like mechanical engineering and packaging. It is, however, fussy about what it buys. Companies on Dynaction's shopping list must be market leaders in their product range, preferably with a healthy export business. Second, they must be cheap, which rules out contested bids. Dynaction rarely pays a price that values its prey at an historic price–earning ratio of more than 6. Dynaction's aim is to float a part of any firm that it buys within four years at twice the price–earnings ratio that it paid.

Their third rule is to let managers manage. It has no centralised cost-control or accounting systems; the executives who run its subsidiaries do almost as they please. Dynaction's approval is required only for big decisions like raising capital or making a significant acquisition. That suits Blanchet and Moretti. Unlike typical tycoons, they admit they hate hard work and sneak off for a game of tennis at their local club as often as possible.

There is a method in this madness. Good managers suffocated by corporate bureaucracy are queuing to join them. Dynaction's bosses reckon they spend about one-third of their time in search of managerial excellence. Once they have found it the challenge is to turn managers into entrepreneurs. So Dynaction gives managers an equity stake of up to 25 per cent in the subsidiaries they manage.

A hands-off strategy also helps to keep costs down. The holding company employs just four people, and operates from two rooms of a house in an unglamorous part of Paris.

What are the snags? If it grows too fast, Dynaction presumably could soon encounter some of the problems that have afflicted more arthritic giants. For a start, the company could lose its valuable *esprit de corps* when its network of business grows. So far, the flair of Dynaction's two founders for choosing the right people has paid off; but, as the company grows bigger, other executives will have to start hiring. If the calibre of managers deteriorates, and problems appear, the holding company would have little choice but to take a stronger hand in its businesses.

A careful look at any of the most successful companies will reveal that buying up other people's companies played a key part in achieving growth. Some companies – Hanson is a prime example – make buying, repackaging and then selling businesses a business in itself.

Licensing

One way to inject accelerated growth into the organisation while minimising the risks associated with either acquisition or new product/service development, is to buy someone else's revenue stream without taking on either their people or premises: the concept is licensing. Here you buy the rights to make and market a proven product or concept that usually has patent, copyright or some other form of intellectual protection already in place.

Shire Pharmaceuticals

Shire Pharmaceuticals was formed in the mid-1980s by a team who broke away from a major multinational pharmaceutical company. They had several product ideas themselves and found backing to take them through the R & D stage and into the market. They sold off one of their products which had world appeal, as they felt too small themselves to properly exploit its potential. The several million they got, along with some venture capital from Schroders, the merchant bankers, allowed them to start building up a UK sales and marketing organisation to exploit their remaining products.

By 1990 it became clear that their present product range was too small to support a national salesforce. Their present force of 20 full-timers and 10 part-timers was about half the size needed to get reasonable hospital and GP coverage. They had done a great job of getting sales up to £3 million but there the business stuck.

In 1991 they recruited an experienced MD from Wyeth Laboratories, the UK subsidiary of American Home Products, the giant American pharmaceutical company. Trevor Davis, the new MD, had a solution, which was to license a complementary range of products from Glaxo. He bid for a package of 20 products, too small to be of strategic interest to Glaxo, with a turnover of £6 million. While that may have been small beer to a multinational, it would triple Shire's business overnight and allow them to recruit a national salesforce through which they could now drive their core products.

Glaxo was offered a deal which allowed Shire to put £1 million on the table and pay the rest as a 'royalty' on the sale of the drugs. That helped Shire's cash flow and gave Glaxo a share in the extra sales of their old products that were generated by having someone give them maximum attention.

There are many sources of licensed products, but perhaps the best source of two-way licensing deals (you can license out anything redundant to your needs, too) is the British Technology Group (BTG).

BTG works closely with universities, colleges, research councils and government research establishments to commercialise the results of their research work. BTG protects the inventions concerned by patenting and other means, identifies potential licensees and negotiates license agreements with manufacturers. Development funds are available to enhance the prospects of successful licensing.

BTG also funds UK companies planning to develop new products and processes based on their own technology. Through its industrial project finance scheme, BTG can provide up to 50 per cent of the funds required for the development and launch of a new product, recovering its investment by means of a percentage levy on sales of the resulting product or process. Equity financing is also available from BTG.

Do not forget that while you are busy adding products and services and making new acquisitions, it may be appropriate to shed some of the old things you were doing.

In the example above Glaxo recognised that its interest and profits were best served by shedding products it could no longer give adequate attention to. This divestment had the double benefit of giving Glaxo's salesforce time to sell more profitable products and kept a growing revenue stream coming in from the old ones. One small shoe manufacturer has kept every product it ever designed in its stock list, and will make any shoe from the list in minimum batches of 10. This Herculean task has held the company in a time warp bogged down by its past and unable to move forward. Its sales plateaued years ago. Still, perhaps in the UK shoe business that is no mean achievement.

Assignment 17

Targeting takeovers

1. Consider whether or not you believe that an acquisition or merger would be desirable at this stage in your firm's life. The deciding question is: 'If we buy a company and it goes disastrously wrong, can we still survive?'.
2. If the answer to the above question is 'Yes', then draw up the profile of your target companies and prepare a plan of campaign along the lines described in this chapter.
3. Consider joint ventures by asking: 'Why shouldn't we start looking for a suitable joint venture partner?'. If you could operate in Europe but do not, the logic of a joint venture is quite compelling. If you have a market opportunity that you need help in exploiting, a joint venture could be a low(ish) risk way in.
4. Consider products, services or business units you should get out of. Remember that to move forward you have to let go of something.

12   *Visionary leadership*

The former manager of the New York Yankees once said: 'If you don't know where you're going, you might end up somewhere else'.

Today, more and more attention is being paid to articulating the business 'vision'. In fact, many people believe that creating and communicating the vision is the most important job of the leader. The editor of *Fortune* magazine has said: 'The new paragon of an executive is a person who can envision a future for his organisation and then inspire his colleagues to join him in building that future' (Dumaine, 1990).

Visions are about dreams, the 'promised land', a destination shared by everyone, and an inspiration to all. The most successful companies are those whose leaders can see and articulate to others the exciting possibilities of the future. Here is Sophie Mirman talking about Trotters, an enterprise she opened in King's Road selling upmarket children's wear: 'We shall keep this company small and keep it private. The service has got to be 100 per cent right. It will be impeccable. We want it to be a small, enjoyable business. We want everyone involved to have fun with it'.

Visionary leaders 'have a dream'. There is nothing Sir Terence Conran hates more than 'unfinished dreams'. The same might be said of Lady Thatcher who, whatever one thought of her politics, was by general consent a visionary of her era. An article describing Sheila Pickles, the woman who transformed Penhaligon's from an ailing perfumery business into an international empire, compared her to Laura Ashley, 'another company built on the nostalgic vision of one woman'. Sadly, the visionary Laura Ashley died in tragic circumstances and there is doubt about whether the company she founded can forge as strong a vision for today in the fickle world of fashion retailing as it did in her time.

There are some interesting as yet unanswered questions around the robustness of vision in some of our most famous established businesses. For example, will Marks & Spencer be able to reinvent their vision for the 21st century? Will the

Branson empire be able to extend itself to have life beyond the vision of one man?

For more recent start-ups, e-business has changed the name of the game for those with a new vision of how to be a global player in a small niche market even when geography is totally against them. Look to Scotland – it has the highest proportion of fully automated businesses in the UK.

Look even further to New Zealand, a tiny country 10,000 miles from LA, 19,000 miles from London, 9,000 miles from the Asian markets, even 3,000 miles from its antipodean cousins in Oz. Try booking yourself a holiday, to find just how Web-centric is even the smallest hotel. Better still, drive past Queenstown, South Island, past the famous 'Remarkables', along the shores of Lake Wakatipu, until you come to a dead end at the head of the valley in a hamlet called Glenorchy. There you will find Glenorchy Fur Products, manufacturing quality possum fur garments, and trading from a brown clapperboard shack about the size of a garden shed. The company will make any article you would like in possum fur, and get it to you fast anywhere in the world. The company's Web site explains why the possum is a pest in NZ, what customers think of Glenorchy Fur Products, and why, if you buy from them, you will be getting something quite different. Look at the organisational facts of life that go with this venture:

- It is environmentally friendly.
- The company has global reach within a niche market.
- There are no grand premises and insignificant overhead.
- There are few direct employees.
- The company has a loose network of suppliers and distributors.
- Those involved have a vision that is passionately held, different, and very clearly explained.

The moral is that in an established business you must constantly communicate, refresh and reinvent your vision, whilst in an e-business start-up, the power and passion of your vision can win you friends/backers and customers unconstrained by geographic limitations.

Those who succeed in business always have strong visions. More than this though, they must be strong visions that are intelligible to other life forms. Recently a VC told us: 'I am sick to death of dot.com businesses set up by 16-year-old teccy whizz kids. They are arrogant, opinionated, ignorant of any business reality and incapable of putting across in plain English what their vision is, and why we should give them our money'. Even dot.coms need to be able to articulate and communicate a clear vision. Being passionate about the product is a great start. Here is how to do it:

Choc Express

Choc Express is passionate about delivered chocolate gifts, anywhere in the world. It is 'totally dedicated to good chocolate' and committed to excellent service in the form of a beautifully packaged chocolate gift, exactly the right size to go through a standard letterbox.

As co-founder and MD Angus Thirlwell says, 'It has been a lot of fun dreaming up ideas and seeing them become products. We like to think that by doing this we can keep people in touch with the power of chocolate'. Like all successful entrepreneurs, Thirlwell is a powerhouse of ideas, anything that excites a chocoholic excites him. His company's Web site isn't just about getting orders; it is about enticing chocolate lovers everywhere to become part of his community. Participating in browsing, tasting, trying new chocolate creations, helping to design new products and fun things, means that Thirlwell is building a club whose members will visit the site even when they are not making a purchase. The Web site has a hot chocolates offer that positively drips off the page! Who could then resist becoming part of the chocolate tasting club (involving scored feedback from customers), or fail to order the 'chocolate labrador looking for a home and willing to share chocolate bones'!

Wardrobe

Look at Wardrobe, started in 1973 by owner/founder Susie Faux and operating a unique fashion business aimed at providing a one-stop shop for businesswomen and non-businesswomen who want to project their individuality. 'You're a brilliantly successfulwoman, do you have time to look the part?'

Or as Susie asks through the Wardrobe Web site (www.wardrobe.co.uk):

'When was the last time you…

Bought a jacket that seemed lined with self-confidence?
Or a trouser suit that shaved inches off your hips?
Or a dress that made you feel good old-fashioned sexy?
Or a pair of shoes that made your legs look as though they should be insured?

Too long? Then make an appointment with Wardrobe.'

With Wardrobe and the previous examples we see a potent mix of passionately held vision, and a joy in breaking convention and doing things in new ways.

It is the power and passion of your vision that will translate paper strategies into a way of life. It is vision which puts your dream to work, by making it something that is shared by everyone, inspirational and clear enough to help people know what kind of decisions not to make in your business. An effective vision centres on people. It also centres on the future and becomes the 'pull-through' for change.

The greatest threat to growing the business comes from the danger that the entrepreneur's thinking and action may be trapped by today's problems, so that the focus is on a 'quick fix' rather than on moving the organisation forward. The challenge is to manage the flow of new ideas against the existing business processes. In this way embryo ideas can be nurtured not squashed, and business processes put in place to fast-track the best ideas into reality.

This chapter aims to help you think afresh about the vision you have for your business, formulate it in such a way that you can get your team on board for the journey and constantly live the values yourself as the ultimate role model. A strong vision will be robust, long-lasting, passionate, inspirational and, above all else, shared.

Developing a vision

When you sit down to write a formal statement of company philosophy you will probably find that 'motherhood' statements are easy, but that it is more difficult to produce a real and relevant vision. It's rather like the chairman of a large company who is reputed to have written the 'shared' values for his 20,000 staff! A statement of vision or values on its own is meaningless unless it is truly shared by everyone in the organisation.

Indeed, in any company with a strong culture any employee at any time can tell you what the company stands for. Developing your business vision isn't therefore a job you can do sitting in splendid isolation; it's an opportunity to involve your people in its design. There are several techniques to help you envision your future with your team:

- organisation pictures;
- culture statements;
- thoughts about effective organisation;
- core mission;
- vision and value statements.

Organisation pictures

In diagnosing the current state of your organisation (in Assignment 10), you drew a picture of how you see your business now. What would your picture of the future look like? Here is Ralph Stayer describing his business to the *Harvard Business Review*:

The image that best captured the organisation end state I had in mind for Johnsonville was a flock of geese on the wing. I didn't want an organisational chart with traditional lines and boxes, but a 'V' of individuals, who knew the common goal, took turns leading and adjusted their structure to the task at hand. Geese fly in a wedge, for instance, but land in waves. (Stayer, 1990)

Other visions of the future we have seen recently include:

● a circus ring: 'Laydeez and Gentlemen, the combined skills, synchronised talents, all under one big top';
● an orchestra;
● a phoenix rising from the ashes;
● a bus with everyone happily on board, knowing the destination;
● a formation of Red Arrows (with ears) flying with safety and precision, a quality organisation – achieved through the involvement of the whole workforce of 350 in teamwork;
● a TQM hospital, compassionate and caring, prevention not cure, open communications, no 'us' and 'them' elitism.

Finally, you and your team will find it useful to put some words around your picture. In the 'best of all possible worlds' what will the future look like, and how will you know when you've got there? When BMW dealers were asked to define their business vision, they considered the following questions in order to define the characteristics of their desired 'end state':

● What is fundamentally different about our business?
● How will staff behave towards customers?
● What will be the customers' image of us?
● What attitude will staff have to their jobs?
● What sort of people will we be recruiting?
● What will be our management style?
● How will staff relate to their managers?
● What training, support and personal development will we offer?
● How will we reward our people?
● How will people work together in team structures?

Culture statements ('the way we do things around here')

In diagnosing your organisation (in Assignment 10), we encouraged you to describe your current culture; historically, as it is now and as you would like to

Historical	Current	Future
• Slightly chaotic but very happy family	• In transition, losing some of our specialness	• International
		• Customer-focused
• Self-centred rather than customer-centred	• Pretty good job with customers, not excellent	• Experienced elder statesmen
• Happy amateurs	• More performance-orientated	• Professional and polished
• Top-line driven		
	• Tolerate failure (which is good)	• Attract and keep terrific people
• Small team playing bar billiards	• Reorganization and management changes	• Attract and keep terrific people
• Passionate attempt to avoid politics		
	• Still a bit disjointed	• Pride and self-worth
		• Spin-off separate units

Figure 2.12.1   Example of company culture: historic, current and future

see it in the future. Brainstorming a list of words and phrases with your team can give you a very powerful insight into the kind of company you want to be. Figure 2.12.1 is an example prepared by the Innovex (now Quintiles) management team during 1990.

Doing some navel-gazing in this fashion helped Innovex to decide which aspects of its past it wanted to retain (for example, being an open, non-political organisation) and which it needed to change (for example, becoming more strongly customer-focused). The words that Innovex used to describe its future actually started to create that future. It provided the management team with a 'vision' of the sort of business they wanted to build and be part of. It helped to contribute to the exceptional performance which resulted in the Innovex/Quintiles merger in the late 1990s. Now as part of the massive Quintiles organisation, a corporate-culture diagnostic carried out in 1998 on a worldwide basis for all 10,000+ staff, has re-affirmed and synthesised a total shared company vision

This approach may seem 'soft'; after all it's about values and attitudes rather than facts and figures. However, if you hadn't once had a 'feeling', a 'dream', would the business exist at all? Get back in touch with your own fundamental beliefs about how you want to run your business. In a seminal article in the *Harvard Business Review* entitled 'Values make the company' (Howard, 1990), the chief executive of Levi-Strauss, Robert Haas, stated that it is values that drive the business: 'It is the ideas of a business which are controlling, not some manager with authority'. This was nicely put earlier by one MD of Glaxo (now

Glaxo SmithKline) when managing his own culture change programme. He said: 'Attitude is like baking powder, it's what makes the cake rise'.

Values help to bring about the kind of business behaviour you need to stay competitive. Levi-Strauss talked about the impact of an uncertain economic climate on their market share in the 1980s and the need to develop 'a whole new set of attitudes and values'. They described these as broadly consisting of moving people's behaviour as shown in Figure 2.12.2:

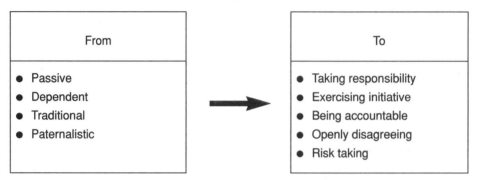

From		To
• Passive • Dependent • Traditional • Paternalistic	⟶	• Taking responsibility • Exercising initiative • Being accountable • Openly disagreeing • Risk taking

Figure 2.12.2　Moving people's behaviour to develop a new set of attitudes and values

Thoughts about effective organisation

In Chapter 5 you benchmarked your business against seven characteristics of effective organisations. Has this given you some clues for how you envisage the future?

Core mission

You may want to revisit your core mission or *raison d'être* to get another view on what your vision is. As Marcus de Ferranti recently said about Brand X (a 90-people business in telecoms transmission capability), 'I would like my mission statement to be to get to a size where we have to be broken up by the Competition Commission' (Pandit, 2000).

The mission statement should, more typically, tell you what's distinctive about your business and the market you operate in. Most important of all, it should give you focus. McKinsey (probably the most prestigious consultancy group in the world) articulate their mission with admirable brevity as: 'To help our clients make positive, lasting and substantial improvements in their performance and to build a great firm that is able to attract, develop, excite and retain exceptional people'.

Vision and value statements

Successful businesses tend to spend a lot of time articulating, communicating and constantly reinforcing their values, business philosophy or credo.

The key job of the chief executive and his or her top team lies in creating and communicating the vision and values. It's very interesting to put these two comments alongside each other. The first is from Deal and Kennedy (Corporate Cultures) and the second from the then ICL (now ICL/Fujitsu). 'The ultimate success of a chief executive depends to a large degree on an accurate reading of the corporate culture and the ability to hone it and shape it to fit the shifting needs of the market place' (Deal and Kennedy). 'ICL is successful because the top people, probably as much by luck as judgment, read the signals right and because there is an emphasis on continuous high profile communication' (ICL).

ICL

The ICL experience is interesting because it illustrates that having a clear management vision and absolute determination is not enough unless you get others on board as well. ICL barely survived the recession of 1980–81. After a large rescue deal put together by the government and the City, it had to demonstrate very different 'ways of doing things around here'. At the start of their culture change process in 1981, there was intense communication and Robb Wilmot as chief executive officer was heavily involved. He issued mission statements, he put together a video, he stood on the top of the ICL organisation with his loudspeaker, he preached the new message on every opportunity and people nodded but ICL realised nothing much was changing.

Wilmot knew that things had to change and he found it immensely frustrating that he couldn't get the organisation to move fast enough. To get change in behaviour, the vision and values must be stated, restated, reinforced and communicated *ad nauseam*. Wilmot had somehow to get his people as familiar with the reasons for change as he was. He put 2,000 of his managers through a core programme, variously knows as 'mind expansion' and 'the sheep dip'. It started top down and ran for three years. The programme lasted 5½ to 6 days. The objective was to get people to realise that things had to change. The event is now viewed as a watershed. People realised that there was a real external threat. The world did not owe them a living. People came away saying, 'I understand the problem' and the programme created a common language for ICL.

Part of this 'common language' was summed up in a glossy brochure distributed by Wilmot, called 'The ICL Way'. It summed up the ICL philosophy in seven commitments. The commitments were to:

- change;
- customers;
- excellence;
- teamwork;

- achievement;
- people development;
- creating a productivity showcase.

The initial reaction was disbelief and cynicism, but later the 'ICL Way' became so accepted that it went out with the offer document to every new recruit.

McKinsey provide a marvellous example of a set of values, which have been strongly and clearly articulated since 1926. Any member of the professional staff who is, or ever has been employed with McKinsey, anywhere in the world, can instantly, seriously and passionately tell you what the company stands for. This is done through a set of 'guiding principles'. These are quoted in full in Figure 2.12.3.

Ericsson, the mighty Swedish telecommunications group, is as lively and enthusiastic as any small entrepreneurial business in stating its values, in the form of three musketeers: 'Perseverance, Professionalism and Respect'. Finally one of the most famous examples of creating and transmitting the vision of the business is Johnson and Johnson. Their credo is reproduced as Figure 2.12.4.

ASPIRATIONS	GUIDING PRINCIPLES
Serve our clients as primary counselors on overall performance	Adhere to the highest professional standards
	Follow the top management approach
	Play an integrative role in problem solving, implementation and capability building
	Build enduring, trust-based relationships
	Strive for superior quality and distinctive impact
Deliver the best of the firm to every client	Serve all clients as Firm clients by leveraging our scale and global network
	Develop and disseminate state-of-the-art management practices
	Manage client and Firm resources in a cost-effective manner
Create an unrivaled environment for superior talent	Develop and excite our people through active apprenticeship and stretching entrepreneurial opportunities
	Foster an inclusive and nonhierarchical working atmosphere
	Uphold the obligation to dissent
	Respect the individual's responsibility for balancing personal and professional life
	Demonstrate care and concern for every individual
Govern ourselselves through a values-driven partnership	Live by the principles of participative partnership
	Benefit from individual freedom and assume the obligations of mutual accountability and self-governance
	Maintain a meritocracy
	Operate as one Firm

Figure 2.12.3 McKinsey's guiding principles

Our Credo
We believe our first responsibility is to the doctors, nurses and patients, to mothers and fathers and all others who use our products and services. In meeting their needs everything we do must be of high quality. We must constantly strive to reduce our costs in order to maintain reasonable prices. Customers' orders must be serviced promptly and accurately. Our suppliers and distributors must have an opportunity to make a fair profit. We are responsible to our employees, the men and women who work with us throughout the world. Everyone must be considered as an individual. We must respect their dignity and recognize their merit. They must have a sense of security in their jobs. Compensation must be fair and adequate, and working conditions clean, orderly and safe. We must be mindful of ways to help our employees fulfil their family responsibilities. Employees must feel free to make suggestions and complaints. There must be equal opportunity for employment, development and advancement for those qualified. We must provide competent management, and their actions must be just and ethical. We are responsible to the communities in which we live and work and to the world community as well. We must be good citizens – support good works and charities and bear our fair share of taxes. We must encourage civic improvements and better health and education. We must maintain in good order the property we are privileged to use, protecting the environment and natural resources. Our final responsibility is to our stockholders. Business must make a sound profit. We must experiment with new ideas. Research must be carried on, innovative programmes developed and mistakes paid for. New equipment must be purchased, new facilities provided and new products launched. Reserves must be created to provide for adverse times. When we operate according to these principles, the stockholders should realize a fair return. *Johnson and Johnson*

Figure 2.12.4 Johnson and Johnson's credo

Building a commitment to a shared vision

One MD outlined his core values as follows:

- being customer-orientated;
- providing quality and value for money;
- being caring and helpful;
- being appreciative;
- being honest, reliable and professional;
- continuously improving.

He went on to explain that 'this is what we called our company philosophy. We've had it for some years but we haven't told anyone about it'. Quite! – Not all that unusual either and what a missed opportunity.

Visionary leadership means somehow taking your vision for growth and making it live in the hearts and minds of all your people. As the *Fortune* article says:

> Yes, a CEO must promulgate a vision, but the most brilliant vision this side of Paraguay won't budge the culture unless it's backed up by action… CEOs encase their mission statements in plexiglass, hand them out and people laugh. You have to change the behaviour of the person who assembles the machine or designs the product. (Dumaine, 1990)

Envisioning the future of your business is one essential of entrepreneurial leadership but it won't get you very far unless you can also inspire your colleagues to join in building that future. A vision statement on its own won't be the magic bullet. Involvement is the rocket fuel that will launch your vision: compulsively communicating your vision. Consult people at all levels in diagnosing your business problems, promoting your vision and values with a large trumpet.

Here are some examples of how other businesses have built commitment to a shared vision within some very different corporate environments:

Jaguar

When Sir John Egan took over at Jaguar cars as chairman and chief executive, he took time to communicate to the workforce the true financial position of the company. The message was, 'It's not going to be easy but we are getting there'. Jaguar ran quality circles as an ongoing way of getting commitment to the need to do things better and differently, and then organised a sporting and social 'Hearts and Minds' programme for Jaguar employees and their families.

ICL

During 1984–85 ICL put an entire division of 600 people through workshops aimed at creating a greater willingness for change and sharing the vision promulgated by Robb Wilmot in his 'ICL Way'. Each workshop involved a cross-functional cross-level group from the most senior director to the youngest, newest secretary. Each workshop identified major business problems and set up 'projects' to try to address the problems. By turning the organisation on its head in this way, Asa Lanum, the America boss of the division, created a powerhouse. Instead of denying the need for change, the new level of business awareness and involvement actually generated internal pressure to grow the business for a different future.

Next Computers

Steve Jobs has proved to be an extraordinarily visionary leader in the computer world. After leaving Apple he started Next Computers. He took the entire management team away for a retreat. During this retreat he argued, shared and fine-tuned so that his vision demonstrably became the team's vision. The only technology they had was a flip-chart board. After Jobs's short presentation on his dream, its importance to him and why he thought it exciting, the flip-chart board was rapidly taken over by the members of the team to demonstrate how they intended to make the vision a reality.

Living the vision

Visionary leaders are ever more important in a world of rapid change. Moreover, different stages of business growth pose different leadership challenges, so you will constantly need to assess how your role should change. At some stage, you yourself may actually be getting in the way of growth and may need to stand aside, and hand the leadership reins to someone better suited to that phase of growth. You may also find that as owner/founder you enjoyed the early entrepreneurial times but get much less enjoyment as the company grows bigger, and ironically becomes more like the Companies you were trying to get away from in setting it up in the first place!

One can sympathise with the search of Anita Roddick (founder and co-chair of Body Shop) for the most appropriate role, now she has brought in a French CEO, and is no longer in the company's driving seat. She explains: 'In the years ahead I see my leadership role as being an irritant, a gadfly – infusing creativity and creating an edge to everything the Body Shop does' (Simms, 2000).

At the same time, there is a view in the City that 'if Roddick got lost in the Brazilian rainforest, the share price would rise'. One analyst is quoted as saying: 'If she were to become any more involved, we would see that as a definite negative'.

The moral is – never think that you are indispensable and know when to go.

On a more positive note, your people will study your every move for a clue about what really matters to you; your example and your strong leadership are crucial to the business of turning vision into action. There are great risks in the old adage 'Don't do what I do, do what I say'. Most of us place much more weight on actions than words. Your team are bound to look to you personally to demonstrate the values which you are professing. In their dramatic 'culture change' programme the mighty BP (then under the leadership of Sir Robert Horton) put tremendous emphasis on what they called 'walking the talk'; that is on senior management demonstrating the new 'OPEN' behaviours in everything they did. (The acronym stands for **O**pen thinking, **P**ersonal impact, **E**mpowerment and **N**etworking.)

You are the 'X factor', it is your personal leadership style which will make all the difference to whether the vision in your head truly becomes the tune to which people's feet are marching. Fortunately, there is a lot to help you develop your visionary leadership. There is also a lot around to get in the way, starting with Machiavelli's definition of leadership in *The Prince* as 'achieving one's ends through guile, deceit and flattery' (1998). There has been much unhelpful mythology around the cult of personality – the leader as 'hero', a great figure with powerful charisma and an ego to match. It was recently stated of a famous business leader, 'He is not held back by a lack of self-esteem'. However, the concept of leader as hero and great man or woman has had its day. These days even Sandhurst relies on methods other than the development of 'officer-like qualities'. Are leaders born or made? Well, some Sandhurst comments (ancient folklore) are salutary: 'Smith is not a born leader yet', 'Men will follow this officer anywhere – out of sheer curiosity'.

The mythology has been exploded; it is not leadership qualities – whatever they are – that makes visionary leaders. In the *Leadership Secrets of Attila the Hun* (Roberts, 1990), Attila advises us that: 'Seldom are self-centered conceited and self-admiring chieftains great leaders but they are great admirers of themselves'. The leader as hero or heroine shouts 'over the top' but he or she might turn around to find that no one is following. The trouble with heroes or heroines is that they create dependency in the organisation. They are playing a losing game. Entrepreneurs quite like to accept responsibility and to see themselves as hero or heroine. There is a certain satisfaction in pulling the rabbit out of the hat yet again, to the cries of amazement from the audience! However, in proving his or her own worth by solving crises, the leader is playing a losing game. By now there's no one around who has any capabilities. Every time this leader pulls the rabbit out of the hat, he or she creates more dependency. That's the trap in becoming a hero or heroine.

The essence of leadership is the activity of orchestrating the resources of others towards solving problems – not in being the hero or heroine oneself. Unfortunately, many entrepreneurial chief executives learn this lesson the hard way. They like to keep on being the hero or heroine. That's one reason why successful CEOs often have to leave at a certain point. They have to leave because there is a dependency on them that they can't shift, and they can't let go. Most entrepreneurs will have to learn the transition from 'meddler' to 'strategist' if they are to avoid being a constraint on the growth of their own organisation. The essence of visionary leadership lies in two aspects, first articulating the vision or direction of the business, second in mobilising the energies of all people towards the vision.

Leadership can best be described not as a quality, or as a combination of technical skills demanded by particular situations, but as an activity. This is why John Adair's 'action-centered leadership' model has proved so successful both in training the officers of Sandhurst and in many walks of business life. The leader must satisfy three distinct but interrelated sets of needs as shown in Figure 2.12.5.

Lao-Tzu said quite a few years ago: 'When the best leader's work is done the people say – we did it ourselves' (Heider, 1985). The idea of leaders as heroes or heroines has been replaced by the concept of leaders as conductors of their orchestra of players.

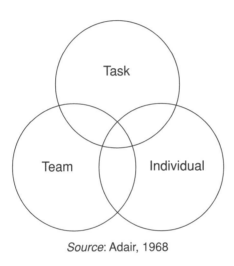

Source: Adair, 1968

Figure 2.12.5   The action-centred leadership model

A very useful guide to assessing your visionary leadership capability is *The Visionary Leader*, a leader behaviour questionnaire by Dr Marshall Sashkin (1995), available in the UK and Europe from MLR Ltd, PO Box 28, Carmarthen SA31 1DT; tel/fax: 01267 281661. This questionnaire helps you to plot where you are on the 'mountain' of leadership from being 'at the Piedmont' through 'on the final ascent' to 'at the summit'. As well as appealing to mountaineering entrepreneurs it also enables you to assess (if you work with feedback from others) just how visionary a leader you are against 10 characteristics which research has shown to be associated with effective leadership. These are:

● *Clear leadership*. Effective leaders focus on a few key issues.

- *Communicative leadership.* Communication skills in getting messages across to others.
- *Consistent leadership.* The leader takes clear positions and avoids 'flip, flop' shifts.
- *Caring leadership.* The leader has genuine concern for others, what Carl Rogers calls 'unconditional positive regard'.
- *Creative leadership.* The leader is willing to take risks and doesn't spend time in 'cover-your-ass' type activities.
- *Confident leadership.* Effective leaders have a sense of self-assurance and a belief that they can make a difference.
- *Empowered leadership.* Effective leaders don't want power for its own sake; they share power to give everyone influence. They 'empower' others.
- *Visionary leadership.* Effective leaders are able to think over relatively long time spans of at least a few years.
- *Organisational leadership.* Effective leaders help the organisation to change.
- *Cultural leadership.* Effective leaders create, articulate and communicate shared visions and values.

Assignment 18

Checking out your leadership ability

1. Develop a statement of your company vision and values, through the involvement of key members of your team and using any combination of the methods described in this chapter, for example:
   - drawing an organisation picture;
   - making a culture statement of what you are moving from/to;
   - thinking about effective organisation (doing your benchmark exercise);
   - revisiting your core mission.
2. Assess your personal leadership capability using the visionary leadership questionnaire.
3. Consider what practical action you can take to involve everyone in the company in enthusiastically understanding and promoting your vision?

Part 3

How will we get there?

Completion of your basic marketing SWOT and CSF analyses, together with reviews of strategic options, and people and financial audits, will have placed you in a strong position to redefine your company's future growth strategy. In the light of the analyses you have undertaken so far, you must begin the third and final phase by revisiting and possibly revising your company's mission statement, first outlined in Chapter 1 (rowing harder does not help if the boat is heading in the wrong direction!), and setting specific objectives to focus your marketing, financial and operation efforts.

Revise the company mission statement

Mission statements do change and should be revisited regularly.

WPP

Martin Sorrell at WPP set out with the mission to 'establish a large multinational marketing services company and to be one of the best', rather than simply being the best boutique agency in London. By the late-1990s the mission statement had altered marginally to be 'the largest multinational marketing services company and the best, by acquisition and adding value to customers' products/services'.

Changing trading and economic conditions will almost inevitably lead to a review and rewriting of mission statements at WPP. In the light of your current trading conditions now, and forecast for the next 18 months, re-examine your mission statement, remembering that it should contain three basic elements:

- A statement of the business you are in and your purpose: eg Connectair stated: 'We are in the commuter/feeder airline business and we want to establish a profitable air-link between Cranfield and Heathrow as a fore-runner for other links'.
- What you aim to achieve over the next one to three years: eg the Metropolitan Police state: 'We aim to maintain a peaceful society, free of fear of crime and disorder' (pessimists may argue that this may take a little longer than one to three years, but it is certainly a desirable aim!).
- How this aim is to be achieved (values and standards): eg Sainsbury's aim 'to be leaders in our trade by acting with complete integrity, working to the highest standards and by contributing to the quality of life in the community'; IBM stating that it wants to achieve its aim 'by dedication to customer service'; Sherry Coutu, founder of Interactive Investor International (iii), stating her aim will be achieved 'by giving private investors an equal footing with investor services' (Vandermerwe and Taishoff, 2000).

Mission statements are important as, unlike specific financial or marketing objectives which may be kept board-level confidential, they are meant to be communicated to all company employees, investors and even customers. But above all, as the management writer Peter Drucker has said:

> A mission statement has to focus on what the company/institution really tries to do so that everybody within the organisation can say, 'This is my contribution to the goal'. No hospital worker can tell you what action or behaviour follows from saying, 'Our mission is healthcare,' but 'it's our mission to give assurance to the afflicted' is simple, clear direction for a hospital emergency room. Every mission statement has to reflect the market opportunity or need, your company competence and gain the commitment of your people. Without all three it will not mobilise the human resources of the organisation to get the right things done. (Drucker, 1978)

The mission must not simply be a statement of good intentions; it must be simple and clear and meet the tasks described above. As new tasks are added, old ones can be removed. Sub-units in a company will have their own unique mission statements, provided they contribute to the overall group mission. This is probably why the group missions most admired by Drucker are the simplest and yet the most motivating; they include the mission of the Salvation Army: 'to make citizens out of the rejected' and of Dr Arnold of Rugby School: 'to make gentlemen out of savages' (like the Metropolitan Police mission statement cited above, Dr Arnold's may be somewhat optimistic!).

Solglas

Solglas Ltd set itself the mission of becoming the largest and most profitable company in the UK glass merchanting and glazing market sector, within five years, by acquisition and commitment to customer service. Its subsidiary company, Autoglass, could contribute to this overall group mission by aiming to become number one in the windscreen and automotive glass replacement business, by similar policies of acquisition and customer service.

Having revised or renewed your group and unit mission statement, you are now able to proceed to set specific targets and goals, to focus your specific marketing, financial and organisational plans.

Set specific objectives and goals

Objectives, goals and tasks flow naturally from the mission statement and contribute to its achievement. Thus, continuing with the Autoglass example, in order to achieve 'the most profitable, number one, position in the windscreen and automotive glass sector', Autoglass needed to set the following realisable objectives:

Autoglass

Objectives

Marketing: to achieve a minimum 25 per cent UK market share, partly by internal growth and own depot expansion, partly by acquisition of competitors.

Financial: to achieve a minimum 20 per cent return on assets, by ensuring new depots and acquisitions matched, within time deadlines, the 25 per cent return on assets achieved in the existing depot network.

Operations: to achieve a basic 30 windscreens fitted per month per employee target, by improved training and recruitment policies.

Social goals: to invest half of 1 per cent of profits in social reconstruction projects, eg Project Fullemploy.

Goals such as these should be specific, measurable and achievable, reflecting quantity, quality and cost-effectiveness. These are as important in non-profit as in profit-related businesses: witness the extraordinary (to businessmen) debate in UK education and health today, in introducing simple objectives and measurement systems. It needs to be done, as Peter Drucker has noted:

> Non-profit organisations find it very hard to answer the question of what 'results' are. Results can be quantified – at least some of them. The Salvation Army is fundamentally a religious organisation. But it knows the percentage of alcoholics it restores to mental and physical health and the percentage of criminals it rehabilitates. It is highly quantitative because it realises that work is only done by people with a deadline. By people who are monitored and evaluated. By people who hold themselves responsible for results. (Drucker, 1978)

Many have argued that, if a venture cannot be measured it should not be undertaken. By setting clear and concise objectives, in accordance with the company's mission, detailed tasks can be assigned to responsible individuals, and the basis of properly managing results and resources can be set in motion. To demonstrate this, see below for more on the Autoglass case study.

To achieve the Autoglass 25 per cent market share objective, tasks would include:

- opening three new depots in the Midlands region, in the next six months;
- initiating discussions with two south-western competitors, to complete national coverage;
- recruiting and training staff to NVQ2 standard for new depot openings;
- developing new promotion material, including a Web site, to help launch new depots and to build additional sales at existing depots.

All of these tasks and actions need to be set down and incorporated with attendant costs and results, in the company's or unit's detailed business plan.

---

13   *The marketing plan*

The final step in the marketing process is completing the marketing plan (see page 25). Your detailed one-year marketing plan (or perhaps covering up to three years for major groups) for each operating unit, should encapsulate much of the analysis and description included so far in this book. In outline it should contain:

- Your company's mission statement plus supporting unit mission statements where relevant. (See Chapter 1).
- A description of market sector (see Chapter 2). This will include size and sector growth rates over the last three to five years (eg windscreen replacement market is currently £30 million per annum, with average growth rate of 3 per cent per annum compound, without inflation); your market share performance to date; and your competitive analysis. All these factors provide evidence for the opportunity you are identifying and forecast you are making.
- Your company's differentiation and marketing mix strengths and weaknesses (see Chapter 3); and marketing options and strategy (see Chapters 8 and 9), to explain the course you have chosen.
- Your marketing objectives, following from your unit mission and SWOT analyses (see Chapter 7).
- The detailed marketing strategy, marketing plan and sales forecast (see below in this chapter).

Throughout this book, we have been emphasising that your unit marketing plan should seek to focus on specific customer segments and demonstrate as far as possible the differentiation of your product or service from competitive offerings.

Marketing strategies for growth

Harvard Professor Michael Porter has described the three basic marketing strategies for growth as overall cost leadership, differentiation and focus (Porter, 1981).

Overall cost leadership

Where markets are large, requiring large-scale capital investment (eg airlines, and in industries such as iron and steel) producing economies of scale from long runs, the winning marketing strategy is frequently to be the most efficient, lowest-cost producer. Tight control, with low margins, creates effective barriers to new entrants and prevents creation of substitutes. Amstrad, for example, is a typical low-cost producer (sourcing computer products from third world countries) and has built a significant market and market share by low pricing.

This is a dangerous marketing strategy, however, for new, small and growing entrants to pursue. Many dot.com start-ups in the late-1990s sought to benefit from the apparent economies available by using Internet technology and concentrated on aggressive pricing to gain market share. Low margins provide little room for manoeuvre when things go awry, as Boo.com found when 30 per cent 'returns' of product (often normal for mail order firms) were not anticipated.

Lack of adequate margins makes funding of growth particularly difficult. It is a characteristic of mature industries where one or two major corporations hold dominant market share (eg Pilkington and St Gobain in glass). This may be seen therefore as a marketing strategy, primarily for world class competitors and matching resources!

Differentiation

By imaginative design, good image, developed networks and high margins, companies able to demonstrably differentiate their goods or services are also able to build brand loyalty by their demonstrated uniqueness. Recent business school studies have noted that in the strongly advertised mineral water market, the manufacturers' brands enjoyed a 22 per cent premium over the own-labels. Evian, the brand leader, had a 19 per cent share against the combined 26 per cent of the own labels. In the less advertised fruit-juice market, some own-labels were dearer than manufacturers' brands!

Companies which complain that in their commodity-like industry it is impossible to create differentiation and get good prices should stop and reflect on the achievements of Perrier with water (surely the most basic commodity business of all!) and Everest with double glazing.

The England rugby team

Clive Woodward, the England rugby coach, has been quietly working to create a 'winning environment' for his product – the England team. Simple actions such as putting players' names on their England jerseys, individual name plaques in the Twickenham changing room, providing each player with laptop computers (from BT) to foster closer communication by e-mail for players when away with their clubs, all aimed to 'differentiate' and provide a better performance from the England team!

Focus

By focusing on one target market at a time, building product differentiation and good margins, focused companies are able to build barriers to entry, frequently in narrow markets unattractive to major competitors (for example Autoglass in the small UK windscreen replacement business). They can do this by creating high switching costs for customers or by erecting distribution barriers. Several examples of well focused companies have emerged in the UK in recent years:

Rohan

Rohan clothing, a UK equivalent to Patagonia in the United States, was developed by founder Paul Howcroft as a provider of lightweight clothing for climbing clubs in the Yorkshire Dales. Supplied by mail order to similar clubs throughout the UK, the light-weight trousers in particular were quickly seen as a boon to travellers, the next target market. With long-lasting zips and ample pockets and attractive design, Rohan's clothing subsequently began to appeal to the fashion-conscious leisure market which led to the opening of retail stores in Covent Garden and Kensington. As a successful, specialist retailer, the company was subsequently acquired by the Clark Shoe and Fashion Group, allowing Howcroft to devote more time to his passion for car rallying!

Ascot Drummond

Cranfield MBAs Humphrey Drummond and Ali Hakeem have used Internet technology to provide an accounting and record keeping service for small businesses. Nearly 500 customers, mostly independent IT consultants, send all their invoices and receipts to Humphrey's London office, where they are scanned in and sent to Ali's tax team in Pakistan. Completed accounts and records are maintained and returned via the Internet. AscotDrummond.co.uk, having proved the system and recently raised £6 million in venture capital, is now seeking further market segments to expand beyond its IT consultants' focus.

While Michael Porter has noted: 'there is no formula for achieving competitive advantage, only approaches that are tailored to individual companies', you can see from the above why the growing business should concentrate on trying to achieve differentiation and customer focus – world class domination by overall cost leadership is for later. Porter added: 'the acid test of strategy is also about what you are not going to do! You can't do everything: you can't offer all features to all men! But you must decide the trade-offs and show how you are unique' (Porter, 1981).

'The five Ps'

In the marketing plan, you should endeavour to follow best practice to maximise your competitive advantage in each of the following key areas: product, price, promotion, place and people ('the five Ps').

Product

We have seen that all products have service elements and vice versa, and in consequence achieving differentiation entails an endless battle or trade-off against cost, quality and service level. In this battle you have to seek improvements along two or even all three dimensions, simultaneously! In the 1960s, British manufacturers, particularly in the automobile industry, appeared to have neglected the quality dimension, in largely the mistaken belief that 'dynamic obsolescence' (the marketing flavour at the moment) was almost good for that industry. The Japanese car manufacturers, in changing their product image within 30 years from 'cheap and cheerful' in the 1960s to reliable and high-performance in the 1990s (proving that quality can be brought back), showed that quality need not be neglected while fighting costs and the rising service levels expected by customers.

Product quality is clearly vital for the growing company. James Koch, in developing the Boston Beer Company, noted that the biggest problem for the new and growing company was in creating in customers' minds an image of product quality. 'You can't sell a product you don't believe in, and in cold-calling the only thing standing between you and the customer's scorn is the integrity of your product' (Koch, 1988).

When looking at companies making pasta, those who believe their pasta is the freshest and best around are likely to be the long-run winners. Product differentiation is important for profits, as the matrix in Figure 3.13.1 shows.

High costs with low differentiation is clearly the box to avoid, confirming again the importance of working with and controlling suppliers' costs, seeking

Differentiation

	Low	High
Low	**OK** eg Pilkington Glass	**Superb** eg Colman's Readymix
High	**Awful** eg high street computer dealers	**OK** eg Everest Double Glazing

Costs (row label spanning the two rows on the left)

Figure 3.13.1   Product differentiation

good design and image (that people buy with their eyes is as true for industrial products as for high street goods), ensuring features and benefits match customers' needs. But, above all, you must ensure that quality is not lost while you integrate these functions. Quality is not, of course, just what you do, but also how you do it, as Jan Carlson of Scandinavian Airlines noted in listing these 'moments of truth' in customer contact (Figure 3.13.2).

Customer contact point	Customer expectation	
Sales	Reliability	
Invoices	Responsiveness	What does the
Telephone, e-mail	Competence	customer think of you at each contact
Reception	Courtesy	point? (Each 'moment of truth'.)
Packaging	Credibility	
Delivery	Security	
	Tangibles	

Figure 3.13.2   'Moments of truth' in customer contact

So, quality is hearts and minds, attitudes and standards, and your product marketing plan must include some quality targets and indications as to how you will audit your performance. Achieving BS 5750, ISO 9000, EN 2900, might be expensive for the growing company, in terms of extra personnel and procedures, but it is now firmly on the agenda of many growth companies, particularly given the quality discipline and assurance it gives to customers, at home and abroad. While many see, for example, BS 5750 as a management control tool designed by large companies to discipline smaller suppliers, smaller growth companies must be familiar with the standards required and be able to demonstrate, via customer reference, their ability to produce the consistent quality required.

Price

Quality and price are closely linked in the minds of most customers. Concentration on good quality should provide greater flexibility in your pricing plan. Differentiation can be achieved by careful focus on the needs of different target groups of customers. Above all, attention has to be paid to the gross margins (ie the gap between sales and variable costs) on each of your product groups. As Brian Warnes has explained in his Genghis Khan guide:

> Ignoring cash and service companies like banks and supermarkets, most manufacturing companies achieving less than about 25 per cent gross margin are likely to fail sooner or later. Companies begin to achieve real strength, cash flow and financial durability once margins get over about 40 per cent. The real high fliers, like properly structured electronics companies, begin to get into their stride at over 60 per cent. (Warnes, 1984)

Many companies survive on smaller margins, but survive is perhaps all they do. Without a good margin there is no overhead room for building further differentiation by extensive promotion, research and development, or distribution experimentation. Goods have to be sold on, with the barest minimum of service, in order to survive. Yet thriving retailers, even in depressed times, concentrate on margins and different target groups of customers by using price and quality across the range:

Choc Express

Choc Express has a range of prices from its 'Fun-Box' (£12.95), through ChocoGram Standard and Super Deluxe up to Champagne and Special Edition (£49.95), all with personalised messages for interested recipients.

The pricing decision has to be revisited regularly, particularly in inflationary times; margins, like quality, must be maintained by constant attention to cost, quality and competition. Price increases should be combined with improvements in quality or service:

Rabone Tools

Rabone Tools commissioned a new corporate design for its wide range of handheld tools. Featuring a single logo, distinctive colour schemes for product groupings, and highlighting new product features, permitted the company to relaunch its existing product range with a 5 per cent price increase, leading to a 60 per cent increase in profits.

Promotion

Advertising (including PR) is a major way for companies to differentiate and focus their activities. In many ways this must be true, if you compare one mineral water with another, or if you try to choose among comparable double-glazing systems; you may choose Perrier and Everest through the sheer weight and differentiation achieved by their distinctive advertising, which their good gross margins permit!

Your promotion plan is in many ways a mini marketing plan. If, as what we have seen suggests, advertising is simply 'an expensive way for one person to talk to another' then, as such, it must be rigorously controlled. Thus, procedures to follow include those recommended by Tim Bell, formerly of Saatchi and Saatchi:

- Set specific campaign objectives (building sales, market share).
- Decide your strategy (budget, media choice, geographical profile).
- Target the audience (market segment, demographic profile).
- Decide the advertising content (specific product/service benefits to highlight).
- Decide execution and style (humour, hard sell?). Ask yourself, if your product/service was a car or a newspaper, which kind of car (a Rolls or a Mini), which kind of newspaper (the *Sun* or *The Times*) do you want it to be seen as?

Leaflets and brochures for exhibitions have to be written with the specific exhibition visitor in mind; press releases are written for professional editors, as Hyde and Partners, advertising agency, explain:

It is the Editor who decides to print, not you, as when you supply and pay for advertisements. You must, therefore, attract the Editor's attention, with a snappy headline
and a stimulating first paragraph. British Rail did it when their PR release entitled
their new rail-airport link at 'Gatquick'. Your release must be short, it must be
factual. It is not a 'sales message'. Print always in double space, to allow the Editor
to make changes.

Issue press releases regularly, to targeted journals and journalists, who may be
invited to product launches or premise openings; include photographs, personality and performance quotations, and write in a sunny story style! Good newspaper or trade journal coverage can provide good copy to help improve the
normally low (2.5 per cent) response rates on direct mail, if you include them in
your mailing.

Make sure your company Web site is not just an online brochure; real e-
commerce solutions allow customers to buy and sell products and services just
as they would in a traditional supply chain. Yet shopping Web sites, updated
daily, can cost 'seven figures in Year 1' (Birch, Gorbert and Schneider, 2000).
Therefore, 'ring-fence' any new e-shopping initiative so that your costs are
known and controlled and ensure at least that your existing site is well designed
(research shows that 'within 3 clicks, visitors must be captured or they will
leave'), with key terms that general search engines can latch on to, with good
banner advertising. Above all, make sure the site is well promoted, along with
your e-mail address, in all company promotional material. Remember that e-
mail is the most widely used Internet function and enables each customer to be
addressed personally, which is good for market segmentation and analysis, as
long as you remember that all e-mail queries should be answered within 24 hours
(best practice is set by Carphone Warehouse where response is within one
hour!).

Above all, monitor carefully the cost/effectiveness of each marketing
campaign undertaken, either by comparing tear-off coupon replies against the
cost of the advertisement, or ensuring customers are questioned, at the till or on
the invoice, as to how they came into contact with your company. Popular
mythology has it that only half of your advertising works, but you must try to
know which half.

Once you are more visible, through good PR, be prepared for 'negative PR'
when things go wrong!

Cobra Beer

Sales of Cobra Beer were severely dented when an article published in *Tandoori*
magazine, sponsored by but only loosely monitored by Cobra, criticised the standard
of waiter service in many of the UK's 8,000 Indian restaurants. As these restaurants

accounted for 90 per cent of Cobra sales, MD Karan Bilimoria was forced not only to suspend the magazine editor, but also to make repeated apologies through all media sources. Sales levels took nearly 12 months to recover!

When subjected to bad PR you may not want to be interviewed, but one rule suggested by news broadcasters is 'always provide a statement. Short factual statements are fine, they will be used by journalists; then you cannot be accused, in your absence, of not saying something – which always looks bad'.

Place

The distribution plan must match the other elements of the marketing mix, noted above, to maintain the differentiation and focus sought by the company. If your product is of the highest quality, with price and promotion to match, it must be available in the major quality stores. Different channels must be used to reach different customer segments, as Table 3.13.1 denotes.

Table 3.13.1   Means of reaching target groups

Company	Channel	Target Group
	Pick your own	DIY
	Farm shop	Commuters/trippers
Market	Mail order/Web site	Specialist interest/Web surfers
gardeners	Specialist shop	Groups (eg health, vegetarian etc)
	Wholesale/retailer	Diverse socioeconomic groups
	Restaurants	Variety of income groups
	Health farms	Health/high income group

The choice of distribution channel, therefore, can make an important contribution to both your company differentiation and to reaching your target group of customers. The chosen channel must be consistent with the differentiation/focus chosen for the company. Distinctive distribution skills can build new customers, eg Federal Express's ability to trace and track packages attracted new customers. Similarly, motor accessory suppliers able to supply parts 'just in time' (JIT) were able to win new business. Remember also, if you are investing in 'safe' property to protect your distribution channel – until very recently the individual who suffered the world's biggest bankruptcy in the *Guinness Book of Records* was the 'owner' of 20,000 Freshwater flats in Central London! Property aspects of distribution are often best left to the real property specialists, particularly in this developing e-tail age!

People

The final ingredient in the marketing plan jigsaw must be quality salespeople who can consistently maintain your key marketing differentiation. It is not entirely impossible! People generally refer to work for quality companies; there are frequent reports among companies committed to quality, like Sainsbury's, of better staff morale, job satisfaction and even admiration of leadership (compared with surveys showing most managers are regarded by staff as being 'misleading'). Attention to maintaining good margins can ensure staff are properly rewarded; as the Relocation Services Institute has observed:

> There is probably, for example, a direct connection between the generally low estate agents' sales fees in the UK (1.5 to 2.5 per cent compared with 7 to 8 per cent in France and the United States) and the low staff performance in the UK, compared with the energetic sales support provided in the US and Continental housing market.

A well-remunerated and motivated staff will act as enthusiastic sales promoters of the quality company as well as being more willing to travel long distances to work and to act as the eyes and ears of the company in the competitive marketplace. None of this will come about simply by accident, as Chapter 14 will explore; but just as customers see quality companies as caring companies, meeting and responding to customer requirements, so, all other things being equal, do employees.

Key company competences

A company marketing strategy of differentiation and focus requires building key skills or 'competences' in all facets of the company's organisation; thus to achieve consistent product or service quality requires continuous employee training plus expertise in buying and managing the supply chain. As we have seen, expertise in distribution skills can help develop new customer segments for the company; equally a sale is not a sale until it is paid for! Thus competence in financial and management control can help accelerate company growth.

Autoglass, while achieving growth through clear focus on meeting insurance company needs, developed a major competence in windscreen and side window computerised stock control and distribution. Consistent use of County Court small-claims departments also impacted in a major way on debtor control. As a result, despite rapid growth, working capital tied up in stock and debtors did not increase in the most recent five years' growth of the company.

Thus, with key competences developing in all aspects of company operations and with all the above 'five Ps' consistently in place in the marketing plan, the basis is set to construct an operations (or people) plan and a financial plan to match the marketing strategy proposed. The natural link with these important activities is the sales forecast.

Sales forecast and control

The sales forecast should be the natural outcome and quantification of the marketing planning. It should reflect:

- The known industry or market segment growth rates. If your growth is to be faster than the industry average growth rate, say 5 per cent versus 3 per cent for your industry sector as a whole, your sales forecast should reflect how you intend to achieve this (perhaps through investment or extra promotional support).
- Estimated own and competitive market shares (with explanations as to why your market share is to increase at the expense of competitors).
- Your own targeted and costed plans to increase market share (for example, new depot openings will add 2 per cent market share).

Comparisons should then be made between the above and the short-term forecasts of your sales team, based on known customer contacts.

Inevitably the smaller, growing business cannot always achieve total levels of precision in all of the above areas; particular attention must be given to making best estimates, nonetheless, and learning from experience.

Autoglass

In making growth plans, the directors of Autoglass were hampered by lack of market information. Through discussions with leading windscreen suppliers it was possible to guess the total size of the UK windscreen replacement market. This was compared with the known average windscreen breakage rate (3.5 per cent per annum) applied to the total car population (17 million) to corroborate market size. The average car population was rowing at 3 per cent per annum, so forecasts of the future replacement market could be made; own unit sales indicated Autoglass market share, and forecasts could be tied to a programme of new depot openings and market growth.

Attention must also be given to:

- known industry production and distribution capacity, with the effect of planned additions or deletions;
- the impact of seasonality and the effect of economic trends on your business;
- your promotional expenditures – timing them so that they relate to planned sales increases and monitoring their impact closely.

The Millennium Dome

How could the forecast of 12 million visitors to the Millennium Dome have been so inaccurate? The MD drafted in, Pierre-Yves Gerbeau, explained that he thought it had been based on costs. The question asked was, 'How many visitors do we need to balance the books?' The answer, 12 million, became a forecast! Gerbeau thought that a total of 6 million would be achieved, although he was hampered by a promotional budget of 2 per cent of the turnover, compared with 8–12 per cent in the entertainment industry generally.

Some companies produce both optimistic and pessimistic forecasts and steer a middle course; conservatism is always recommended, particularly where new products are involved, especially because, as a rule, less than 20 per cent of your first customers will become repeat clients. Sometimes even the past can be a poor guide to the immediate future:

Coldshield Windows, as one of the first national double-glazing companies, grew at annual interest rates of between 25 and 30 per cent throughout the early 1970s, benefiting from customer concern with the first oil price rise and the rapid spread of central heating. Attempts were made to correlate the percentage of homes with central heating (60 per cent by 1979) and the low percentage of homes with double glazing (under 10 per cent in 1979), to show that growth could continue at these rates throughout the early 1980s. Depot expansion plans were developed and promotional expenditure committed on this basis. The sharp economic downturn of 1980–82 halted market growth completely, and only the more conservatively planned double-glazing companies remained in the black!

So, do not let the natural optimism of the sales team outweigh the careful reasoning and logic of the marketing plan, or ignore the economic cycle (as mentioned earlier, check the second issue of *The Economist* each month, which summarises economic forecasts 18 months ahead for all major European countries). Ensure that your control system regularly monitors the effectiveness of your marketing efforts, regularly recording, for example, the cost of promotional sales leads, or sales per sales person, to give some early indication of market maturity or turn-down. Continuing the Coldshield example:

Recording promotional expenditure per sales lead was introduced in 1980 and showed an average cost of £40 per direct newspaper lead; this compared with under £10 cost per sales lead for Wallguard's new company in France. The disparity emphasised the growth of UK competition in double glazing as well as the maturity of the market, and this showed in static sales figures.

Armed with a sensible marketing plan and a conservative sales forecast, you are now able to develop your matching operations (people) and financial plan.

Assignment 19

Prepare your marketing plan

1. Summarise your unit mission statement.
2. What has been your average percentage industry/market growth rate in the last three to five years, and what is your current market share percentage compared with main competitors?
3. What SWOT conclusions have most relevance for your marketing plan (strengths to build on, weaknesses to repair), what strategic role is your unit performing (invest/disinvest), what opportunities are there for you to increase productivity, improve sales volume in your business?
4. How will your company be different from your competition in terms of product, price, promotion, distribution and selling methods?
5. What distinctive competences/skills has your company developed to keep it ahead in the future?

14 *The people plan*

Where people fit into the business plan

If the business plan describes the journey you intend to make, the people plan explains how you will get your team on board to turn intention into reality. A vital part of your business plan will be the power of the executive summary, in which a description of the management team and the company's culture and history will be essential to the 'feel' of what you're trying to do.

Equally important will be the evidence that you have assessed and are using current organisation capability as fully as possible. At the same time you need to spell out in detail the management and staffing strategies which will be needed for future growth: numbers, skills mix, and how you will recruit, retain and reward.

You may have carried out the most sophisticated environmental scan, financial forecasts and marketing SWOTs, but if you haven't put in place the organisation and people to make it happen, then you haven't got a business plan. Organisation is strategy. To be a superb strategist you need both environmental responsiveness and flexible organisation resource. This chapter aims to help you plan to get resource in place. None of it comes about by accident, and unfortunately every source of people resource (recruitment, training, re-skilling) tends to take a lot of money, effort and most important, time, to get in place.

Your people objectives

Where you put your people is the direction in which your business will move. In carrying out earlier work of organisational diagnosis, you have assessed your people, structure and systems, the potential fits and misfits with your plans for growth and the key items on your organisational agenda for change. Life in the e-world will affect every aspect of your people planning, from getting a dedication to customer service through to orchestrating an integrated customer response from departments who have long been in conflict. It will mean being able to put flexible project teams together around customer needs and empowering your employees to give the best possible levels of service.

Joseph A Hey and Son

Take the Web site www.funeralassist.co.uk – a business-to-business Web site launched by funeral directors Joseph A Hey and Son. MD Robert Morphet, in an interview with the *Director* magazine in spring 2000 describes how 'funerals and monumental masonry are probably the least likely business sector to come to mind when considering e-business. We provide the ultimate crisis purchase and we are by our very nature a most conservative industry'. This has not stopped him launching a Web site to bring together every aspect of bereavement, and invite every funeral director and heads of associated trades to join. Here is a 100-year-old business challenging every aspect of its organisation, and breaking away from 'the constraints that restrain the majority of business today'. These constraints include short-term vision, lack of imagination, a refusal to consider anything other than what has gone before, and most of all the inability to trust and empower staff.

What are the organisational levers that you will need to pull to achieve change? Are they primarily to do with people, or process, or changing your structure? Your people objectives are likely to include some, or all, of the following:

- recruiting new skills;
- developing the management team;
- building your company culture and identity;
- reviewing 'people systems' such as appraisal, career planning, selection processes;
- rewarding your people;
- setting up processes for communication and coordination as the organisation grows;
- changing the organisation structure.

Key elements of the people plan

Having decided your primary people objectives, you are in an excellent position to outline the initiatives you intend to take to turn a paper business plan into an organisational reality. The following elements will be key:

- vision and values;

- recruitment and selection;
- retaining and motivating staff;
- appraisal;
- recognition and rewards;
- roles and responsibilities;
- communication and team building;
- a training and development plan.

Vision and values

Your business plan needs to excite both your management team, who will make your money for you, and the potential backers who will give you more. No one wants to put their life or their money into a business that's as boring as Scunthorpe on a rainy day. A mission statement is vital evidence of a clear focus, but it is a passionate and inspirational vision of what's special about you and your company philosophy that will bring in the punters. The product branding which you sell to customers is nothing without the 'internal' branding. The executive summary of the business plan is the perfect opportunity for flaunting your company vision and showing how every aspect of your organisation supports it. For example, if your vision is about customer excellence, then is this obsession with the customer reflected in everything you do? – Is it the first item on every board meeting? Do senior managers spend a lot of time in front of customers? Do you have processes for customer feedback?

Recruitment and selection process

Recruitment is perhaps the biggest worry for growing businesses. Increasingly there are worrying skills shortages which will affect your ability to recruit, particularly in the IT sector. People are choosy and you will need to sell them on your business vision, values and ethos. Your Web site can be a potent vehicle in helping here. A Cranfield survey has identified the problems of small businesses (see Table 3.14.1).

Table 3.14.1   The key problems of small businesses

Key priorities	Percentage of respondents
Recruiting key staff	83
Finding customers	59
Raising new finance	31
High interest rates	27
Red tape	21

Source: Cranfield Working Papers, 1992

Getting the right people is difficult, time-consuming and expensive. Getting it wrong is even more expensive and can be extremely painful. Few growing businesses can claim not to have fallen into this trap. However, you can increase the odds on success by putting in place some basic process and discipline which is likely to include:

- Deciding on the numbers and skills mix you are going to need over the next one to three years.
- Preparing job descriptions as a guide to recruitment, covering job title and purpose, to whom responsible, for whom, limits of authority and main tasks.
- Preparing a person specification, outlining the sort of person you think is likely to be effective in the job. (The seven-point plan covers physical make-up, attainments, general intelligence, special aptitudes, interests, disposition, and circumstances.)
- Sourcing your requirements creatively, through networks of contacts, employment and search agencies, newspaper advertisements, hotel wine evenings etc.
- Weeding out from application forms or CVs those who don't fit the job description and person specification.
- Using psychometric tests to supplement your interview process. A huge range of tests covering aptitude or ability is available; tests of general intelligence, tests of attainment, personality inventories. You can locate the appropriate test for your business through the British Psychological Society (0116 254 9568) or the Chartered Institute of Personnel Development (020 8971 9000).

Retaining and motivating staff

Having got the right people to implement your strategy, the problem is to keep them. In a service business, all you have is your people, and demotivated people will walk. We all live with the expectations not of our own generation, but our children's and they care about different things, and will be motivated by different things. In a knowledge economy, more workers have choice over where they work; some of them may not even be on your firm's headcount. How do you motivate people who are not your employees? How do you make them feel that they belong? If morale and levels of job satisfaction are low, then performance will suffer, the team will be affected and often people (usually those you want to keep!) will leave. 'Holcot Press is a service business', Richard Meredith says, and 'keeping people and good morale is crucial to our business'.

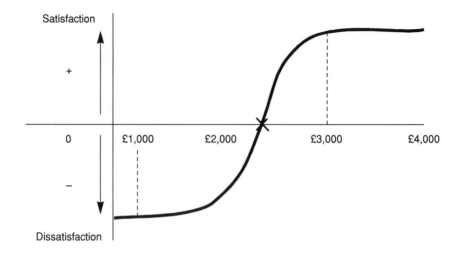

Figure 3.14.1 The effect of a salary increase on job satisfaction

One of the biggest mistakes you can make is to assume that money alone is the way to motivate staff. See Figure 3.14.1, which provides a graphic example of how minor is the motivating effect of a salary increase by itself.

In fact, it's not so much the amount of money awarded that is important – expectation is all. The 'S' shaped curve shows that the effect of a salary increase on job satisfaction and therefore performance depends on what you expected. Thus, if you expected a salary increase of £2,000 and this is what you got, then the effect is zero. If you expected an increase of £2,000 and were given £3,000, then your job satisfaction will increase. You will have a warm glow but the feeling soon tails off. Similarly, if you expect £2,000 and are given £1,000, you will be actively demotivated.

Maslow's famous hierarchy of needs shows just how many other factors are involved in job satisfaction, from physiological, through security and social needs to the needs for self-esteem and self-actualisation. In fact, the problem isn't so much that of motivating people, but of avoiding demotivating them! If managers can keep off the backs of employees, it is quite possible that they will motivate themselves. After all, as Herzberg established years ago in his interviews at Pittsburgh Iron and Steel, most of us want the same things: a sense of achievement or challenge, recognition of our efforts, an interesting and varied job, opportunities for responsibility, advancement and job growth.

You can gain a lot of mileage by arranging the context of work so that people can find more motivators in the jobs they do. You will also keep them longer and they will be more likely to empower the business change you are seeking.

Question	Rating 0...5...10	Comment
1. How would you assess your morale right now? Please explain why.		
2. What action would help to move your score up and increase your job satisfaction?	_Comment only_	
3. How well does the management team manage?		
4 How effective are our internal communications up, down and across? What improvements would you suggest?		
5. How clear are you about what is expected of you (targets, etc)?		
6. How adequately are you rewarded and recognised for good performance?		
7. How well does the appraisal process work? Any recommendations?		
8. How fully are we using all your talents? How could we do better?		
9. What do you most like about working for this business? (What's special about us?)	_Comment only_	
10. To what extent do you feel part of the total team? How could we involve you more?		

Figure 3.14.2 Some ideas on a simple attitude survey (to use as an annual benchmark)

To benchmark the morale of your people, carry out these key activities:

● monitor labour turnover regularly;
● carry out exit interviews;
● survey levels of job satisfaction.

Attrition rates need to be assessed against industry or regional norms.

Braxxon

Braxxon, a technology consulting company to the City, was concerned to see its labour turnover rising above its 10 per cent per annum measure. To make sense, this figure needed to be looked at in the context of London norms, other consultancy retention rates, and also the volatile and seductive financial sector of the square mile. Braxxon concluded that less than 10 per cent attrition was desirable but ambitious, but more than 20 per cent was unacceptable and would flag a morale issue.

When anyone leaves, it is a good idea to get a reliable and trusted member of staff to carry out an exit interview. In this way you can discover the real reasons why people are leaving and identify sources of internal dissatisfaction. If every one or two years you carry out a simple internal survey of staff attitudes, you will be able to pinpoint problem areas in the parts of your business which you can't reach (see Figure 3.14.2 for a sample survey questionnaire). Even a simple 0–10 scale will give valuable information. For example, Holcot Press management team defined their morale and the morale of those under them on a simple scale, reproduced in Figure 3.14.3. The difference in rating indicates the work they had to do in 1990 to bring the motivation of all employees up to the level of the management team.

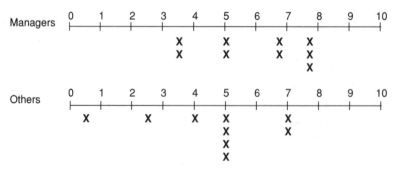

Figure 3.14.3 The morale of Holcot Press management team and their subordinates

Appraisal

Appraisal lies at the heart of assessing, improving and developing people's performance for the future of the business. However, to be an effective tool, appraisal needs to be approached seriously and professionally by all involved. It must start to appraise people against the new competences needed in the e-world. Increasingly we will need to appraise people against their 'soft' skills, for example their ability to communicate with colleagues, live the vision, empower and coach their people. It is no longer possible in most organisations for individuals to do their own thing without regard to others in the delivery process. This will mean that the appraisal process expands beyond the traditional boss to subordinate one on one, to encompass the feedback of peers and employees and also to give feedback to bosses.

Innovex

Take Innovex (now part of the Quintiles Group): in the early 1990s, it began to create more sophisticated processes in anticipation of significant growth through merger and acquisition. At the time, Innovex had a fairly half-hearted appraisal system. Not all managers carried out appraisals, some interviews took only half an hour or so, assessment of areas for improvement was distinctly lacking, there were no clear objectives, people were assessed against personality characteristics (such as 'common sense') rather than results. Yet the great issue for Innovex was the lack of depth of management resource. This could easily become a limitation on its phenomenal growth plans. There were no obvious successors to the top players, and managers were already 100 per cent stretched in their current jobs. The requirement was to grow people capable of running businesses in the UK and Europe. There were significant gaps between the management 'animal' of the current business and the one Innovex would need for the future. As Barrie Haigh said, 'The key is to look hard at our people, look hard and develop'. He recognised that the mechanism for doing this was appraisal.

Innovex then put all its managers and secretaries through appraisal interview training (using video), took a good look at its appraisal system and revamped it to try to make the appraisal interview:

- A 'talk between people who work together'.
- An open two-way discussion, which both appraiser and appraisee prepare for in advance and which is expected to take around one and a half hours on average.
- Results-orientated rather than personality-orientated. The appraisal interview will start with a review against objectives and finish by setting objectives for the year to come.
- A process kept separate from salary review.
- A process that starts with performance and only later moves on to reviewing potential.

- A narrative rather than an exercise with tick boxes and ratings, covering discussion of achievements, areas for improvement, overall performance, training and development and career expectations.
- An activity carried out at least once a year, with more regular quarterly reviews.
- An opportunity to identify training needs and act upon them.

Recognition and rewards

As a business grows it is common to find that rewards are encouraging the performance needed in the past rather than the performance needed now. Different stages of growth demand different reward packages, from the hands-on commission-based, sales-linked rewards of a Phase 1 business, through the cost and budget management of Phase 2, into the challenges of giving the whole management team a share of the future which comes in Phase 3.

As the business grows up the Greiner curve (see Greiner, 1972) it is likely that the recognition and reward package will need to be slanted to:

- encourage genuine 'ownership' of and commitment to the business;
- provide some element of reward for team performance as well as individual success;
- demonstrate a direct relationship to performance.

Roles and responsibilities

Although managers, and certainly consultants, are often over-enthusiastic in pulling the lever for change that is marked 'structure', you will need to consider whether the current structure of your business is a constraint on growth. For example, if you have a traditional, functional, hierarchical structure with lots of layers of management, it is very likely that it will preclude you from exploiting new market opportunities. Unfortunately, restructuring means more than just rewriting the 'organisation chart' of today. It means getting people to behave in new ways. The dedication to customer service that is demanded in e-commrce means that the old functional divisions, for example between sales and production, must be broken down and employees enabled to work in a coordinated fashion with their colleagues. Aligning the whole organisation with its customers requires new roles and new skills. Far more employees than before will be in touch with customers, at some stage in the delivery process. They all need to be immersed in the corporate vision, informed about the customer base, and empowered to act. They will need interpersonal skills to form effective relationships externally and internally, they will need to be able to contribute to temporary project teams, and not be threatened when these teams dissolve. Some employees will have to learn the subtleties required in handling cross-cultural relationships, for example, how to handle the requirements of a German or an Algerian client from a UK Web site.

If you want to get people to behave differently, rather than telling them to do so, it's usually much more effective to give them different things to do. This is why realigning individual roles and responsibilities can be a powerful force for change.

Glaxo

In writing behavioural guidelines as an outline for the working practices needed to achieve the strategic plans of the 1990s, Glaxo UK (now Glaxo SmithKline) defined five parameters represented by the acronym 'RATIO'. Two of these five principles refer specifically to realigning roles as a powerful force for change:

Role clarity – clear definition of job parameters so that each individual's contribution to outputs and objectives is understood and overlapping responsibilities are minimised.

Accountability – clear definition of responsibilities so individuals understand both their contributions to achieving business goals and the scope of their decision making.

Communications and team building

The young, entrepreneurial business needs to give little attention to its internal communication. Its people tend to be a highly motivated small team, spending a lot of time together at work and socially. As the business grows in numbers, sheer size will start to crack the foundations of its camaraderie; the introduction of new people without the original motivation will change the flavour of relationships. It is at this point that you will find yourself consciously having to introduce ways and means of getting the team together and keeping them facing the right way. Involving your team in the preparation and presentation of the business plan can, in itself, be a good way of enabling motivation and coordination.

In addition you will probably have to start putting in processes to address what happened quite naturally in Phase 1 growth. It's amazing how many business-people expect a group to work as a team without any practice. After all it (presumably!) doesn't work this way for football teams. The way to build a team is to find many formal and informal ways of bringing them together: cascade briefings, state of the nation addresses, lunches, social events, special project teams, happy hours. Fun is actually quite compatible with profit. The importance of informal contact between people, as a way of building productive networks, cannot be over-emphasised, but it won't happen without the mechanisms to make it happen.

It's absolutely clear that the more you are trying to grow and change the business, the more you will have to communicate. Briefing groups are an excellent discipline for downward communication but there's a lot more to it than that. You need processes to ensure upward communication and especially to coordinate across the barriers that your organisation will establish as it grows. There are plenty of examples to help here and plenty of ways of building your team: for example, outward bound programmes, internal team-building events – giving everyone the same language.

The Belbin team profiles, for example, are particularly useful as a way of identifying individuals' preferred team roles, accepting that difference is essential to effective teamworking and learning to live with each other. Belbin suggests that successful teams need a mix of roles (see Figure 3.14.4). For more information, visit www.belbin.com.

Training and development plan

It is inevitable as the business grows that through no fault of their own, people's knowledge and skills, which were once adequate, become inappropriate for the next phase of growth. One option is to get rid of people with obsolete skills and bring in new ones. But this is expensive, time-consuming and very disruptive to team identity and culture. Clearly a preferable option is to keep training and developing your existing people resource (see Figure 3.14.5). Sometimes people have a good knowledge base, but the wrong attitude: this is a motivation issue. Sometimes they are willing but inexperienced: this is a training issue; and sometimes they are both negative in their attitude and unskilled, in which case why keep them?

Even those who have been recruited with the skills they need, require training to do things your way, which may not be the way they have been taught in the past. Figure 3.14.6 is a typical training 'menu' resulting from a training needs analysis within a small publishing business.

Unfortunately, when asked what training they need, most people find it difficult to answer. It is therefore essential to spend time identifying training needs for your team, for each key individual and also for yourself. Training needs are the gap between performance now and the performance you would like in the future. Perhaps you have historically employed managers with a sales background, whereas what you need for the future are strong all-round businessmen who can run bits of a growing business. The appraisal interview provides one good opportunity for identifying training needs; another approach is to carry out a training needs analysis. This analysis depends on interviewing members of staff to determine key issues such as their background, role, skills needed in the job, strengths and weaknesses, and career aspirations. A good survey will also include a discussion of changing business requirements and the gap between these demands and present capability.

Chair/team leader	**Company worker**
Stable, dominant, extrovert	Stable, controlled
Concentrates on objectives	Practical organiser
Does not originate ideas	Can be inflexible but likely to adapt to
Focuses people on what they do best	established systems
Plant	**Monitor evaluator**
Dominant, high IQ, introvert	High IQ, stable, introvert
A 'scatter of seeds', originates ideas	Measured analysis not innovation
Misses out on detail	Unambitious and lacking enthusiasm
Thrustful but easily offended	Solid, dependable
Resource investigator	**Team worker**
Stable, dominant, extrovert	Stable, extrovert, low dominance
Sociable	Concerned with individuals' needs
Contacts with outside world	Builds on others' ideas
Salesperson/diplomat/liaison officer	Cools things down
Not original thinker	
Shaper	**Finisher**
Anxious, dominant, extrovert	Anxious, introvert
Emotional, impulsive	Worries over what will go wrong
Quick to challenge and respond to challenge	Permanent sense of urgency
Unites ideas, objectives and possibilities	Preoccupied with order
Competitive	Concerned with 'following through'
Intolerant of woolliness and vagueness	

Figure 3.14.4   Belbin's team profile

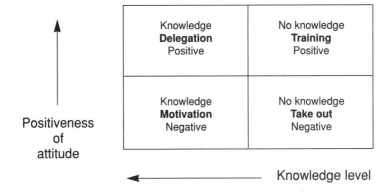

Figure 3.14.5   The role of training

Technical/Job related	• Accounting or sales skills • Negotiation skills • Computer skills
Management skills (existing and potential managers)	• Leadership and motivation • Teambuilding • Appraising, counselling and disciplinary interviews • Managing change • Recruitment and selection • Training and developing staff
Business	• Basic finance • Principles of marketing • Putting together the business plan • Understanding strategy

Figure 3.14.6 An example of a training menu

Whilst some training needs are certainly to do with learning new skills, much will be to do with changing attitudes and mindsets to cope with a global world of massive customer expectation, continuous technological change, team performance and total uncertainty about the future.

The former Training and Enterprise Councils, now called Learning Skills Councils, may be able to help you in training development. Please consult their Web site: www.lsc.gov.uk.

Checklist: minimum requirements for people systems

Recruitment and selection:

- job descriptions for all roles;
- person specifications;
- an application form;
- an advertising/sourcing procedure.

Retaining and motivating (including staff appraisal):

- monitoring annual labour turnover;
- exit interviews;
- annual survey of staff attitudes (you can do it yourself);
- appraisal interviews – once a year at least – an opportunity for two-way discussion available to all staff;
- appraisal format covering objectives, performance, training needs and review of potential.

Reward:

- a pay system which distinguishes good performers from poor performers (and rewards the behaviour you want!);
- a pay system comparable with the going rate in the market place;
- recognition of team performance (at a local and/or corporate level);
- 'Little, immediate and often' reward and recognition.

Training and development plan:

- a training plan that specifies the needs of the total team;
- training-needs analysis of key individuals' strengths, weaknesses and requirements (appraisal will help);
- a self-development plan for you.

Communications:

- a monthly management meeting;
- twice-yearly 'state of the nation' talks when you bring everyone together to put across the realities of the business and its performance;
- a cascade system for briefing downwards (the Industrial Society will advise);
- informal/social/cross-functional meetings (ie weekly happy hour, peanut party or lunches).

Assignment 20

Putting the people plan in place

Prepare a people plan for your business based on:

1. Your vision (see Assignment 18).
2. Key people objectives (developed from your agenda for change, Assignment 12 – the structure, people or systems levers you need to pull).
3. The people plan.

Topic	Action	Who will do what by when?
Recruitment and selection (Getting the right people)		
Retaining and motivating (Keeping them)		
Appraisal (Assessing them)		
Recognition and rewards (Rewarding them)		
Communication and team-building (Team involvement)		
Roles and responsibilities (Structure change)		

Figure 3.14.7 Sample people plan

15 *Managing change*

Managing change effectively is intrinsic to the business plan. Only if your business plan uses existing resources to the full and only if it gains the commitment of those who have to implement it will it become a reality. When examining the present state capability in Assignment 12 you will have already identified items on your organisational agenda for change. The question this chapter addresses is how best to manage people through the transition state in order to achieve the future state of your business plan.

Change is no longer a matter of gradual and cosy adaptation. Nor is it a matter of planning for a particular change, and then expecting a period of consolidation. There are no stable states any more; the pace of technology change has forced us all to live in a world where the only constant is radical change. Figure 3.15.1 shows the constant process of change in a business.

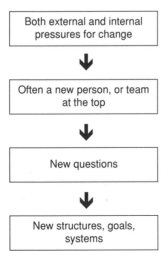

Figure 3.15.1   Ongoing changes in a business

Change hurts

Change is an unavoidable fact of life. The pace of change is accelerating without periods of remission. Yet the paradox is that whilst we all have to change, fast and constantly, most of us don't like change, and will resist it as far as we can. We have only to observe people in a meeting or the staff canteen or relaxing in the pub to know that the human being is a creature of habit, who likes familiar patterns: the same bar stool, the same group of friends to talk to over lunch. We like things to stay the same. By definition change means the unknown; it's risky, uncertain and worrying, and that applies to organisational change just as much as to personal changes such as divorce.

ICL

In 1983 ICL (now ICL/Fujitsu) was rescued from the brink of disaster by a combined City and government deal. Sir Michael Edwardes was put in as the new man at the top. Of his earlier experience in British Leyland he had written: 'It is easier to lead a defence of the status quo than to lead people into something new with all the attendant uncertainties and the innate fear of the unknown which change implies'.

Thus, even while Robb Wilmot, then MD, was announcing that 'every part of our business has changed, is changing and will continue to change', people within ICL perceived change as a temporary and unnecessary disruption of the status quo. They believed that once management got it 'right', change would go away and their lives could get back to normal. They didn't really want to see how inevitable change was for ICL's survival – the costs were too great.

Of course, change has productivity costs, but change also costs emotionally – it hurts. Here are some comments from ICL from the 1983–84 period:

Fear: '[I] don't think the company realise how frightened people are.'
Loss: '[We see] teams broken, relationships broken, lack of commitment to keeping our unit.'
Discomfort: 'We feel very battered.'
Stress (causing personal overloads): 'In the past we worked hard and played hard, and people laughed – they don't any more.'

Individual resistance to change shouldn't be a surprise, it's the normal reaction. Resistance stems from:

- fear of the unknown;
- lack of information;
- threats to status;
- threats to established skills and competences;
- fear of failure;

- reluctance to let go;
- lack of perceived benefits;
- threats to the power base;
- low trust organisational climate;
- history and previous custom;
- fear of looking stupid;
- feeling vulnerable and exposed;
- threat to self-esteem;
- loss of control of one's own destiny;
- loss of team relationships;
- high anxiety;
- stress.

The predictable process of change

Almost any major change will make things worse before it makes them better. The concept of the productivity curve means that the immediate impact of change is a decrease in productivity as people struggle with new ways of doing things, cope with their own learning curve and desperately try to 'keep the shop open'. It may be months or even years before productivity recovers let alone exceeds original levels (see Figure 3.15.2).

Unfortunately, the inevitable fall-off in production increases the likelihood that managers who have an unrealistic expectation of how long change will take to achieve, panic and pull the plug on the change just when they are about to start to see the pay-off! This phenomenon is well described by John Philipp and Sandy Dunlop, adapting an idea from Darryl Connor and depicting it as 'the long dark night of the innovator' (see Figure 3.15.3).

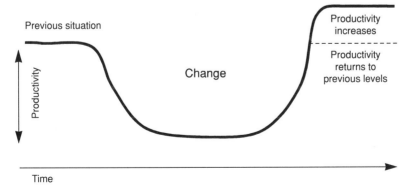

Figure 3.15.2   The productivity curve

Figure 3.15.3 A map of the organisational energy during any major transition programme

Everything looks like a failure halfway through. It takes courage to stay with the vision during this period, to persevere, to maintain enthusiasm and commitment. Here's one company that didn't make it:

ABC Retail

ABC Retail is part of a US consumer chain. It has been established in the UK for many years. It employs over 2,000 staff in the UK with almost 150 branches. After pressure from its parent company a new French chief executive was appointed. His job was to implement a vast programme of change, moving the organisation from formal traditional values towards greater delegation of authority levels and greater personal responsibility. He said it would take time. One and a half years later, the shareholders concerned about low profits, forced the new CEO out. A CEO was brought over from the United States to undo the changes made by his predecessor and to 'bring the UK operation back into the family'.

Change always takes longer than you think. For example, it is said that a major programme of attitude change in a large organisation will take five years. One or two of the big and extremely prestigious Swedish banks maintain that it has taken them the best part of 20 years to turn unwieldy organisations around to be decentralised and customer responsive. Even in a small responsive business, the temptation is to assume that change can be made to happen overnight. For example, one chief executive we know asked his consultant to devise a totally new 'culture' and to have it in place by the next board meeting.

The risk of not allowing sufficient time for the change to 'bed down' is that the embryo change plant will be pulled up and thrown on the rubbish heap, to be succeeded by yet another change and another after that – all equally likely to meet the same fate. The change process predictably takes time, costs money and effort, and causes an immediate fall-off in productivity. Perhaps by expecting this scenario, the entrepreneur can help to maintain his or her cool and ride the rapids.

In responding to a significant change, people also go through a predictable pattern of personal response. This has been described as a transition curve, showing an individual's response to change over time (see Figure 3.15.4).

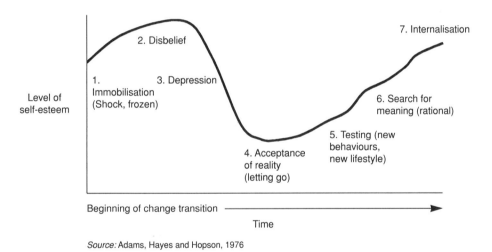

Source: Adams, Hayes and Hopson, 1976

Figure 3.15.4   Self-esteem changes during transitions

Similarly, Fink, Beak and Taddeo describe a four-stage process through which people typically pass in learning to adjust to a personal change such as bereavement or an organisational change such as a relocation, redundancy or restructuring (see Figure 3.15.5).

The most important lesson for anyone who is trying to grow a business is that change doesn't happen automatically. The way in which the CEO handles innovation and change will have a critical effect in helping people to go through the change process as rapidly and painlessly as possible. Managerial support is crucial, just as support for a grieving spouse is crucial. It's an interesting but sad fact that most people who are trying to cope with bereavement get the support

1. Shock
2. Defensive retreat
3. Acknowledgement
4. Adaptation

CHANGE

Figure 3.15.5 Typical response to significant change (organisational or individual)

from friends and family when they least need it, in the early stages of shock. When they most need encouragement, months later, most of the relatives have gone home!

Identifying and managing resistance

Like sales objections, resistance to change should be expected and even welcomed. By expressing their resistance people can convert themselves into believers and create their own momentum for change. Any organisational change will have pros and cons, it is the balance between the driving forces and the resisting forces that will determine whether change happens. This balance can even be expressed as an equation, which states that unless the weight of dissatisfaction with what you've got (A), plus the desirability of the proposed change (B), plus its practicability (D), exceeds the cost of change (X), the change won't happen (see Figure 3.15.6).

$$C = (A\ B\ D) > X$$

C	=	Change
A	=	Dissatisfaction with status quo
B	=	Desirability of proposed change
D	=	Practicability of change (minimum risk/disruption)
X	=	Cost of changing

Figure 3.15.6 Managing resistance

For example, you may see a house that you find very desirable. But unless you are pretty dissatisfied with the one you've already got (let's say it has too few bedrooms) and unless the move is practicable (it doesn't disrupt school arrangements for example) then the 'cost' of changing will outweigh the benefits and you won't do it. The same applies to organisational change. Consider the following examples.

An oil company in the United States decided to reorganise into independent oil and gas companies. The change involved relocation, causing geographic and personal dislocation for hundreds of people. Senior managers were surprised by 'significant resistance' from employees. Given the following comment from their consultants should they have been surprised by strong resistance? 'The rationale for change was obscure since the existing organisation was very profitable and displayed no obvious evidence of the need for transformation.'

Kurt Lewin's force field analysis is a useful technique for assessing the forces for and against the change in such a way that you may be able to change the balance between them (see Figure 3.15.7 on page 292). After all, if the driving forces and the resisting forces are opposite and equal, then even a non-scientist can see that no movement will take place.

In this second example the technique is applied by John Elliot, owner/founder of EBAC Ltd, to a stock control problem.

1. *What is the problem?* Poor stock control.
2. *Where are we now?* Production stoppages due to shortages but high stock levels.
3. *Where do we want to get to?* Low stock and no stoppages.
4. *What are the driving forces?* (See Figure 3.15.8 on page 293 for an example.)
5. *What are the resisting forces?* (Again, see Figure 3.15.8.)
6. *What action can we take?* We need to devise a solution, devise a detailed plan and describe as clearly as possible the system as it should be.

Interestingly, the evidence is that in handling resistance there may be greater benefit in eliminating the negative rather than accentuating the positive. Thus, rather than putting on his boxing gloves in an effort to outweigh resistance by hammering the positive benefits of change, the manager may do better to adopt a more laid-back, judo approach, allowing people to express their resistance – the Zen rather than the macho approach. It pays to resist rushing into aggressive mode and to spend some time listening and understanding. As in the ethos of the Samaritans, merely expressing a problem may help in coming to terms with it.

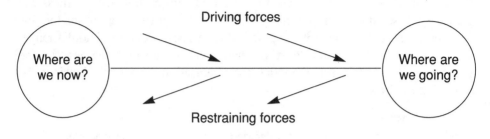

The process of force field analysis

1. What is the problem?
   (Write it down and define it in specific terms: who is involved, what is the magnitude?)

2. Where are we now?

3. Where do we want to get to? (Define the desired end result and try to make it measurable)

4. What are the things going **for** us? – Driving forces
   (List all the forces, organisational, individual, motivational, which are helping the change along)

5. What are the things going **against** us? – Restraining forces
   (List all the sources of resistance to the change)

6. What **action** can we take to maximise the driving forces and minimise the restraining forces?

Figure 3.15.7 Kurt Lewin's force field analysis

There are already some clues for the manager who is concerned with handling the inevitable resistance and increasing the odds for successful change. These include:

● involving people as early as possible in the change;

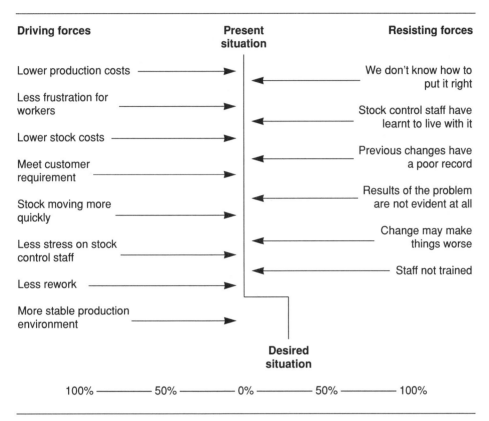

Driving forces	Present situation	Resisting forces

Lower production costs ⟶   ⟵ We don't know how to put it right

Less frustration for workers ⟶

⟵ Stock control staff have learnt to live with it

Lower stock costs ⟶

⟵ Previous changes have a poor record

Meet customer requirement ⟶

⟵ Results of the problem are not evident at all

Stock moving more quickly ⟶

⟵ Change may make things worse

Less stress on stock control staff ⟶

⟵ Staff not trained

Less rework ⟶

More stable production environment ⟶

Desired situation

100% ——— 50% ——— 0% ——— 50% ——— 100%

Figure 3.15.8 A sample force field analysis

- anticipating the impact on people – anticipating who will perceive themselves as winners and who will see themselves as losers;
- not underestimating resistance;
- identifying the key influencers;
- using coalitions and alliances to build critical mass for change;
- expecting organisational inertia.

When considering organisational inertia it is worth reminding ourselves that resistance to change isn't just an individual phenomenon. Organisations resist change too. For example, here are Rosabeth Moss Kanter's Ten Commandments (Kanter, 1985) for making sure that innovation never happens in your business!

1. Regard any new idea from below with suspicion because it's new, and it's from below.
2. Insist that people who need your approval to act first go through several other levels of management to get their signatures.

3. Ask departments or individuals to challenge and criticise each other's proposals (this saves you the job of deciding; you just pick the survivor).
4. Express your criticisms freely, and withhold your praise (this keeps people on their toes). Let people know they can be fired at any time.
5. Treat identification of problems as signs of failure, to discourage people from letting you know when something in their area isn't working.
6. Control everything carefully. Make sure people count anything that can be counted, frequently.
7. Make decisions to reorganise or change policies in secret, and spring them on people unexpectedly (this also keeps people on their toes).
8. Make sure that requests for information are fully justified, and make sure that it is not given out to managers freely (you don't want data to fall into the wrong hands).
9. Assign to lower-level managers, in the name of delegation and participation, responsibility for figuring out how to cut back, lay off, move people around, or otherwise implement threatening decisions you have made, and get them to do it quickly.
10. Above all, never forget that you, the higher-ups, already know everything important about the business.

Diagnosing readiness for change

Greiner puts particular emphasis on organisational readiness for change existing when there is both considerable external pressure for change (eg from new market or technology trends) combined with internal pressures (eg from low morale or pressure for profits). A certain entrepreneur we know has really decided that this year he will lose weight! Despite years of external pressure from his wife, his doctor and his friends to lose weight, he stayed the same. It was only when the external pressure for change was equalled by the internal pressure to maintain his image on the ski-slopes that he really changed! Similarly, the greatest organisational readiness for change exists when, for example, the external pressure from disgruntled shareholders is echoed by internal pressure, for example, from an attitude survey indicating dissatisfaction. Readiness for change is greatest where there are neither very high security levels, nor very low security levels. If people are too insecure then they tend to dig in, retrench and resist change; when they are too secure, for example some insurance companies, then it is difficult for the organisation to see the warning signal that times may be changing.

The likely commitment, or readiness for change of key individuals can also be plotted using the technique of 'commitment charting' (Beckhard and Harris,

1987). Clearly, there is a critical mass of individuals or groups whose active commitment is necessary to provide the energy for the change to occur. Before this time, the change leaders may find they have few friends; afterwards everyone climbs aboard. The steps in developing a commitment plan are:

1. Identify target individuals or groups whose commitment is needed.
2. Define the critical mass needed to make change happen.
3. Develop a plan for gaining commitment of the critical mass.
4. Monitor progress.

Commitment charting will help you to form a diagnosis and an action strategy for the key players you need to gain critical mass. The technique works on the assumption that for each key player it is necessary to gain some degree of personal commitment or the change won't happen. To make a commitment chart, list all the members or groups who are part of the critical mass on the vertical axis of the chart. Then consider the degree of commitment you must have from each (see Figure 3.15.10, page 296). Possibilities are that key players have:

- no commitment;
- enough to let it happen;
- enough to help it happen;
- enough to make it happen.

In Figure 3.15.10, the 0 indicates the minimum commitment you need, the X indicates where you think that person's commitment is at the moment. When the 0 and the X are in the same box, breathe a deep sigh of relief; where they are not draw an arrow connecting the two – this will give you a map of the work to be done.

Bruce Elliot, when he ran Elliot Brothers, used commitment charting as a way of looking at whether he had the momentum within his team to move the company culture nearer towards 'growth through delegation'. His force field analysis is shown in Figure 3.15.9, page 296. We have already looked at his commitment chart – Figure 3.15.10.

These pose some interesting issues for Bruce. Should he back off from trying to drive the change through? How to increase the 'buy in' of two key members of the team, how to persuade Chris not to be too enthusiastic?

Unfortunately, managing people through organisational change isn't a straightforward step-by-step process. It's messy and it involves doing lots of things at the same time. The change star model (Figure 3.15.11) has proved a useful framework to help get people through the change process as quickly and painlessly as possible.

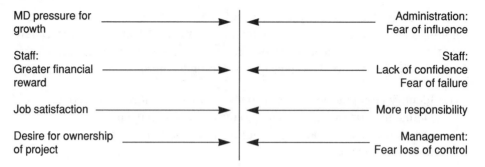

MD pressure for growth	→ ←	Administration: Fear of influence
Staff: Greater financial reward	→ ←	Staff: Lack of confidence Fear of failure
Job satisfaction	→ ←	More responsibility
Desire for ownership of project	→ ←	Management: Fear loss of control

Figure 3.15.9 Elliot Brothers' force field analysis: growth through delegation retaining existing strengths

Key players	No commitment	Let it happen	Help it happen	Make it happen
Bruce			0 ←	X
Guy	X →	0		
Stewart	X →		0	
Andrew	X →		0	
Julie		X →	0	
Chris		0 ←		X
Steven		0 ←	X	
Stuart		(X 0)		
David	X →		0	

Figure 3.15.10 Elliot Brothers' commitment chart

It starts from the belief that if an entrepreneur has to make an assumption about how people react to change, it is wisest to assume that change hurts. The change star model provides four 'pointers' to help you convert the perception that 'change hurts' into the perception that 'our business is change'.

There is no right place to start on the change star; it is an iterative model. 'Tell them why' may seem the obvious start point but unless you have 'made it manageable' it may be that the resistance you will meet later on will make the change too hot to handle. Similarly, you can't afford to wait until the later stages of the change to adopt a 'shared approach'; this must come right at the

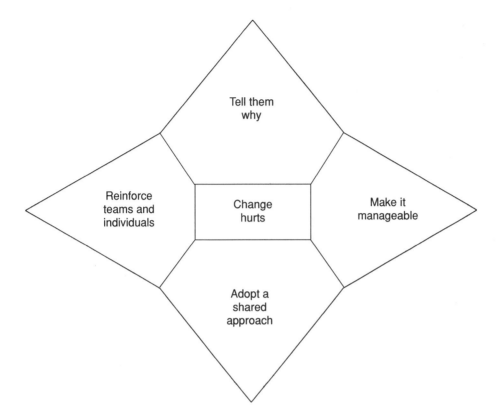

Figure 3.15.11 The change star model

beginning. The fourth pointer of the star talks about the need to 'reinforce teams and individuals' in order that people feel safe enough to take the risks of change. This climate of positive thinking and a 'people matter' approach cannot be built overnight. If you have a punitive culture where people 'keep their heads below the parapets' and come out of every meeting with their boss feeling uncomfortable, then it will be a long time before they feel they can risk making mistakes without being cut off at the knees.

Here is a checklist of questions to help anticipate the size/potential impact of a change on your people:

- How far do people see the need for change?
- How many people will be affected by the change?
- Will existing teams be broken up?
- Is a change of boss involved for anyone?
- Will retraining be needed?
- How many people will perceive themselves as losers?

- What levels of resistance do you anticipate?
- How will career opportunities be affected?
- How long will the change take to achieve?
- Will relocation be necessary?
- What are the effects on travel time to work, social and domestic arrangements?
- How much will customers be affected?

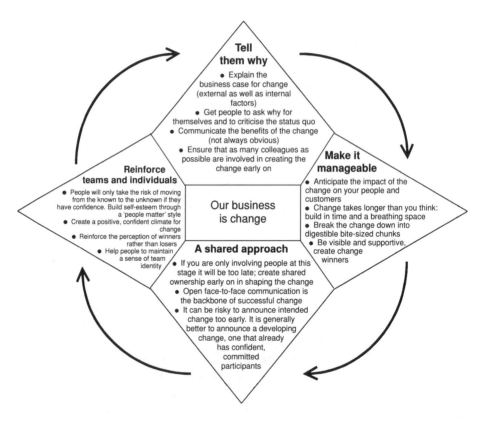

Figure 3.15.12 Using the change star

A cautionary tale

John Squires ran a successful software house employing 150 people based near Reading. He was committed to growth in a market place which presented many opportunities. He had set the business up six years previously and 'lived, ate and breathed it'. The business consisted of three separate teams, one based in Bracknell doing 'leading edge' work, one near Reading covering routine operations and a new business start-up outside Henley. Over the last year or so he had begun to see a strong argument for co-locating the teams on one office site which had become available in the centre of Reading. It made good business sense to him and he had tossed the idea around in his mind for many months. He didn't want to get the grapevine working overtime so he kept things to himself and refined his plans.

At last arrangements were finalised. On the Friday afternoon he called in his three direct reports to tell them the news. They were not pleased. Fred Jackson, who ran the Bracknell operation, asked him to work through the implications for staff and reconsider. But Bracknell is only 23 miles from Reading and John Squires couldn't see the problem. He left in his new Porsche for an urgent meeting in London, after instructing his secretary to place this announcement on the noticeboard:

> As from 10 December, Project Teams A, B and C will relocate in the newly acquired office in Queens Road, Reading. The revised organisation chart is attached. There will be no available car parking spaces so you are asked to make alternative arrangements.

Over the weekend, lines between the Squires' employees buzzed angrily. On the Monday morning, Fred Jackson gave in his resignation and that of two of his key systems analysts. One was a divorced woman, living in a Bracknell flat with a handicapped child. She said she would now find it impossible to get home at lunchtime and to shop conveniently, and would rather find another job than make the move. The other, who had recruited many of the bright young team at Bracknell, said that he wasn't prepared to see his people absorbed by the Reading group – who did most of the 'bread and butter work', were not of the same calibre and would only degrade the prestige of his group. By Monday lunchtime, John Squires was ruefully considering what had gone wrong with a change which, to his mind, made so much sense.

Assignment 21

Planning for change

1. Complete a force field analysis related to a major problem/change issue associated with implementing your business plan.
2. Complete a commitment chart of the key people within your business team, outlining what movement of attitude will be needed to achieve your business plan.
3. Produce a plan for change, identifying key change issues and outlining actions within the change star framework:
   - consider how to ensure that your business plan can be implemented by the people you have (when under fire);
   - list the likely change issues for people (ie resistance levels, winners and losers);
   - outline a change plan for achieving 'buy in'.

1. What is the problem/change issue?	
2. Where are you now?	
3. Where do you want to get to?	
4. What are the things going for us	Driving forces Present Resisting forces status quo
5. What are the resisting forces?	
6. What action can minimise resisting forces and maximise driving forces?	

Figure 3.15.13   Force field analysis template

Key players	No commitment	Let it happen	Help it happen	Make it happen
1.				
2.				
3.				
4.				
5				
6.				

X = The level of commitment of that key player right now
0 = The minimum commitment you will need to make the change happen

Figure 3.15.14   Commitment chart template

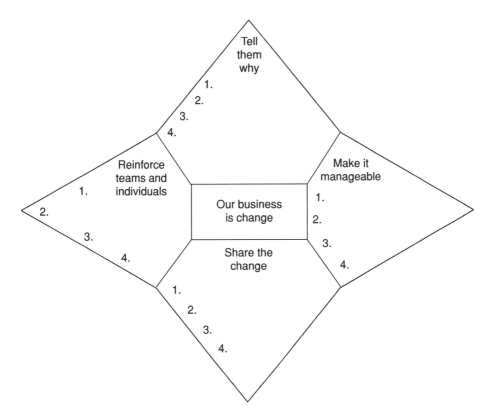

Figure 3.15.15 Change star template

16 *The financial plan*

Financial objectives are both the starting and finishing point of a good business plan. At the outset you need specific objectives covering such areas as return on capital employed, profit growth, gross margin, gearing and liquidity (see Chapter 4), to achieve which you must develop new marketing strategies and improve performance in your existing areas of business.

The financial plan seeks to reflect the financial implications of your marketing, people and operational plans in the form of profit-and-loss accounts, cash flows and balance sheets. In this respect it will be an iterative process as different strategies or variations of existing ones are tested to validate their effect on the company's financial performance (see Figure 3.16.1).

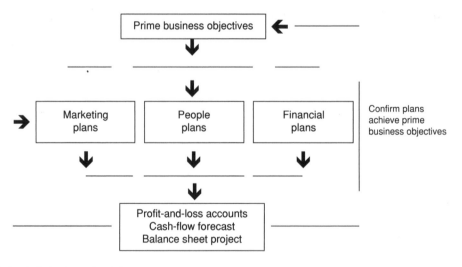

Figure 3.16.1   The financial plan: an iterative model

So, for example, a particular marketing strategy might have a satisfactory effect on profit growth and meet marketing objectives such as market share, but strain cash flow critically or cause the gearing ratio to become unacceptably high.

Financial plans also have a strategic dimension of their own which is reflected in the amount of extra funds the company is prepared to commit to achieve growth and the balance of where those funds will come from – for example, debt versus equity (see Chapter 10).

Before looking in detail at the financial plan, it will be useful to see why financial data is such an important element of the business plan, and what sort of information on financial performance is needed.

The sales forecasts are the essential input from which financial projections contained in a business plan are made. These projections are not the business plan, rather they should be viewed as the financial consequences of pursuing a particular course of action. Every business plan should contain them. If additionally you can demonstrate a sound grasp of financial matters, you will be talking the same language as financiers, which has to be an advantage in any negotiation for funds. But more importantly, the financial reports used for planning the business are also used for monitoring results and controlling events once the venture is under way.

Liquidators, who ought to know why businesses fail if anyone does, have at the top of their reasons for failure: 'lack of reliable financial information'. Many failed entrepreneurs believe accounting to be a bureaucratic nuisance carried out for the benefit of the Inland Revenue alone. These same people, who would never drive a car without a fuel gauge, speedometer or oil pressure indicator, frequently set off at breakneck speed running their business with only a 'gut feel', or perhaps the annual accounts to guide them. For them the end of the first year is often the end of the business. Financiers recognise this syndrome only too well, which is one reason why they take the 'financials' so seriously. The other reason is that it is their money that is at stake.

Taking the analogy further, a motorist must also plan ahead to arrive successfully at his or her goal: to reach the destination safely on time. The success of any journey, particularly a long one, depends very much on the care taken at this stage. The preparation must centre around three distinct areas:

● The car: making sure it is serviced, filled with fuel, and generally in a fit state to make the journey.
● The route: choosing one that takes account of the traffic, possible roadworks, and en route facilities such as petrol, refreshments, etc. The driver should also choose the route which is both the shortest practical one, and which is familiar.

- The travellers: ensuring that everyone is prepared for the journey. This may mean seeing games and toys have been packed for the children to keep them occupied on the journey. It will also mean ensuring that the luggage is packed and loaded into the car, and the house is left secured.

If this stage is accomplished with reasonable care and attention, the travellers and their vehicle have a very good chance of success in the next phase, which is the journey itself.

The soundest approach to any journey is to calculate the distance to be travelled to determine an average travelling speed that is maintainable and safe, and from these two to calculate the time needed to travel this distance. Working back from when they want to arrive at your destination and allowing a margin of safety for petrol stops, refreshments, etc, they can calculate when they should set off.

The rest of the journey, given that Phase 1 has been carried out properly, should be very straightforward provided they follow their plan, follow the map correctly and take account of the warning signs along the route. In all probability they will arrive at your destination safely and on time.

There are many parallels between the planning, information needs and decisions made by the safe motorist and the successful entrepreneur's business plan, as the financial reports described below will illustrate.

Planning assumptions

The believability of any business plan will depend greatly on the assumptions that underpin it. These assumptions should cover the key areas of the business and its operating environment. You also need to assess the downside risk and show how far things can go before new action has to be taken. Your assumptions can be recorded and monitored using a device like Table 3.16.1 on page 306.

These assumptions may be slightly different for each major objective/strategy. An example of these assumptions, which may be slightly different for each major objective/strategy is given in the extract from a business plan below.

Celtic Carveries

Celtic Carveries will set up and operate a small chain of carvery restaurants in Scotland. These will provide traditional food in a relaxed atmosphere offering value-for-money food in the middle price market.

The carvery is already a proven concept in parts of England, serving roast meals on a quick throughput basis but without the 'fast food' image. Labour costs are low and, with a limited menu, waste is avoided and in turn makes value for money possible.

One carvery has been in operation for six months in Stirling, so the following assumptions have been drawn partly from experience and partly from market research.

Profit-and-loss assumptions

(a) Sales

Carveries in operation will be:

Year 1	2
Year 2	4
Year 3	7
Year 5 onwards	10

Opening six days a week, meals sales will be:

Year 1	40 per day
Year 2	50 per day
Year 3 onwards	60 per day

Sales value per meal will be:

Food	£6.50
Drink	£2.50

(b) Cost of sales per meal:

Food	£1.75
Drink	£1.00
Labour	£2.70
	£5.45

This equals 61 per cent of sales.

(c) Wages: each carvery will employ seven staff at a cost of £42,600 per annum (labour costs = 30 per cent of sales, which compares favourably with a general restaurant's 40 per cent).

(d) Directors: paid £15,000 in first year, rising to £20,000 from year 3.

(e) Administrative staff: needed mainly from year 2. Costs will rise from £5,000 to £40,000 over seven years.

(f) Rent and services: £30,000 per carvery per annum.

(g) Alterations, equipment and decoration: £40,000 per carvery.

(h) Advertising: £2,000 per carvery per annum.

(i) Inflation: all income and expenditure is stated at current prices.

Cash-flow assumptions

(a) No debtors – all meals paid for in cash.

(b) Salaries and wages paid monthly.

(c) Purchases paid monthly.

(d) Rent paid half-yearly.

(e) Rates paid monthly.

(f) Loan interest paid quarterly from month 1.

(g) Overdraft interest paid quarterly from month 3.

(h) Sales spread evenly over each month of year (sensitivity analysis described later shows how this assumption can be varied).

Balance sheet assumptions

(a) Closing stock: building up to six weeks' sales.

(b) Depreciation of fixed assets: improvements and office, 20 per cent per annum; fixtures and fittings, 25 per cent per annum.

(c) Creditors: equivalent to one month's cost of sales.

Table 3.16.1 Assumptions underpinning your objectives and strategies

Key assumptions	Basis of assumption	Confidence in assumption	What will happen if assumption proves incorrect	When contingency action can be taken, and when it should be taken
1				
2				
3				
4				
5				

The cash-flow forecast

The acid test of whether or not your growth strategies are desirable and achievable will show up in the long-term cash-flow projections.

In practical terms, the cash-flow projections and the profit-and-loss account projections are parallel tasks which are essentially prepared from the same data. They may be regarded almost as the 'heads' and 'tails' of the same coin: the profit-and-loss account showing the owner/manager the profit or loss based on the assumption that sales income and the cost of making that sale are 'matched' together in the same month; and the cash-flow statement looking at the same transactions from the viewpoint that, in reality, the cost of the sale is incurred first (and paid for) and the income is received last, anywhere between one week and three months later. Obviously, the implications for a non-cash business of this delay between making the sale and receiving the payment and using a service/buying goods and paying for them are crucial, especially in the early years of the business and when your business is growing quickly.

Celtic Carveries' cash-flow projection for one year is shown in Table 3.16.2. Cash inflows are at the top and outflows below, with the next monthly and cumulative position to date shown at the bottom. From this we can deduce that, despite a fairly hefty injection of funds, they expect to end up with an overdraft of £6,063 at the year end, and a worst cash position in month 1 of £17,046. An overdraft facility of around £20,000 should be included in the business plan proposal. The negative figures at the bottom show how much money you will need to fund your growth plans – and when and for how long you will need the funds.

In practice you will find it desirable to produce your long-run cash-flow projection on a quarter by quarter basis.

The profit-and-loss account

So much for cash flow. It is also important that your strategies are delivering the desired profit, growth and the appropriate margins.

You now need to match income and expenditure to the appropriate time periods, ignoring the cash implications. For example, if a customer orders and takes delivery of your goods and service, but does not pay for 100 days, the figure will not appear in the first quarter's cash flow, but it will form part of the income for profit-and-loss purposes. The same applies to expenses incurred, whether paid for or not.

Table 3.16.3 shows Celtic Carveries' history and projection. A couple of years' history on the same chart with the projections can make your growth plans

Table 3.16.2 Celtic Carveries' cash flow, Year 1

Month	1	2	3	4	5	6	7	8	9	10	11	12	Totals
Receipts													
Cash sales	18,667	18,667	18,667	18,667	18,667	18,667	18,667	18,667	18,667	18,667	18,667	18,667	224,004
Owner's capital introduced	15,000												15,000
Other capital introduced	30,000												30,000
Loans capital	42,258												42,258
Total Receipts	105,925	18,667	18,667	18,667	18,667	18,667	18,667	18,667	18,667	18,667	18,667	18,667	311,262
Payments													
Capital expenditure	90,000												90,000
Food and wine	5,703	5,703	5,703	5,703	5,703	5,703	5,703	5,703	5,703	5,703	5,703	5,703	68,436
Wages, cooks, etc	5,680	5,680	5,680	5,680	5,680	5,680	5,680	5,680	5,680	5,680	5,680	5,680	68,160
Rent	12,000						12,000						24,000
Rates	500	500	500	500	500	500	500	500	500	500	500	500	6,000
Advertising	4,000												4,000
Overheads	2,500	2,500	2,500	2,500	2,500	2,500	2,500	2,500	2,500	2,500	2,500	2,500	30,000
Administration	400	400	400	400	400	400	400	400	400	400	400	400	4,800
Drawings	1,250	1,250	1,250	1,250	1,250	1,250	1,250	1,250	1,250	1,250	1,250	1,250	15,000
Loan interest	938			938			938			938			3,752
Overdraft medium-term loan interest			891			707			881			696	3,175
Total payments	122,971	16,033	16,924	16,971	16,033	16,740	28,971	16,033	16,914	16,971	16,033	16,729	317,323
Cash-flow surplus/deficit (–)	–17,046	2,634	1,743	1,696	2,634	1,927	–10,304	2,634	1,753	1,696	2,634	1,938	–6,061
Opening cash balance	0	–17,046	–14,412	–12,669	–10,973	–8,339	–6,412	–16,716	–14,082	–12,329	–10,633	–7,999	
Closing cash balance	–17,046	–14,412	–12,669	–10,973	–8,339	–6,412	–16,716	–14,082	–12,329	–10,633	–7,999	–6,061	

Table 3.16.3 Celtic Carveries: profit-and-loss account for the year to 31 October

£000	2 yrs ago	Last yr	Year 1	Year 2	Year 3	Year 4	Year 5
Sales income	224	504	995	1,432	1,600	1,685	1,685
Cost of goods sold	137	307	623	874	976	1,028	1,028
Gross profit	87	197	372	558	624	657	657
Expenditure							
Administration	5	28	30	30	40	40	40
Rent	24	48	84	120	120	120	120
Rates	6	12	21	30	30	30	30
Advertising	4	8	14	20	20	20	20
Overheads	30	60	105	150	150	150	150
Depreciation	22	38	61	77	63	50	39
Total	91	194	315	427	423	410	399
PBIT (Profit before interest and tax)	–4	3	57	131	201	247	258
Interest	7	8	18	26	11	10	0
Taxation	–1	5	28	55	80	92	95
Directors' emoluments	15	18	20	25	25	25	25
Profit and tax	–25	–28	–9	25	85	120	138

much more clear. The date at the top of the profit-and-loss account shows the period over which income and expenditure has been measured, in this case a year. For your business plan the earlier years should be shown in greater detail: either quarterly or preferably monthly for year 1 at any rate, quarterly for year 2, and annually for years 3 to 5 should be acceptable.

The balance sheet

The balance sheet shows what assets we will deploy and how those will ideally be financed for each year of the plan. So in the Celtic Carveries example in Table 3.16.4, you can clearly see that additional capital is required to fund the fixed asset improvement programme, essential to the success of the restaurant group.

Sensitivity analysis

While you have been realistic in preparing your forecasts of sales and related costs, it is highly probable that actual performance will not be as expected over the planning horizon. This could be for one or more reasons, such as resistance to innovation (if a new product is involved), over-estimate of market size, change in consumer demand, slow take-up of product etc. All these could mean that sales forecasts are significantly wrong. It is advisable to pre-empt any potential investor's question, such as 'What happens if your sales are reduced by 20 per cent?' by asking yourself the question first and quantifying the financial effects in your business plan. You need not go into any great detail; it is sufficient to outline one or two scenarios.

Celtic Carveries' sensitivity analysis

In arriving at sales forecasts, estimates were made by comparison with the accounts of X Ltd who have a similar operation. If, however, these estimates were incorrect and our sales were 20 per cent lower, turnover would be £180,000 with costs of sales falling to £110,000 and the company would still produce a gross profit at the end of year 1 of £70,000. Given a fixed cost of £90,000, our first year loss would be extended from £4,000 to £20,000. This position could be largely offset by cutting the directors' pay for that year.

Table 3.16.4 Celtic Carveries: balance sheets at 31 October

	This year	Year 1	Year 2	Year 3	Year 4
Net assets employed					
Fixed assets					
Improvements	48,000	86,400	141,120	184,896	147,916
Fixtures and office	30,500	43,900	82,995	97,051	85,631
	78,500	130,300	224,115	281,947	233,547
Current assets					
Stock	1,887	38,425	72,819	109,250	109,250
Cash	0	2,366	2,029	10,863	120,641
	1,887	40,791	74,848	120,113	229,891
less					
Current liabilities					
Creditors	11,383	25,617	48,546	72,833	72,833
Overdraft	6,063	27,929	60,974	45,657	0
Tax	0	4,000	25,000	58,000	80,000
	17,446	57,546	134,520	176,490	152,833
= Net current assets	(15,559)	(16,755)	(59,672)	(56,377)	77,058
Total assets *less*					
current liabilities	62,941	113,545	164,443	225,570	310,605
Financed by:					
Share capital					
Owners	15,000	15,000	15,000	15,000	15,000
Other directors	10,000	10,000	10,000	10,000	10,000
New venture					
capital	20,000	90,000	120,000	150,000	150,000
Profit/loss for year	(24,317)	(28,455)	(8,557)	25,570	85,036
Retained earnings/					
reserves	–	–	–	–	25,569
	20,683	86,545	136,443	200,570	285,605
Loan capital					
Long term	25,000	25,000	25,000	25,000	25,000
Medium term	17,258	2,000	3,000	–	–
	42,258	27,000	28,000	25,000	25,000
TOTAL	62,941	113,545	164,443	225,570	310,605

Summary of performance ratios

When you have completed your pro forma profit-and-loss accounts for years 1 to 5, together with your pro forma balance sheets for years 1 to 5, you should prepare a summary of your business's performance in certain key areas (see

Table 3.16.5). This summary will help both you and any potential outside investor to compare your business's performance in the different years.

- One year against the next: for example, has gross profit grown or declined between years 1 and 5?
- Against other similar businesses, for example: does your business give as good a return on investment as others?
- The ratios can be used as an aid in making future financial projections. For example, if you believe it prudent to hold the equivalent of a month's sales in stock, once you have made the sales forecast for future years the projections for stock in the balance sheet follow logically.

Table 3.16.5 Summary of Celtic Carveries' performance ratios

Year	1	2	3	4	5
Gross profit (%)	39	39	39	39	39
Total expenditure (%)	41	38	33	30	26
Profit before tax (%)	(10)	(5)	2	6	10
ROI (%)	–	–	–	13	30
Gearing (%)	67	24	17	11	8

This summary of key ratios should include the following:

- Sales: actual sales, to be used as the base figure for all other calculations.
- Cost of goods sold: expressed as a percentage of sales to highlight any increase/decrease in this key area over the period.
- Total expenditure (expenses): expressed as a percentage of sales to indicate how well these have been controlled over the period.
- Profit before tax. Expressed as a percentage of sales to show how well sales have been converted to bottom line profit. Perhaps the key measure of operational performance (add back tax to profit after tax).
- Profit growth: experience as a percentage year on year.
- Net worth: this is actual investment in the business, ie share capital plus reserves, which on its own gives a valuable measure of absolute growth.
- Return on net worth: this is also referred to as return on investment (ROI), and is undoubtedly the key measure of profitability used by outsiders to compare your business with others. It is calculated by taking your net

profit (after tax and before dividends) and dividing this by the average value of your share capital and reserves.

● Debt to equity: frequently referred to as 'gearing', this is calculated by taking total borrowings (both long and short term) divided by total capital and reserves (net worth) and expressing the result as a percentage. This ratio is, however, a double-edged sword in that, if your gearing is high (ie you are mainly financed by borrowings), potential investors will see high rewards, assuming your business performs well, but if you are asking a bank or similar institution for interest-bearing funds, it will normally expect to see low gearing, to show a certain level of your commitment, expressed as share capital, to reduce the risk of it not being able to recover its loans.

● Net current assets: this is calculated by subtracting current liabilities from current assets, thereby giving creditors an indication of your liquidity or ability to meet current liabilities when they fall due.

● Current ratio: this is calculated by dividing current assets by current liabilities and expressing the result as a ratio, thereby giving an indication of your ability to meet short-term obligations as they become due. It is often refined to include only those current assets 'quickly' convertible to cash (ie excluding stocks) and all current liabilities repayable within 12 months. In this form it is known as a quick ratio.

There are three other useful working capital ratios which reveal the strength of financial control in a business plan and can be used in financial forecasting. These are:

$$\text{Average debtor collection period} \quad = \quad \frac{\text{Debtors}}{\text{Sales}} \times 365$$

This gives a guide as to how long you expect to take (or have taken) in getting back money owed to you.

$$\text{Days stock held} \quad = \quad \frac{\text{Stock (or inventories)}}{\text{Cost of goods sold}} \times 365$$

This shows the stock level held, in proportion to your sales. This is more useful than comparing figures alone, as you would expect levels to change with increases or decreases in sales.

$$\text{Average credit period taken} \quad = \quad \frac{\text{Creditors}}{\text{Purchases}} \times 365$$

This shows how much credit you are taking from your suppliers. As a rough guide, if you are allowing your customers 30 days to pay then you should be looking for that credit period yourself.

Look back to Chapter 4 for further classification of key ratio calculations. If your accounting is a little rusty, read *Financial Management for the Small Business* (Barrow, 2001).

Financing requirements

Your business plan may look very professional, showing that you have a very high probability of making exceptional returns, but it will fall at the first hurdle if your funding requirements have not been properly thought out and communicated to potential investors. It is not sufficient for you to look at your pro forma cash flow statement and, taking the maximum overdraft position, say:

> The management require £150,000 to commence business, which may come either from bank loans or from a share capital injection. The cash-flow projections show that if the funding was by way of loan it would be repaid within three years. If the funding came from an issue of share capital an excellent return would be available by way of dividends.

Such a statement leaves many questions unanswered, such as:

● Why do you need the money?
● When will you need it?
● What type of money do you need?
● What deal are you offering your investors?
● What exit routes are open to your investors?

Let us examine each of these questions in turn, as your business will have to include answers to them.

Why do you need the money?

You probably have a very good idea of why you need the funds that you are asking for, but unless the readers of your business plan have plenty of time to spare (which they have not) and can be bothered to work it out for themselves (which they cannot), you must clearly state what you will use the funds received for. See Table 3.16.6 for an example.

Table 3.16.6   A breakdown of funds needed

	£
To purchase:	
Motor vehicle	5,000
Plant and equipment	100,000
To provide:	
Working capital for first 6 months	75,000
Total requirement	180,000
Less investment made by (you)	30,000
Net funding requirement	150,000

This statement clearly tells the reader how the funds will be used and gives clear pointers as to appropriate funding routes and timing of the funding requirements.

When will you need it?

In the example above a net investment of £150,000 is required, which is likely to come from several different funding routes, depending on how it is to be used. However, one thing is apparent: the whole £150,000 is not needed immediately or even at the same time, so do not ask for it all to be provided at the same time.

The £100,000 for plant and equipment will be needed several weeks or months before trading can begin, and the £5,000 for the motor vehicle can in all probability be left to closer to the time at which you will need it. The working capital requirement of £75,000 is needed in varying amounts over the first six months or so of trading. Your funding request should clearly show this 'timetable of anticipated funding'. See Table 3.16.7 for an example. The statement should be carried on for as long as external funding is required and shows that:

1. An equity investment of £100,000 is made three months prior to implementing your growth plan and remains in the business for the medium- to long term.
2. A bank overdraft facility of £75,000 is required, which is first used during month 3, reaches a peak of £70,000 during month 5, and is cleared by month 9 (ie the sixth month of trading). Note that the full £75,000 facility appears not to be needed but it is advisable to obtain more than is required to cover the unforeseen.
3. An HP loan of £5,000 is required in month 3, and is repaid over three years.

Table 3.16.7   Example timetable of anticipated funding

Date	Requirement per cash-flow forecast £000	Anticipated funding			
		Share issue £000	Your cash £000	Bank loan £000	HP loan £000
Pre commencement of growth plan					
Month 1	100	100	30	–	–
2	5		–	–	–
3	70			45	5
Commencement of growth plan					
Year 1 Month 4	20			60	4.85
5	10		–	70	4.70
6	(5)		–	65	4.55
7	(20)		–	45	4.40
8	(21)		–	24	4.25
9	(25)		–	–	4.10
10	(20)		–	–	3.95
11	(10)		–	–	3.80
12	(10)		–	–	3.65

What type of money do you need?

The amount of money you need and what you require it for will help you to decide what type of money you need to finance growth. Two points need stressing here; they have already been covered in Chapter 6, but are so crucial as to be worth revisiting.

Gearing. Do not allow your business to have more debt than equity over the whole horizon of your business plan. Highly geared companies, unless the risks are minimal, are simply fruit machines which ultimately will not shell out as much money as you put in (see Chapter 10).

'Giving away' equity. This is always a contentious issue with successful entrepreneurs. For many the problems start with the idea of giving away a share of their business because they feel that they are losing control by so doing. The problem can be alleviated by looking at other successful business people who have already been down this route: Anita Roddick, founder of the Body Shop, and Richard Branson of Virgin are minority shareholders in their companies, yet nobody would dispute that they are in control.

The deal on offer

People can and do sell off varying amounts of their business to raise funds. While ideally you should retain 51 per cent of the voting power in your company, it is possible to achieve this by owning less than 51 per cent of the shares. Part of the negotiating process will hinge on voting rights of shares, and it is not uncommon for outside investors to accept restricted voting rights on their shares. Do not forget that you want their money and you have got to give up something in return.

So far the question of how much the business is worth has been avoided and, since this is what will determine how much equity you will need to sell to raise the required funds, it needs to be answered. There is no one way to value a business and once you start to try, you will find it is more of an art than a science, but you can begin to get a feel for value using the present value formula. The formula used to calculate it is quite simple, but the factors used in arriving at the valuation are somewhat subjective. However, a simple valuation of a company by way of an example is shown below.

Cranfield Engineering Ltd

Cranfield Engineering Ltd (CEL) is a new start-up business which needs a £200,000 equity injection to achieve its business plan objectives. Table 3.16.8 gives a brief summary of its financial projections.

Table 3.16.8   Cranfield Engineering Ltd financial projection

	Turnover £	Profit after tax £
Year 1	200,000	(25,000)
Year 2	500,000	100,000
Year 3	750,000	200,000

Assuming that a P/E ratio (the ratio of a share's price to its earnings) of 10 is used as the accepted multiplier of earnings in their industry, then using the formula:

$$\text{Present value (PV)} = \frac{\text{Future valuation (FV)}}{(1 + i)^n}$$

where

FV = maintainable profits times applicable P/E ratio;
i   = required rate of return (to investor);
n   = number of years until date of forecast earnings, used to calculate valuation.

Assuming that the figures provided by CEL are accepted at face value (which is unlikely) and that maintainable profits are achieved in Year 2, and that our investor is seeking a 60 per cent return (because of the high risk involved), then the valuation of the company would be as follows:

$$PV = \frac{£100,000 \times 10}{(1 + 0.60)^2} = \frac{£1,000,000}{2.56} = £390,625$$

If the company is valued at £390,625 and CEL requires £200,000, the percentage of the equity that the investor will acquire will be 200,000/390,625, which is 51.2 per cent. Obviously, while the above is mathematically correct there would be much negotiation about the acceptability of the factors being used and perhaps which year's profits represent 'maintainable profits'. In the above example, if year 3 had been used, the investor's share of the equity would have fallen to 41 per cent.

Exit routes

Exit routes for investors also have to be considered at the point of raising funds. This matter is dealt with in Chapter 18.

Assignment 22

Pulling together the financials

1. Prepare a 3–5 year profit-and-loss account projection based on your marketing strategy for growth.
2. Indicate the key assumptions that underpin your projections.
3. Reflect the cash flow and balance sheet implications and calculate key ratios to show how your business performance helps to meet your key business objectives. You may find a spreadsheet or a business plan writer helpful.

Figure 3.16.9 Summary of ratios

Ratio	3 years ago	2 years ago	Last year	This year	Average % growth	Main competitors	% Difference from our performance	Action required*
1. Percentage sales growth								
2. Percentage profit growth								
3. Headcounter growth								
4. $\dfrac{\text{Sales}}{\text{No of employees}}$								
5. $\dfrac{\text{Profit}}{\text{No of employees}}$								
6. Value added per employee								
7. ROCE: $\dfrac{\text{Profit before interest and tax}}{\text{Capital employed}}$								
8. ROSC: $\dfrac{\text{Profit after tax}}{\text{Share capital and reserves}}$								

Figure 3.16.9 Summary of ratios (*continued*)

Ratio	3 years ago	2 years ago	Last year	This year	Average % growth	Main competitors	% Difference from our performance	Action required*
9. Gearing: $\dfrac{\text{Share capital and reserves}}{\text{All long-term capital}}$								
10. $\dfrac{\text{Operating profit}}{\text{Loan interest}}$								
11. $\dfrac{\text{Gross profit}}{\text{Sales}}$								
12. $\dfrac{\text{Operating profit}}{\text{Sales}}$								
13. $\dfrac{\text{Net profit}}{\text{Sales}}$								
14. Current ratio: $\dfrac{\text{Current assets}}{\text{Current liabilities}}$								
15. Quick ratio: $\dfrac{\text{Debtors and cash}}{\text{Current liabilities}}$								
16. Average collection period: $\dfrac{\text{Debtors}}{\text{Sales}} \times 365$								

Figure 3.16.9 Summary of ratios (*concluded*)

Ratio	3 years ago	2 years ago	Last year	This year	Average % growth	Main competitors	% Difference from our performance	Action required*
17. $\dfrac{\text{Creditors}}{\text{Purchases}} \times 365$								
18. $\dfrac{\text{Stock}}{\text{Cost of sales}} \times 365$								
19. $\dfrac{\text{Sales}}{\text{Working capital}}$								
20. $\dfrac{\text{Sales}}{\text{Fixed assets}}$								
21. Other key ratios								
22.								
23.								
24.								

* You do not have to wait to the bitter end to take steps to improve performance. So if, for example, you see your sales per employee is way out of line with the norm in your industry, jot down any ideas for improvement as you go along.

17 *Writing and presenting your business plan*

Up to now the assignments have focused on gathering and analysing data needed to validate and confirm your strategy for growth, to assess your business team's capability to implement the chosen strategy and to quantify the resources needed in terms of staff, machinery, money and management.

Getting the data together along the lines we have suggested can take anything between 200 and 400 work hours, depending on the nature of your business and how much data you already routinely gather. Your task will have been made that much easier if you have involved all your staff in gathering and analysing the information, and in writing up the business plan. They will also be that much more committed both to implementing the ensuing strategy and to preparing future business plans.

However onerous the overall task of preparing a new business plan, it is essential if you are to shift the business through from being almost exclusively entrepreneurial and opportunity-driven to having a strategic focus that allows the whole management team a share in the future of the firm. (Remember Greiner!)

Benefits from having a current business plan include the following:

- Few businesses can grow without additional finance. While it would be an exaggeration to say your business plan is a passport to sources of finance, without it you will not really know how much money you need to finance growth and no one today will lend or invest in a business without a plan.
- A systematic approach to planning enables you to make your mistakes on paper, rather than in the marketplace. One potential entrepreneur made the discovery while gathering data for his business plan that the local competitor he thought was a one-man band was in fact the pilot operation

for a proposed national chain of franchised outlets. This had a profound effect on his marketing strategy!

Another entrepreneur found out that, at the price he proposed charging for a new product, he would never recover his overheads or break even. Indeed, 'overheads' and 'break even' were themselves alien terms before he embarked on preparing a business plan. This naïve perspective on costs is by no means unusual.

● Your business plan will make your management team more confident that they can achieve the strategic goals set. They will be better able to communicate the company's strategy to others in a way that makes it easier for them to understand and appreciate the reasoning behind your plans. This will give both the appearance and substance to your having management in depth: absolutely essential for organisations moving along the continuum from one-person outfit to major enterprise.

Remember: the secret of making money is to make others content to make it for you.

Now the information gathered so far in carrying out the assignments has to be assembled, collated and orchestrated into a coherent and complete written business plan aimed at a specific audience.

In this chapter we will examine the six activities that can make this happen:

● packaging;
● layout and content;
● writing and editing;
● who to send the plan to;
● the oral presentation;
● what financiers look for in a business plan.

Packaging

Every product is enhanced by appropriate packaging and a business plan is no exception. The panellists at Cranfield's enterprise programmes prefer a simple spiral binding with a plastic cover on the front and back. This makes it easy for the reader to move from section to section, and it ensures the plan will survive frequent handling. Stapled copies and leather-bound tomes are viewed as undesirable extremes.

Using a good, letter-quality finish, together with wide margins and double spacing, will result in a pleasing and easy-to-read document.

Layout and content

There is no such thing as a 'universal' business plan format. That said, experience at Cranfield has taught us that certain layouts and contents have gone down better than others. These are our guidelines to producing an attractive business plan which tries to cover both management requirements and the investor's point of view. Not every sub-heading will be relevant to every type of business, but the general format can be followed, with emphasis laid as appropriate.

First, the cover should show the name of the company, its address, phone number, e-mail address, Web site and the date on which this version of the plan was prepared. It should confirm that this is the company's latest view of its position and financing needs. If your business plan is to be aimed at specific sources of finance, it is highly likely that you will need to assemble slightly different business plans, highlighting areas of concern to lenders as opposed to investors, for example.

Second, the title page, immediately behind the front cover, should repeat the above information and also give the founder's name, address and phone number. A home number can be helpful for investors, who often work irregular hours – as you probably do. He or she is likely to be the first point of contact and anyone reading the business plan may want to talk over some aspects of the proposal before arranging a meeting.

The executive summary

Ideally consisting of one, but certainly no more than two pages, this should immediately follow the title page. Writing up the executive summary is not easy, but it is the most important single part of the business plan; it will probably do more to influence whether or not the plan is reviewed in its entirety than anything else you do. It can also make the reader favourably disposed towards a venture at the outset, which is no bad thing.

These one or two pages must explain the following:

- The current state of the company with respect to product/service readiness for market, trading position and past successes if already running, and key staff on board.
- The products or services to be sold and to whom they will be sold, including details on competitive advantage.
- The reasons customers need the products or services, together with some indication of market size and growth.
- The company's aims and objectives in both the short and longer term, and an indication of the strategies to be employed in getting there.

- A summary of forecasts, sales, profits and cash flow.
- How much money is needed, and how and when the investor or lender will benefit from providing the funds.

Obviously, the executive summary can only be written after the business plan itself has been completed. The summary below, for instance, accompanied a 40-page plan.

Pnu Cleen

Pnu Cleen will assemble and market an already prototyped design for a vacuum cleaner. The design work was carried out by myself and my co-director when we were at Loughborough University taking a BSc course in design and manufacture. The prototype was made during my postgraduate course in industrial design engineering at the Royal College of Art in London.

The vacuum cleaner is rather special. Its design, powered by compressed air, is aimed at the industrial market and fulfils a need overlooked by cleaning equipment manufacturers.

The vacuum cleaner offers to the customer an 'at-hand' machine that can be used by their employees to keep their workplace or machine clean and tidy during production. This produces a healthier and more productive environment in which to work.

The vacuum cleaner is cheaper than electrical vacuum cleaners and more versatile. It is also far less prone to blockage which is especially important considering the types of material found in manufacturing industry.

The vacuum cleaner can be produced at low unit cost. This, together with the market price it can command for what it has to offer, will mean that only a small turnover is needed for the company to break even. However, with the prospect of a sizeable market both in this country and abroad, the company has the chance of making substantial profits.

The company will concentrate on this product for the first five years to ensure that it reaches all of its potential market and this will make a sound base from which we can either expand into other products or incorporate the manufacturing side of the product into our own capabilities.

The financial forecasts indicate that break even will be achieved in the second year of operations, and in year 3 return on investment should be about 40 per cent. By then sales turnover will be a little over £1 million, gross profits about £400,000, and profit before tax but after financing charges around £200,000.

Our P/E ratio from year 3 will be 10 to 1, which should leave an attractive margin for any investor to exit, with comparable stock being quoted at 19 to 1.

We will need an investment of £300,000 to implement our strategy, with roughly half going into tangibles such as premises and stock, and the balance into marketing and development expenses. We are able and willing to put up £100,000. The balance we would like to fund from the sale of a share of the business, the exact proportion to be discussed at a later stage.

The table of contents

After the executive summary follows a table of contents. This is the map that will guide the new reader through your business proposal and on to the inevitable conclusion that they should put up the funds. If a map is obscure, muddled or even missing, the chances are you will end up with lost or irritated readers unable to find their way around your proposal.

Each of the main sections of the business plan should be listed and the pages within that section indicated. There are two valid schools of thought on page numbering. One favours a straightforward sequential numbering of each page. This seems to us to be perfectly adequate for short, simple plans, dealing with uncomplicated issues and seeking modest levels of finance.

Most proposals should be numbered by section. In the example that follows, the section headed The Business and its Management is Section 1, and the pages that follow are listed from 1.1 to 1.7 in the table of contents, so identifying each page as belonging within that specific section. This numbering method also allows you to insert new material during preparation without upsetting the entire pagination. Tables and figures should also be similarly numbered. Individual paragraph numbering, much in favour with government and civil service departments, is considered something of an 'overkill' in a business plan and is to be discouraged, except perhaps if you are looking for a large amount of government grant.

The table of contents below shows both the layout and content which in our experience is most in favour with financial institutions. Unsurprisingly, the terminology is similar to that used throughout the book. For example, Chapter 2 covers the items covered in 3.2 in the sample table of contents below. For competitive strengths and weaknesses you can look back to Chapter 3 for guidance and inspiration. Performance ratios mentioned in 8.1 are explained in Chapter 4. If in doubt use the index, which will guide you to relevant areas of the text.

Table 3.17.1   Sample table of contents

Appendices should include:
Management team biographies
Names and details of professional advisers
Technical data and drawings
Details of patents, copyright, designs
Audited accounts
Consultants' reports or other published data on products, markets etc
Orders on hand and enquiry status
Detailed market research methods and findings
Organisation charts

Writing and editing

You and your colleagues should write the first draft of the business plan yourselves. The niceties of grammar and style can be resolved later. Different people in your team will have been responsible for carrying out the various assignments in the workbook, and writing up the appropriate section(s) of the business plan. This information should be circulated to ensure that everyone is still heading in the same direction and nothing important has been missed out.

A 'prospectus', such as a business plan seeking finance from investors, can have a legal status, turning any claims you may make for sales and profits (for example) into a 'contract'. Your accountant and legal adviser will be able to help you with the appropriate language that can convey your projections without giving them contractual status. This would also be a good time to talk over the proposal with a friendly banker or venture capital provider (VC). Either can give an insider's view of the strengths and weaknesses of your proposal.

When your first draft has been revised, then comes the task of editing. Here the grammar, spelling and language must be carefully checked to ensure that your business plan is crisp, correct, clear and complete – and not too long. If writing is not your trade then, once again, this is an area in which to seek help. Your local college or librarian will know of someone who can produce attention-capturing prose, if you do not.

However much help you get with writing up your business plan, it is still just that – *your plan*. So the responsibility for the final proofreading before it goes out must rest with you. Spelling mistakes and typing errors can have a disproportionate influence on the way your business plan is received.

The other purpose of editing is to reduce the business plan to between 20 and 40 pages. However complex or sizeable the venture, outsiders will not have time to read it if it is longer, and insiders will only succeed in displaying their muddled thinking to full effect. If your plan includes volumes of data, tables, graphs etc, then refer to them in the text, but confine them to an appendix. The text (not the table or appendices) of your final business plan should be eminently readable if you want to stay out of the reject pile in lenders' and investors' offices.

The Fox Index can help you make sure the business plan is readable. Research into the subject has shown that two things make life hard for readers: long sentences, and long words. Robert Gunning, a business language expert, has devised a formula to measure just how tough a letter, report or article is to read (Gunning, 1981). Called the Fox Index, it takes four simple steps to arrive at.

1. Find the average number of words per sentence. Use a sample of at least 100 words long. Divide the total number of words by number of sentences to give you the average sentence length.
2. Count the number of words of three syllables or more per 100 words. Do not count: (a) words that are capitalised; (b) combinations of short, easy words – like 'bookkeeper'; (c) verbs that are made into three syllables by adding 'ed' or 'es' – like 'created' or 'trespasses'.
3. Add the two factors above and multiply by 0.4. This will give you the Fox Index. It corresponds roughly to the number of years of schooling a person would require to read a passage with ease and understanding.
4. Check the results against this scale:
   - 4 and below, very easy: perhaps childish
   - 5, fairly easy: tabloid press, hard sales letters
   - 7 or 8, standard: *Daily Mail*, most business letters
   - 9–11, fairly difficult: *The Times*, good product literature
   - 12–15, difficult: *The Economist*, technical literature
   - 17 or above, very difficult: *New Scientist* – no business use, except to bamboozle.

Who to send the business plan to

Now you are ready to send out your business plan to a few carefully selected financial institutions who you know are interested in proposals such as yours. This will involve some research into the particular interests, foibles and idiosyncrasies of the institutions themselves.

If you are only interested in raising debt capital, the field is narrowed to the clearing banks for the main part. If you are looking for someone to share the risk with you then you must review the much wider field of venture capital. Here, some institutions will only look at proposals over a certain capital sum, such as £1 million, or will only invest in certain technologies. It is a good idea to carry out this research before the final editing of your business plan, as you should incorporate something of this knowledge into the way your business plan is presented. You may find that slightly different versions of 'the deal on offer' have to be made for each different source of finance to which you send your business plan.

Do not be disheartened if the first batch of financiers you contact do not sign you up. One Cranfield enterprise programme participant had to approach 26 lending institutions, 10 of them different branches of the same organisation, before getting the funds she wanted. One important piece of information she brought back from every interview was the reason for the refusal. This eventually led to a refined proposal that won through. It is well to remember that financial institutions are far from infallible, so you may have to widen your audience to other contacts.

Body Shop

Anita Roddick, the Body Shop founder, was turned down flat by the banks, and had to raise £4,000 from a Sussex garage owner. This, together with £4,000 of her own funds, allowed the first shop to open in Brighton. Today there are hundreds of Body Shop outlets throughout the world. The company has a full listing on the Stock Exchange and Roddick is a millionaire many times over – at least one Sussex bank manager must be feeling a little silly!

Finally, how long will it all take? This depends on whether you are raising debt or equity, the institution you approach and the complexity of the deal on offer. A secured bank loan, for example, can take from a few days to a few weeks to arrange. Investment from a VC will rarely take less than three months to arrange, more usually six or even nine months. Two Cranfield Business Growth participants raised substantial six-figure sums of venture capital during a recession and both took 13 months from first approach to getting the cheques in the bank!

Although the deal itself may be struck early on, the lawyers will pore over the detail for weeks. Every exchange of letters can add a fortnight to the wait. The 'due diligence' process in which every detail of your business plan is checked will also take time, so this will have to be allowed for in your projections.

Having said that, some deals are done very fast. One Internet start-up in the UK, Clickmango.com succeeded in raising £3 million from Atlas Venture in just eight days. Such was the enthusiasm for the natural health products Web site venture that an earlier meeting with another VC resulted in an offer of £1 million in just 40 minutes. However, as the business folded within three months when no offers of second stage financing were forthcoming, it can reasonably be assumed that the VCs had learnt their lesson, albeit the hard way.

The oral presentation

If getting someone interested in your business plan is half the battle in raising funds, the other half is the oral presentation. Any organisation financing a venture will insist on seeing the team involved presenting and defending their plans – in person. Financiers know that they are backing people every bit as much as the idea. You can be sure that any financiers you are presenting to will be well prepared. Remember that they see hundreds of proposals every year, and either have or know of investments in many different sectors of the economy. If this is not your first business venture they may even have taken the trouble to find out something of your past financial history.

Keep these points in mind when preparing for the presentation of your business plan:

- Be well prepared, with one person (you) orchestrating individual inputs. Nevertheless, you must also come across as a team.
- Use visual aids and rehearse beforehand.
- Explain and, where appropriate, defend your business concept.
- Listen to the comments and criticisms made and acknowledge them politely. You need to appear receptive without implying you have too many areas of ignorance in your plans.
- Appear businesslike, demonstrating your grasp of the competitive market forces at work in your industry, the realistic profits that can be achieved, and the cash required to implement your strategies.
- Demonstrate the product or service if at all possible, or offer to take the financiers to see it elsewhere. One participant on a Cranfield enterprise programme arranged to have his new product, a computer-controlled camera system for monitoring product quality in an engineering process, on free loan to Ford for the three months he was looking for money. This not only helped financiers to understand the application of a complex product, but the benefit of seeing it at work in a prestigious major company was incalculable.
- Work on increasing the financiers' empathy with you. You may not be able to change your personality but you could take a few tips on public speaking. Eye contact, tone of speech, enthusiasm and body language all play their part in making the interview go well, so read up on this, and rehearse the presentation before an audience.

What financiers look for in a business plan

If you are to succeed in raising funds, it is important to examine what financiers expect from you.

It is often said that there is no shortage of money for new and growing businesses – the only scarce commodities are good ideas and people with the ability to exploit them. From the potential entrepreneur's position this is often hard to believe. One major VC receives several thousand business plans a year. Only 500 or so are examined in any detail, less than 25 are pursued to the negotiating stage, and only six of those are invested in.

To a great extent the decision whether to proceed beyond an initial reading of the plan will depend on the quality of the business plan used in supporting the investment proposal. The business plan is the ticket of admission giving the entrepreneur his or her first, and often only, chance to impress prospective sources of finance with the quality of the proposal. We have established that, to have any chance at all of getting financial support, your business plan must be the best that can be written and it must be professionally packaged. But when evaluating your business plan before sending it out to sources of finance, it may help to try to get under the skin of those financiers.

In our experience at Cranfield, the plans that succeed meet all of the following requirements.

Evidence of market orientation and focus

Entrepreneurs must demonstrate that they have recognised the needs of potential customers, rather than simply being infatuated with an innovative idea. Business plans that occupy more space with product descriptions and technical explanations than with explaining how products will be sold and to whom usually get cold-shouldered by financiers. They rightly suspect that these companies are more of an ego trip than an enterprise.

But market orientation in itself is not enough. Financiers want to sense that the entrepreneur knows the one or two things his or her business can do best, and that the entrepreneur is prepared to concentrate on exploiting these opportunities.

Blooming Marvellous

Two friends who eventually made it to an enterprise programme – and to founding a successful company – had great difficulty in getting backing at first. They were exceptionally talented designers and makers of clothes. They started out making ballgowns, wedding dresses, children's clothes – anything the market wanted. Only when they focused on designing and marketing clothes for mothers-to-be which allowed them to feel fashionably dressed was it obvious they had a winning concept. That strategy built on their strength as designers, their experiences as former mothers-to-be, and exploited a clear market opportunity neglected at that time by the main player in the marketplace, Mothercare.

From that point their company made a quantum leap forward from turning over a couple of hundred thousand pounds a year to being in the several million pound turnover league in a few years.

Evidence of customer acceptance

Financiers like to know that your new product or service will sell and is being used, even if only on a trial or demonstration basis.

Solicitec

Solicitec is a company selling software to solicitors to enable them to process relatively standard documents such as wills. The founder had little trouble getting support for his package house conveyancing once his product had been tried and approved by a leading building society for their panel of solicitors.

If you are only at the prototype stage, then as well as having to assess your chances of succeeding with technology, financiers have no immediate indication that, once made, your product will appeal to the market. Under these circumstances you have to show that the 'problem' your innovation seeks to solve is a substantial one that a large number of people will pay for.

One inventor from the Royal College of Art came up with a revolutionary toilet system design that as well as being extremely thin, used 30 per cent of water per flush and had half the number of moving parts of a conventional product, all for no increase in price. Although he had only drawings to show, it was clear that with domestic metered water for all households a distinct possibility, and a UK market for half a million new units per annum, a sizeable acceptance was reasonably certain.

As well as evidence of customer acceptance, entrepreneurs need to demonstrate that they know how and to whom their new product or service must be sold, and that they have a financially viable means of doing so.

Proprietary position

Exclusive rights to a product through patents, copyright, trademark protection or a licence helps to reduce the apparent riskiness of a venture in the financier's eyes, as these can limit competition, for a while at least.

One participant on a Cranfield enterprise programme held patents on a revolutionary folding bicycle he had designed at college. While no financial institution was prepared to back him in manufacturing the bicycle, funds were readily available to enable him to make production prototypes and then license manufacture to established bicycle makers throughout the world.

However well protected legally a product is, it is marketability and marketing know-how generally that outweigh 'patentability' in the success equation. A salutary observation made by an American Professor of Entrepreneurship revealed that less than 0.5 per cent of the best ideas contained in the US *Patent Gazette* in the last five years have returned a dime to the inventors.

Believable forecasts

Entrepreneurs are naturally ebullient when explaining the future prospects for their businesses. They frequently believe that 'the sky's the limit' when it comes to growth, and money (or rather the lack of it) is the only thing that stands between them and their success.

It is true that, if you are looking for venture capital, the providers are also looking for rapid growth. However, it is as well to remember that financiers are dealing with thousands of investment proposals each year, and already have money tied up in hundreds of business sectors. It follows, therefore, that they already have a perception of what the accepted financial results and marketing approaches currently are, for any sector. Any company's business plan showing projections that are outside the ranges perceived as acceptable within an industry will raise questions in the investor's mind.

Make your growth forecasts believable; support them with hard facts where possible. If they are on the low side, approach the more cautious lending banker, rather than VCs. The former often sees a modest forecast as a virtue, lending credibility to the business proposal as a whole.

Due diligence

VCs will go through a process known as 'due diligence' before investing.

This process involves a thorough examination of both the business and its owners. Past financial performance, the directors' track records and the business plan are all subjected to detailed scrutiny, usually by accountants and lawyers.

Directors are then required to 'warrant' that they have provided ALL relevant information, under pain of financial penalties. The cost of this process will have to be borne by the firm raising the money, but will be paid out of the money raised, if that is any consolation.

Assignment 23

Write up your three-year plan for business growth.

18

Exit routes

The routes to realising the value of your business are many and the one chosen will probably be governed by a number of factors, some personal and some economic. Below are listed and described the principal exit routes open to entrepreneurs.

Types of sale

Trade sales

The vast majority of companies are sold to other companies – usually larger ones, and often ones quoted on the Stock Exchange. Because the shares of small independent unquoted companies are 'illiquid', that is they cannot be bought and sold easily, they are viewed as being less valuable than shares of a similar type of larger quoted company.

So whilst a quoted company's shares might trade on a P/E (price/earnings) ratio of 12, a similar unquoted company would be more likely to be valued on a P/E of 8. Thus, if your profits were £250,000 and your company was unquoted, it might be valued at £2 million (8 × 250,000) whilst a public company undertaking identical activities could be valued at £3 million (12 × 250,000).

Were a public company to buy your unquoted company for £2 million and absorb its profits into its own, the value of the acquiring company could rise by £3 million, without any change in the level of business undertaken. That is £1 million more than they paid in the first place. So much for the 'magic' of multiples.

Here are some examples of companies' reasons for selling up.

Scientific instruments

From its origins in a garage, one small British manufacturer of scientific instruments managed to finance expansion from retained profits. Despite all the efforts of its management, however, the company faced three seemingly insuperable barriers to growth.

It lacked the resources to develop its own computer systems; it was unduly dependent on an overseas supplier; and it was unable to break into the US market because its products were not sufficiently competitive. These problems were compounded by a new product which suffered from technical and design failings.

By the time the company was employing 20 people, it appeared to have reached a limit to its growth. It was helped out of this impasse when it was acquired by a larger company. This allowed the smaller firm to finance a new research and development programme and invest in production capacity.

With the help of its larger parent, the smaller company has since grown to turnover of £11 million and a workforce of 245. Some 70 per cent of its production is exported and it spends 12 per cent of turnover on R & D.

Thomas Goode

After 164 years in business, Thomas Goode's 60 family shareholders decided that the company, which has been financially weakened in recent years by failed diversifications and a rough retailing market, could best be taken forward as part of a larger organisation. They also wanted to realise some of the capital tied up in the business, which they hoped would fetch about £10 million.

Hambros Bank was asked to look for suitable buyers and very quickly received several preliminary offers from potential purchasers in the UK as well as from the United States, Japan and continental Europe.

The business started in 1827, when Thomas Goode opened a china store in Hanover Square. The shop moved in 1845 to a site in South Audley Street and consists of an enticing maze of small showrooms displaying ornate glassware, porcelain and fine china.

Mrs Robinson, a former executive editor of *Vogue* magazine who also worked as a main board director at Debenhams, gradually transformed the business after her appointment as MD and also brought in outside professional managers. They modernised the shop, speeded up service, introduced computer technology, achieved faster stock turn-round and improved the availability of goods. They also introduced a range of branded goods, ranging from pottery to playing cards, and are looking at further licensing and franchising opportunities. Thomas Goode has retained three royal warrants, which are proudly on display near the entrance. Other precious objects are also on show and two seven foot high Minton china elephants stand guard in the window.

However, the company reached an impasse, finding it hard to expand without further injections of cash. The company was hit badly by the collapse of a pottery manufacturer it ran in Stoke-on-Trent and an unfortunate – and expensive – attempt to stage an exhibition in the United States on the day that Wall Street dived by 5 per cent.

Like many other UK retailers, Thomas Goode suffered from the harsh trading climate in a recession and was further hampered when some large orders from Kuwait and Iraq were cancelled because of tensions in the Middle East. Sales in the company's final independent trading year rose from £3.4 million to £3.6 million, but the company still made a small loss at the pre-tax level.

Technophone

Finland's largest private company, Nokia, became the world's second biggest manufacturer of cellular telephones after Motorola of America when it paid £34 million for Technophone, a British company set up seven years ago with a share capital of just £3.3 million The agreement made Hans Wagner, Technophone's chairman, and Nils Martensson, MD, millionaires many times over. Together, they held 60 per cent of the share capital. Martensson remained in charge of Technophone and joined the board of Nokia-Mobira, the cellular telephone arm of Nokia.

The deal was the fruit of more than 12 months of talks between the companies. It put Nokia in a position to take advantage of the expected rapid expansion in demand for cellular telephones – expected because of a recent agreement on common European technical standard; and fast-rising usage of the equipment worldwide. Martensson claimed at the time that both companies would benefit from economies of scale as production volumes increased, and from shared research and development.

Technophone was set up in Camberley, Surrey, and quickly established a reputation for innovative lightweight telephone designs.

Management buy-in (MBI)

MBIs happen where a capital provider, usually a VC, backs an entrepreneur to buy into a company and effectively take it over. Usually the VC will have had a satisfactory relationship with the buy-in candidate in some other venture.

Amtrak

A former mail sorter who set up his own parcel delivery company with a £15,000 loan 11 years ago has sold up for £86 million.

Roger Baines, who left school at 15 to work for Hanson Parcels in Bristol, agreed to sell his Amtrak Holdings in a deal arranged by 3i, the venture capital firm. Baines built the company into what is now the country's eighth-largest parcel delivery company, with a nationwide network of 330 franchises delivering 50,000 parcels a day. He has now retired to Jersey.

Being brought in to run Amtrak as head of 3i's management buy-in team is Mick Jones, the ousted chief executive of Business Post, one of Amtrak's fiercest rivals. Jones fell foul of a boardroom coup orchestrated by Business Post's Peter and Michael Kane after the brothers – who own 51.9 per cent of the company – returned from semi-retirement in Guernsey to take operational control of the company. They are now chief executive and MD respectively. Jones said: 'I was sent home from Business Post on gardening leave in August and I have been sitting at home since, maybe playing the occasional round of golf. 3i had been scanning the newspapers, called me up and asked me if I would be interested. I immediately accepted – it's the perfect job'.

Jones was due to stay on Business Post's payroll for another nine months but went on to sever all ties with the company to work at Amtrak.

Very small firms can often find it difficult to attract much venture capital interest in funding a buy-out. The reason is usually that the VC believes the owner/manager makes all the key decisions, leaving the management to 'obey orders'. As the VC has no intention or desire to manage the business, it will need convincing that the existing management team can really run the business.

Management buy-out (MBO)

This term is applied to the sale of a business to its existing management team. Buy-outs are where most VCs put most of their money: upwards of 80 per cent of all venture capitalist investment goes into MBOs. It is not hard to see why they are so popular. The typical MBO is brought about by a large firm divesting peripheral activities to concentrate on its core business. The business being divested is usually well established and profitable, and the people in the best position to run the business are probably there already. Properly incentivised with shares and options, the existing team, now turbocharged, yields more profit than ever before. The result is much happiness – and wealth all round.

Glass's Guide

The bible of Britain's secondhand car industry, *Glass's Guide*, was sold to an American investment company as part of a deal worth £126 million in August 1998. The Glass's Group, which publishes the guide, was bought by Dallas-based Hicks, Muse, Tate & Furste.

Almost every motor dealer in Britain carries a copy of the guide, which lists the value of thousands of different vehicles by age and model.

It was originally the brainchild of enthusiast William Glass, who began noting down the value of sales at early car markets in the 1920s.

MD Robin Oliphant said: 'It was a time when the first cars where changing hands and there was no market or methodology to the pricing'.

The guide grew in popularity and Glass established a business to publish it in 1933, which he ran until 1954. His family then managed the company for a few years until it was sold to the publishing giant Thomson.

The guide changed hands again in 1995, when a management buy-out team led by Mr Oliphant acquired the business. Management still controls between 20 per cent and 30 per cent of the company – a stake worth about £25 million to £35 million.

The group provides software and databases which predict the value of cars in the future. It also helps businesses manage their vehicle fleets by forecasting costs for maintenance and accident repair.

Oliphant said he expected the takeover to provide extra funds for expansion into Europe: 'We've always had ideas which have exceeded our shareholders' ability to fund them'.

BIMBOs

This strange sounding title stands for buy-in management buy-out. This occurs when some of a company's existing management team join with a new incoming MD backed by a VC to buy the business. These are attractive deals for VCs as they get the best of several worlds. They get to put their own man in to run an established business, who is in turn supported by people who should know where the bodies are if anyone does.

Sale to the workers

This is not exactly the most popular notion in entrepreneurial circles, but the case below makes interesting reading.

Tullis Russell

Tullis Russell has 1,200 employees making every sort of specialist paper, from that required to insulate high-voltage cable to that used for postage stamps. David Erdal, the sixth generation of the Erdal family to run the company, spent a year on the factory floor before going to Harvard Business School where he was the resident left-wing 'weirdo' in an annual intake of 800. He was appointed chairman of the company at the age of 37. The only one of fourteen of his generation of the family working in Tullis Russell, he was determined to hand it over to the employees and he spent the next nine years doing this.

His job was to reconcile the interests of the family (25 interested parties) who had not been able to sell their shares since 1874 and who wanted to get their money out, and the future interests of the employees who were both suspicious and sceptical.

There was nothing the matter with capitalism, he had decided, the problem was it created very few capitalists. 'A lot of rubbish is talked about capital taking the risk, therefore it must get the rewards. All managers know that a large part of their role is to shift the risk away from capital to the employees. If the share price is in danger of going down, you cut their wages or sack them.' Erdal's problem was how to hand the company over. Fewer than a third of family businesses survive to the third generation. It is estimated that 30,000 independent private companies are lost in Europe each year because the owners fail to make proper arrangements.

Erdal was very glad that he had been to Harvard Business School. He was attacked by City analysts who could conceive of nothing better than to employ them at enormous fees to sell the company to a multinational. He talked to other institutions and what they came up with was daylight robbery.

The first thing Erdal did was talk to everyone in the company personally in groups of 20 over six weeks. He claimed that if he had said to them, 'Would you like to buy shares?' Ten per cent of them would have bought them, but he was saying; 'We are forcing you to take these shares out of profits. They are free'. (Even then, 12 employees refused them.)

The workforce were pretty sarcastic when they got their first dividend cheque, which in many cases was for £1. By 1987 they were beginning to cheer up a bit. With the AGM and the annual report and better dividends, they were beginning to think about business. They began to see that, if costs were reduced, they would benefit.

In 1993 it was decided to introduce a new shift system so that the machines could run for 50 weeks without stopping. Erdal sent a team of senior management and union representatives to look at several paper mills in Europe. Normally there would have been tremendous opposition, the changeover would have taken two years and job increases in that area would have been 66 per cent. As it was, people worked harder for an increase in pay, no new employees were needed and the changeover was completed in six months.

There are two far-sighted provisions in the 1989 and 1994 Finance Acts which made the deal work for both sides. The family could sell their shares to a qualifying employee share trust (Quest), financed by the company, and reinvest the £19.3 million they received without paying capital gains tax. Had they sold for cash to an outside bidder this tax would have come to about £7 million. By forming a Quest the employees could finance the buy-out from pre-tax profits, all money, capital as well as interest, being allowable against tax. If there had been a management buy-out, the company would have had to repay the debt from after-tax money, which would have cost another £6 million. As it was, the employees put up no money. The family also agreed to give the buy-out a fair wind by allowing them to spread the payments over nine years.

The employees and the employee benefit trusts now control Tullis Russell, owning 60 per cent of the shares. The rest are owned by the charitable trust set up after the war. This charitable trust, Erdal claims, gives stability to the company because it is a genuine long-term holder of shares. It has the power of veto over the future sale of the company, and it can veto the choice of directors put forward by the board (of which Erdal is still non-executive director).

The company is still very clearly management led, which is the single most important factor in any business. Generally, non-management employees cannot decide which markets to go for, or how to launch a new product. What they can do is say: 'If we operated this machine differently, it would be less wasteful', and they can make complex decisions about work scheduling.

Employees are allotted shares, 50 per cent of which are based on salary and 50 per cent equally per head. These shares may only be sold on the internal market and, if an employee leaves, must be sold within 10 years.

On retirement they should have not only a separate pension but also a nest egg of at least a year's wages – £16,000. The average sum they have in shares has now risen to almost £4,000. (The majority of people in the UK retire with no capital at all; 50 per cent of households have less than £500 in liquid assets.)

At Tullis Russell things are going from triumph to triumph. 'It patently works without me', Erdal is on record as saying. The executive car park has gone and so have salads for lunch in the canteen (due to market forces – nobody ate them). Profits have quadrupled over the last few years to more than £7 million, after £2 million of profit sharing. The management hopes to increase production to 200,000 tons a year in five years without buying any new paper machines, up from 117,000 tons this year, and 64,500 four years ago. This is among the fastest growth rates in the industry.

Family takeover

If you have children or other family members involved in the business, they may well be the right people to take it over. Even if there is no obvious family succession candidate, it might be worth casting your net beyond the immediate family. One person attending the Cranfield Business Growth Programme wrote to all his relations, asking if anyone would like to join him. A stepdaughter accepted the challenge and quickly became a key member of the management team.

But you will need to plan how you will extract any value you want or need from takeover by a family member. It may be that you can allow your relative to pay for the company over a number of years – ideally before they take over. You might be content to retain a shareholding and take your reward by way of a dividend. On balance, a clean break is usually best, but in any event clear arrangements for payments agreed in writing is a prudent arrangement to ensure family peace.

Reed Personnel

Alec Reed, chairman of Reed Personnel, says the recruitment industry hardly changed at all during his first 35 years in the business. But now there is a great change in the recruitment industry, sparked off initially by recession and hastened by the new technology, Reed Personnel is moving into a new era, with the appointment of Alec's son James, as chief executive. The founder, who learnt his business and management acumen in the School of Life, is passing on the baton to the Oxford- and Harvard-trained new generation.

Alec Reed says Gillette, the toiletries giant, has never stopped paying his salary. He left Gillette 38 years ago, where he had risen from junior clerk to become divisional accountant. His former employers became his first client, and have remained with the company ever since. Reed, like all successful entrepreneurs, was in the right place at the right time.

'When I opened the first branch in my home town of Hounslow, it went like a bomb, and at first I didn't realise why,' Reed says, 'it was right in the middle of the battlefield for labour between traditional employers along the Great West Road and London Airport, which had just opened and had a huge demand for staff.'

Local companies were happy to give Reed their vacancies because they paid only for success, and Reed delivered the staff they wanted. Now the company has 250 branches in prime high street locations, and covers 14 recruitment specialisms from accountancy to paramedics.

Alec Reed, whose company has a turnover of £226 million generating a personal fortune estimated at around £45 million, still sees Reed Personnel as a small business. 'Being a big business is all in the mind,' he argues. 'I thought we'd got big when we achieved 10 branches. Now we've 250 and we're a substantial recruitment company, but the business still runs as a multiplication of small units.'

Reed says there was never an assumption that any of his three children would join the business, but he concedes that there are undoubted advantages for everyone to keep the executive reins in the family. 'A family business is focused on the long-term view rather than making a quick buck, and so it creates stability for the staff and share-holders,' he argues. 'An employed chief executive may be in the company for less than a decade and has to make his name in a short space of time, perhaps to the detriment of the ultimate value for the company.'

'Having a family member at the top also cuts out a lot of management politics. You know the MD won't be headhunted, and there's no chance of forming factions because the next chief executive won't come in for 30 years. Clients appreciate that we're putting our money where our business is, and so everything depends on our offering them a good service.'

Having handed over the daily running of the business, Alec Reed has more time to pursue his many interests, including the family charity, which is involved with a number of good causes.

Reed started his company with some idea of the basics of business, but knew nothing about personnel and recruitment. 'I picked it up as I went along. I'm not any good as a day-to-day manager, though I'm a great delegator.'

Comparing his own style 'undisciplined and floppy' with the formal style of the new chief executive, Reed senior says: 'James is a more cerebral manager'. In saying this, he encapsulates the difference between himself, the founder–entrepreneur, and the business-school-trained executive.

James Reed grew up aware of the family business, recruiting temporary and perma-nent staff. But a job with the family firm was by no means a foregone conclusion.

After graduating he worked at the Body Shop and Saatchi & Saatchi before joining the BBC as a trainee television producer. He might have continued a successful career on the small screen, but for his inheritance.

'I knew whatever I did I ultimately wanted to be in charge,' James Reed says. 'Reed had reached an interesting stage of development in a business that was changing very quickly. Like my father at Gillette I was feeling frustrated at the time, and he made the prospect of working in the firm seem very attractive.'

James was conscious there could be charges of nepotism when he joined. 'It was important for me to be well qualified, so that I could justify my existence,' he says. A Harvard MBA gave him an American taste for innovation, and he has introduced leading edge technology to improve the company's recruitment service. Reed's Web site was used at a US conference as an example of how to use the Internet.

It is difficult to separate family and working life when it is your own business. But James Reed sees it as a bonus: 'There's the motivation to make it as successful as you can because your name is above the door'.

Succession planning in a family business can be difficult. One organisation which can help is the Stoy Centre for Family Business, 8 Baker Street, London W1U 3LL; tel: 020 7893 2171; fax: 020 7487 3686; e-mail: scfb@bdo.co.uk; Web site: www.scfb.co.uk

Michael Thornton, grandson of the founder of Thorntons PLC, has this advice to offer on making a family business successful:

- Insist on regular and disciplined family gatherings to address critical family issues.
- Consider establishing a family council with away days for the whole family.
- Have a written statement of family value policies and aspirations for the business including a written policy on the procedure for the admission of a family member into the business.
- Set up really good lines of communication across the family.
- Diversify with caution: 'stick to the knitting'.
- Bring non-family members into the board – even at non-executive director level they bring an independent view and fresh ideas and help to calm the family emotion.

When Thorntons floated, its shares were eight times oversubscribed.

Who can help

If you plan to exit by way of a flotation or a management buy-out then you will have a fairly predictable route. The path to flotation is covered in Chapter 10. For a buy-out you will in all probability start by discussing financing the deal with the bank or a VC.

For a trade sale the options on advice are a little broader. You could just wait for people to approach you. However, as with selling anything, if you can get people to bid against each other you can usually get a better price.

But if you invite people to bid, you have to provide the appropriate information – and this will be pretty well everything. That information will be shared liberally to attract as many bidders as possible. It will reveal your weaknesses as well as your strengths, and it will indicate future plans. All in all, this is very valuable information, particularly to a competitor, and it is one of those who is most likely to end up buying the business.

Managing the auction

You will probably require an accounting firm or a business broker to manage the 'auction' process. Such brokers operate on a mixture of upfront fee (usually small, or perhaps even non-existent in some cases) and a sliding scale of commission payable on a successful result.

The brokers prepare a memorandum describing your business. Often a business plan can substitute for an offer memorandum. Readers expect a business plan to be prepared by management; they expect an offer memorandum to be written by the broker. A business plan is particularly appropriate if you are not enthusiastic about being openly for sale. An offer memorandum suggests you plan to sell the business, and to do so soon. A business plan sends no such message, and it does not have to be prepared in secret.

The business broker shows the offer memorandum or business plan to anything from a dozen to over a hundred prospective buyers. Those tentatively agreeing to value the business highest are invited to study more detailed information, and three or four are allowed to tour the facilities and meet key managers. Then, if all goes well, the remaining few bid against one another.

Confidentiality

Confidentiality agreements are usual before information is provided. The protection provided is not watertight, but large organisations want to avoid litigation. And the financial community is a relatively small one, sharing its information and gossip quickly in a way that makes or breaks reputations. You will also want to include in any confidentiality agreement an assurance that would-be suitors do not offer jobs to your key staff for a period of, say, two years after a failed bid.

Due diligence

Once both sides are in general agreement over the terms of the sale, your business will be reviewed in detail. This will ensure that the buyer gets what he thinks he is getting. The ownership of assets, patents and copyrights will be examined, as will employment contracts, the customer terms and conditions and so on. The basis of plans and projections will also be reviewed. If you think your annual audit is an intrusive experience, due diligence is more like invasive surgery.

Just in case the prospective buyer has missed anything, you will be asked to 'warrant' the deal. This basically means that if any material liability is uncovered after the sale that was not either uncovered in the due diligence or included in your offer memorandum, you pick up the bill. The buyer may well expect a sum to be set aside to cover any such eventuality for a period of months – or even years.

If the due diligence uncovers problems, there are usually only four options:

● If the buyer is very keen to buy, he or she can be asked to 'live with it'.
● If the buyer is less keen, the price can be adjusted to reflect the potential problem.
● Specific guarantees or indemnities can be offered to protect the buyer from potential problems. This may include retentions of some of the purchase monies.
● The deal is off.

'Dressing to kill'

To avoid horrors being uncovered in the due diligence, you may need to 'clean' the company up beforehand. A change of auditors may be necessary, if you have been using a sleepy small local firm, especially if they have become particularly friendly. In preparing for a sale you would be wise to select a more inquisitive and thorough firm, with a reputation that is likely to be known to and respected by potential buyers.

Private businesses do tend to run expenses through the business that might be frowned upon under different ownership. One firm, for example, had its sale delayed for three years while the chairman's yacht was worked out of 'work in progress'. There can also be problems when personal assets are tucked away in the company, or where staff have been paid rather informally, free of tax. The liability rests with the company, and if the practice has continued for many years the financial picture can look quite messy.

The years before you sell up can be used to good effect by improving the performance of your business relative to others in your industry. Going down the profit-and-loss account and balance sheet using ratios such as those covered in Chapter 4 will point out areas for improvement. Once the business is firmly planted on an upward trend, your future projections will look that much more plausible to a potential buyer. You should certainly have a business plan and strategic projections for at least five years. This will underpin the strength of your negotiations by demonstrating your management skills in putting together the plan, and showing that you believe the company has a healthy future.

Some entrepreneurs may wonder if such an effort is worthwhile. Perhaps the following example will show how financial planning can lead to capital appreciation for the founder.

A 34-year-old owner–manager built up a regional service business in the United States that had a 40 per cent compounded annual growth rate for the five most recent years. He employed an experienced CPA (chartered accountant) as his chief financial officer. This person developed budgets for one- and three-year periods and a detailed business plan charting the company's growth over the next five years. The owner's objective stated to his directors was to be ready to sell his business when the right offer came along.

A UK company interested in acquiring a leading service company in the region and finding a manager with the potential for national leadership carefully analysed the company and came away impressed with management's dedication to running its business in a highly professional manner. Because the previous year's after-tax profits had been $500,000 on sales of $10 million, the UK company offered $4.5 million on purchase and $4.5 million on attainment of certain profit objectives (well within the growth trend). The transaction closed on these terms.

The $9 million offering price, representing 18 times net earnings, was 50 per cent higher than the industry norm and clearly justified the owner's careful job of packaging his business for sale.

Valuing the business

There are no mathematical or accountancy based formulae that will produce the correct value for your business. There are some principles that can help, but the figure you end up with will in all probability have more to do with your negotiating skills than with audited accounts.

Connectair

Robert Wright, a Cranfield MBA who started up his venture, Connectair, immediately after completing his MBA in 1985, provides a cautionary tale. He sold out to Harry Goodman, late of International Leisure fame in 1989 for around £7 million. Not bad for just under five years' work. However, negotiations with Goodman took up nearly a year, and his opening offer was under £1 million.

Robert did rather better when he sold his business for the second time, after buying it back from receivership. This time the sale, at the end of 1998, was to British Airways and the sum from the deal was £75 million.

The starting point has to be how much you want to make from the sale. If you are planning to retire you will be unpleasantly surprised to discover exactly how much cash you need now to produce anything resembling a decent salary for the next 20 years. If inflation runs its historic course you can expect the value of your nest egg to halve every seven years.

The next task is to revalue your assets for sale rather than their continued use in the business. It seems incredible, but companies still leave assets at book value when planning to sell up. Quite recently there was widespread publicity about the sale of a major advertising agency where the buyer found he was able to recoup a large chunk of the sale price by selling off an undervalued office building in Tokyo. Good news for the buyer, galling for the seller.

Using a formula to set the selling price

It will always be helpful to develop some logic for setting the selling price. The net present value (NPV) technique involves using a formula with logic behind it, which can provide the basis for a rational rather than a purely emotional discussion with prospective buyers. The formula used to calculate it is quite simple, but the factors used in arriving at the valuation are somewhat subjective. An example of a simple valuation of a company is shown at the end of Chapter 16.

It is much more likely that negotiations will centre on the price/earnings (P/E) ratio described earlier. For public companies, who are most likely to be the buyers, this ratio is vital in their relationship with the City. The higher that ratio the more highly rated the firm is in the eyes of the financial community.

The factors that drive the P/E ratio are growth, security and potential. So a company that has grown rapidly, has great potential for future growth and always hits its profit forecast will have its shares much sought after.

The P/E ratio will also be affected by the prevailing economic climate.

Afterwards

What happens afterwards rather depends on your goals in selling up. If you are retiring, your plans should be well laid beforehand. If you are staying on as a member of a larger group, as Technophone's Nils Martensson did, then you need to be prepared for a corporate rather than entrepreneurial life. This can be hard, and few people make the transition successfully.

If you are walking away with a large cheque, as Robert Wright did, your experiences may bear a close resemblance to a bereavement. He, and many others who have sold up, have taken years to find the right opportunity to get back into business. What they have found helpful is to set themselves up as a sort of one-man venture capital and management consultancy business. By putting the word out that they are interested in buying or backing ventures in the field they understand best, they receive a steady stream of proposals and presentations, from which they hope to fund their next venture.

Demon Internet

Cliff Stanford began Demon Internet in the boiler room of a Southend cinema 13 years ago. He sold the business to Scottish Telecom, part of Scottish Power for £66 million in 1998.

Stanford promptly launched a new venture – a brand called Redbus, which he will attach to any promising businesses he can find.

Stanford hopes Redbus will become a Virgin-style umbrella brand for a range of activities. He has set aside £15 million of his own cash to buy something and intends to lobby VCs for further funds. 'This brand will become very, very well known. I want it to be linked with innovation and Britishness.'

All business opportunities will be considered 'from information technology to soft drinks'. The main asset of Redbus is Stanford's business expertise. 'I understand what customers want. I know how to negotiate and how to get sound deals.'

Martinelli

Getting a foot in the right proverbial door can often set a small business owner on the road to a fortune. Such was the case for Martin Gill, a serial entrepreneur who is now building his third business.

Gill's first taste of success came when he left his job as Brooke Bond's marketing director to launch The London Tea & Produce Company. He later sold the firm, founded The London Herb & Spice Company, which he also sold, and then launched Martinelli, a brand-creation business that counts among its names The London Gin Company and The Loch Ness Whisky Company. He leaves manufacturing to others.

Gill joined Brooke Bond in 1967 but by 1973 had become disillusioned with working for a large organisation. With Brooke Bond's financial controller he bought a defunct business, The London Tea & Produce Company, for a few hundred pounds, set up in Welbeck Street, London, and began blending and packing teas from India, Sri Lanka and Kenya, selling them at a 25 per cent premium to Twinings.

A key early contract came from Air France which, he discovered from a friend at Maison Fauchon, France's equivalent to Fortnum & Mason, was hunting for teas for Concorde's inaugural commercial flight. He began by supplying 20 cases a month and was stunned when, after six months, the order came back with two extra zeros added – Air France wanted 2,000 cases. He thought it was a mistake but it turned out that Air France's MD had tasted the tea on Concorde and had liked it so much he insisted it be served throughout the fleet.

This gave London Tea & Produce a big revenue boost, solved some cash flow problems and began the process by which the business became an international brand selling in 12 countries.

After two years Gill was making a £100,000 profit on sales of £6 million, but he still had cash flow problems and he decided his company needed to be part of a bigger group. Thus he sold to Argyll Foods for £1 million and moved into the then-embryonic herbal-tea sector by launching The London Herb & Spice Company. In 1988, when sales had reached £5 million, Gill sold to Premier Brands for £5 million and after a short period he took early retirement.

But serial entrepreneurs do not make happy pensioners – they get bored, as Gill discovered. In 1998 he started Martinelli with £130,000 of savings and a £400,000 investment from 3i and Foreign and Colonial Ventures. The venture capitalists advanced a further £400,000. His latest product is Sin & Tonic, a low-alcohol gin-and-tonic mix, which he dreamt up after losing his driving licence.

Professional advice

Nothing said in this chapter should be construed as a substitute for taking professional advice. Most people only sell a business once in their lives. The best professional advisers in the field sell a dozen or so each year. A good tax and pension strategy can double the end value you receive and legal advice on warranties can make sure you get to keep the money.

You could do worse than put yourself in your potential buyer's mind by re-reading Chapter 11, but reversing roles.

References

Adair, J (1968) *Training for Leadership*, John Adair MacDonald & Co, London

Adams, J, Hayes and Hopson (1976) *Transitions V: Understanding and managing personal change*, Martin Robertson, Oxford

Ansoff, I H (1986) *Corporate Strategy*, Sidgwick and Jackson

Barrow, C (2001) *Financial Management for the Small Business*, 5th edn, Kogan Page, London

Beckhard, R and Harris, R T (1987) *Organizational Transitions: Managing complex change*, Addison Wesley, MA

Belasco, J A (1990) *Teaching the Elephant to Dance*, Hutchinson Business Books Ltd, London

Belbin, M (1981) Management Teams: Why they succeed or fail, Butterworth-Heinemann

Birch, A, Gorbert, P and Schneider, D (2000) *The Age of E-Tail*, Capstone Publishing, Oxford

British Venture Capital Association (1998) *Guide to Venture Capital*, BVCA, London

Churchill, N C and Lewis, V L (1983) The Five Stages of Small Business Growth, *Harvard Business Review*, May/June

Cranfield Working Papers (1992) *How Small Firms Recruit Key Staff*, Cranfield School of Management, Cranfield

Cranfield Working Papers (1993) *3i/Cranfield European Barometer*, Cranfield School of Management, Cranfield

Cranfield Working Papers (2000) *Barriers to Growth*, Cranfield School of Management, Cranfield

Datastream/ICV (1999) *Financial and Statistical Services*, Princeton University Library, September

Drucker, P F (1978) *Age of Discontinuity*, HarperCollins

Dumaine, Brian (1990) Creating a New Company Culture, *Fortune*, January

European Venture Capital Association (1999) Annual Survey of Venture Capital in Europe, European Venture Capital Association, Brussels, Belgium

Galbraith, J K (1975) *Money*, Andrew Deutsch, London

Greiner, L E (1972) Evolution and Revolution as Organisations Grow, *Harvard Business Review*, July/August

Gunning, R (1981) *Business Week*, July 6

Handy, C (1989) *The Age of Unreason*, Arrow Books, p 7

Heider, J (1985) The Tao of Leadership, Gower Publishing, Abingdon, Oxon

Howard, R (1990) Values Make the Company: An interview with Robert Haas, *Harvard Business Review*, Sept/Oct

Jones, T O and Sasser, W Earl (1995) *Harvard Business Review*, November/December

Kanter, Rosabeth Moss (1985) *The Change Masters: Corporate entrepreneurs at work*, Unwin Publications, London

Kirchhoff (1994) *Entrepreneurship and Dynamic Capitalism*, Quorum Books, Westport, CT

Koch, J (1988) *INC Magazine*, March

Machiavelli, Niccolò (1998) *The Prince*, reissue edn, Penguin Books, Harmondsworth

McClelland, D C (1992) *Achievement Motive*, Irvington Publishers

McDonald, M (1990) *Marketing Plans*, Heinemann, Oxford, p 159

McDonald, M (1994) Developing the Marketing Plan, *The Marketing Book*, Butterworth-Heinemann, London

McKinsey (1990) *McKinsey Quarterly Review*, Winter

Melkman, A (1979) *How to Handle Major Customers Profitably*, Gower Press

Observatory for SME Research (1997) *Fifth Annual Report*, EIM Small Business Research Consultancy, The Netherlands

Ohmae, K (1988) Getting back to strategy, *Harvard Business Review*, November/December

Olins, W (1989) *Corporate Identity*, Thames and Hudson, London

Pandit, M (2000) Article in the 'People' section, *The Director*, September

Peters, T and Waterman, R H (1985) *In Search of Excellence*, HarperCollins, New York

Peters, T and Waterman, R H (1985b) *In Search of Excellence* (video), Video Arts Ltd, London

Porter, Professor Michael E (1981) *Competitive Strategy*, Collier Macmillan, London

Roberts, W (1990) *The Leadership Secrets of Attila the Hun*, Bantam Books, London

Roddick, A (1991) *Body and Soul*, Ebury Press, London

Roddick, A (2000) *Business As Unusual*, Thorsons, London

Sashkin, Marshall (1995) *The Visionary Leader*, Human Resource Development Press Inc, Amherst, MA

Simms, J (2000) The Queen of Green, *The Director*, September

Stayer, R (1990) How I Learned to Let My Workers Lead, *Harvard Business Review*, Nov/Dec

Vandermerwe and Taishoff, M (2000) *Interactive Investor International Case*, part 5, European Case Clearing House, Cranfield University, Cranfield

Venture Economics (2000) *National Venture Capital Yearbook*, Venture Economics, Newark, New Jersey

Warnes, B (1984) *The Ghenghis Khan Guide to Business Survival*, Osmosis, London

Wong, Saunders and Doyle (1989) *Association of MBA's Journal*, AMBA, London

Index

Are you making the most of your IT investment?

BT knows that information technology is only as useful as you make it. That's why we are working with Cisco Systems to help thousands of small businesses get a return on their IT investments. For hardware or advice on installation and on-going support from one experienced team, *Freefone 0800* **7836306** or visit **www.bt.com/sme**

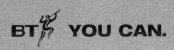